Windows 8 Hacks

T0373233

Preston Gralla

O'REILLY®

Beijing · Cambridge · Farnham · Köln · Sebastopol · Tokyo

Windows 8 Hacks

by Preston Gralla

Printed in the United States of America.

Published by O'Reilly Media, Inc., 1005 Gravenstein Highway North, Sebastopol, CA 95472.

O'Reilly books may be purchased for educational, business, or sales promotional use. Online editions are also available for most titles (*http://my.safaribooksonline.com*). For more information, contact our corporate/institutional sales department: 800-998-9938 or *corporate@oreilly.com*.

Editor: Nan Barber
Production Editor: Kristen Borg

Proofreader: nSight, Inc.
Indexer: Jay Marchand
Cover Designer: Karen Montgomery
Interior Designer: David Futato
Illustrator: Rebecca Demarest

December 2012:   First Edition

Revision History for the First Edition:
2012-11-27   First release

See *http://oreilly.com/catalog/errata.csp?isbn=9781449325756* for release details.

ISBN: 978-1-449-32575-6

[LSI]

Table of Contents

Preface

Windows 8 represents one of the biggest changes to Windows ever undertaken by Microsoft, with a new tiled main interface that works equally well via touch or keyboard and mouse. But one thing hasn't changed from previous versions—it's eminently hackable.

As you'll see in this book, you can hack just about anything. Want to hack the new Start screen and tiles, the new Lock screen, the new tile-based apps, or the automatic notification information? Yes, you can do that. How about running other operating systems inside Windows 8, running Windows 8 on a Mac, or hacking SkyDrive and social media? I'll show you how to do that as well.

And yes, I'll even show you how you can bring back a version of the old standby Start menu that Microsoft killed off in Windows 8, or bypass the new Start screen and boot directly into the Desktop.

You'll find over a hundred great hacks in this book. Some are simple enough that you can do them in a few minutes. Some take some serious time and thought. But all of them are useful or entertaining. You'll learn how to get far more out of Windows 8, and have fun in the process.

The hacks you'll find inside are useful, frequently entertaining, and will save you countless hours at the keyboard. Whether you want to speed up your PC, customize the Windows interface, hack your wired and wireless network, get more out of the Web, make better use of email, use the Registry to bend the operating system to your will, or use Windows for countless other useful tasks, you'll find what you're looking for here. And each hack doesn't just show you *how* to do something; it also teaches *why* it works. Each hack is a starting point, rather than an ending point, so that you can apply the knowledge you've gained to create new hacks of your own.

How to Use This Book

You can read this book from cover to cover if you like, but each hack stands on its own, so feel free to browse and jump to the different sections that interest you most. If there's a prerequisite you need to know about, a cross-reference will guide you to the right hack. If you're not familiar with the Registry yet, or you want a refresher, you might want to spend some time in Chapter 11 to get a good grounding.

How This Book Is Organized

This book is not a mere tips-and-tricks compendium that tells you where to click, where to drag, and what commands to type. It takes advantage of Windows' flexibility and new features, recognizes that there are specific tasks you want to accomplish with the operating system and related hardware and software, and offers bite-size pieces of functionality you can put to use in a few minutes. It also shows how you can expand on their usefulness yourself. To give you this kind of help, the book is organized into 11 chapters:

Chapter 1, Setup and Startup Hacks

Want to disable or hack your way through the Lock screen, speed up boot time, refresh your PC by reinstalling Windows without touching your data, run Windows 8 on a Mac, or run other operating systems inside Windows 8? You'll find those along with plenty of other hacks.

Chapter 2, Hacking the Start Screen, the Windows 8 Interface, and Apps

Windows 8's biggest change, as compared to previous versions of Windows, is the new tile-based Start screen, as well as the Windows 8 native apps built specifically for it. (The interface and apps for it were previously called Metro, but Microsoft has abandoned that name.) This chapter shows you how to bend the Start screen and Windows 8 native apps to your will. Here you'll find out how to hack the Start screen and individual Windows 8 native apps, get access to Windows 8 power tools from the Start screen, track app use with the Task Manager, and much more.

Chapter 3, Hacking the Desktop

Even if it's no longer center stage, your old favorite the Desktop still lives in Windows 8, and I'll show you how to hack it. Here's where you'll learn to bring a Start menu back to Windows 8, and even boot directly to the Desktop rather than the Start screen. You'll also find out how to bring back the Quick Launch toolbar, run Desktop apps and Windows 8 native apps side by side, make the Desktop more tablet-friendly, and control the Control Panel. I'll even show you how to turn on Windows 8's hidden "God Mode."

Chapter 4, Productivity and System Performance Hacks

When it comes to PCs, there are only three important speeds—fast, faster, and fastest. This chapter shows you how to make sure that your PC always runs in the fastest lane. You'll discover hidden tools for juicing up performance and tracking down bottlenecks, peer deep into your system with various Windows 8 monitors, speed up performance using the Task Manager, and use File History to recover deleted files or get back previous versions of files. And the chapter also includes a comprehensive list of Windows 8 keyboard shortcuts. Those with tablets or touchscreen devices will be pleased to see its comprehensive list of touchscreen gestures.

Chapter 5, Cloud and Social Networking Hacks

Windows 8 is the first version of Windows designed from the ground up for the cloud and social networking, and this chapter shows how you how to hack them. Here you'll find plenty of ways to hack SkyDrive, including making it play nice with your other Windows folders and using it to sync files on all of your Windows 8 devices as well as with other versions of Windows and Macs. I'll also clue you in to other free file-syncing services, and show you how to get the most out of Windows 8's People app and make it work with Facebook and other social media services.

Chapter 6, Music, Media, and Video

Windows 8 is a multimedia powerhouse, and this chapter shows you how to get more out of it. It shows you how to improve watching DVDs and TV shows in Windows 8, use Windows 8 with your Xbox 360, organize your photos with metadata, burn recorded TV shows directly from Windows Media Center to DVD, and more. There's even a hack that shows you how to convert vinyl LPs and tapes to MP3 files.

Chapter 7, Networking, the Web, Wireless, and the Internet

Face it: you live on the Web, Internet, and wired and wireless networks, so why not make the most of it? In this chapter, you'll find plenty of ways to improve your life online, including making Windows 8 play nice with your home network, hacking DNS to speed up Web browsing, and hacking Windows 8's Wi-Fi, wireless, and network settings. You'll see how the Task Manager can track bandwidth use of individual apps and your entire network. And there are also several hacks that show you how to use powerful networking command line tools like `netstat`, `ip config`, `ping`, `tracert`, and `pathping`. You'll find out how to extend the range of your wireless network, troubleshoot bad wireless connections, and how to keep your home network safe and secure.

Chapter 8, Security

It's a nasty world out here. There are snoopers, intruders, and malware writers looking to turn your PC into a spam-spewing zombie. But this chapter helps you fight them off and also shows how to customize how you use security. You'll see how to encrypt your PC and set up your own virtual private network (VPN), as well as tell Windows 8 not to snoop on your location. You'll find out how to create a picture password for even more Windows 8 security. Don't like the way that User Account Control (UAC) works? No problem—I'll show you how to hack it. You'll also find out how to unlock Windows 8's super-secret Administrator account, punch an escape hole through the Windows 8 firewall, and protect your privacy by removing Windows 8 metadata.

Chapter 9, Email

Email—can't live with it, can't live without it. In this chapter, you'll learn many ways to get more out of it. Here's where you'll find out how to trick the Windows 8 email app into using POP mail, use different live tiles for different email accounts, bypass limits on sending large email attachments, hack Microsoft's Outlook.com web-based mail service, turn Gmail into a universal inbox, stay off spam lists, and more.

Chapter 10, Hardware

Hardware hacks: just the though of them can make grown men and women shiver. But they're easier than you think. I'll show you how to use Windows 8's new Storage Spaces feature to combine storage from many different devices into one big virtual disk as well as how to hack Windows 8's power plan, extend Windows 8 across multiple monitors, troubleshoot hardware woes, get a comprehensive list of all your drivers, and more.

Chapter 11, The Registry and Group Policy Editor

If you're going to hack Windows 8, you'll need to use the Registry. It's that simple. This chapter goes beyond merely teaching you how to use the Registry and how it's organized (although it covers that in detail). It also shows you how to hack the Registry itself—for example, by offering hacks on how to use *.reg* files to edit the Registry safely. Additionally, you'll find out how to use the Group Policy Editor for hacking.

Conventions Used in This Book

This book uses the following typographical conventions:

Italic

Used to indicate new terms, URLs, filenames, file extensions, directories, and folders.

`Constant width`

Used to show code examples, verbatim searches and commands, the contents of files, and the output from commands.

Constant width bold

> Shows commands or other text that should be typed literally by the user.

Constant width italics

> Used in examples, tables, and commands to show text that should be replaced with user-supplied values.

Pay special attention to notes set apart from the text with dashed lines:

Tips, suggestions, and warnings appear between dashed lines. They contain useful supplementary information or an observation about the topic at hand.

Using Code Examples

This book is here to help you get your job done. In general, you may use the code in this book in your programs and documentation. You do not need to contact us for permission unless you're reproducing a significant portion of the code. For example, writing a program that uses several chunks of code from this book does not require permission. Selling or distributing a CDROM of examples from O'Reilly books does require permission. Answering a question by citing this book and quoting example code does not require permission. Incorporating a significant amount of example code from this book into your product's documentation does require permission.

We appreciate, but do not require, attribution. An attribution usually includes the title, author, publisher, and ISBN. For example: "*Windows 8 Hacks*, by Preston Gralla. Copyright 2013 Preston Gralla, 978-1-4493-2575-6."

If you feel your use of code examples falls outside fair use or the permission given above, feel free to contact us at *permissions@oreilly.com*.

Safari® Books Online

 Safari Books Online (www.safaribooksonline.com) is an on-demand digital library that delivers expert content in both book and video form from the world's leading authors in technology and business.

Technology professionals, software developers, web designers, and business and creative professionals use Safari Books Online as their primary resource for research, problem solving, learning, and certification training.

Safari Books Online offers a range of product mixes and pricing programs for organizations, government agencies, and individuals. Subscribers have access to thousands of books, training videos, and prepublication manuscripts in one fully searchable database from publishers like O'Reilly Media, Prentice Hall Professional, Addison-Wesley Professional, Microsoft Press, Sams, Que, Peachpit Press, Focal Press, Cisco Press, John Wiley & Sons, Syngress, Morgan Kaufmann, IBM Redbooks, Packt, Adobe Press, FT Press, Apress, Manning, New Riders, McGraw-Hill, Jones & Bartlett, Course Technology, and dozens more. For more information about Safari Books Online, please visit us online.

How to Contact Us

Please address comments and questions concerning this book to the publisher:

O'Reilly Media, Inc.
1005 Gravenstein Highway North
Sebastopol, CA 95472
800-998-9938 (in the United States or Canada)
707-829-0515 (international or local)
707-829-0104 (fax)

We have a web page for this book, where we list errata, examples, and any additional information. You can access this page at *http://oreil.ly/win8hacks*.

To comment or ask technical questions about this book, send email to *bookques tions@oreilly.com*.

For more information about our books, courses, conferences, and news, see our website at *http://www.oreilly.com*.

Find us on Facebook: *http://facebook.com/oreilly*

Follow us on Twitter: *http://twitter.com/oreillymedia*

Watch us on YouTube: *http://www.youtube.com/oreillymedia*

Acknowledgments

Thanks as always to my editor Nan Barber, and to senior editor Brian Sawyer. And I'd like to thank Jason Schneiderman, who proofread the manuscript; Kristen Borg, who shepherded this book through production; Ron Bilodeau for the layout of the book; and my technical editors, Jason Arnold and Sander Berkouwer, for saving me from making disastrous errors.

Finally, as always, thanks go to my wife Lydia, my daughter Mia, and my son Gabe. Without them, is anything worth hacking?

1

Setup and Startup Hacks

Install Windows 8, start it up, and start using it. What could be simpler? What's there to hack?

Plenty, as it turns out. If you don't like Windows 8's Lock screen, you can bypass it or make it work more the way you want it to. You can speed the Windows 8 boot, or even make startup faster. And you're not stuck with a single Windows 8 installation. You can install and run Windows 8 on a Mac, and run other versions of Windows inside Windows.

There's all that, and plenty more, in this chapter.

HACK 01   Disable Windows 8's Lock Screen

> Tired of being forced to click through Windows 8's lock screen before you get to the Start screen? Here's how to bypass it.

Boot your PC or wake it from sleep, and you go straight to Windows 8's lock screen, which looks more like the screen you'd expect to see on your smartphone than on a PC. It tells you the time and date, and a variety of timely information—meetings taken from your calendar, updates from social networking sites, an indication of your power level, email notifications, and other similar information.

That's all very nice, but if you're on a PC, you probably want to get straight to work. And that means getting to the Start screen faster. If you like, you can bypass the Lock Screen.

Note: If you're using a Windows 8 tablet, you may find the Lock screen more useful, since you may want to glance at your calendar or social networking sites while you're on the go.

To do it, you use the Local Policy Editor. Launch it by pressing Windows key+R to open the Run bar, type **gpedit.msc**, and press Enter or click OK. The Local Policy Editor launches (Figure 1-1).

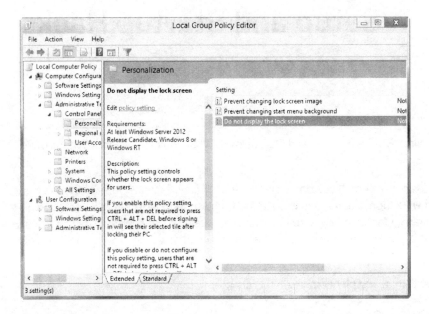

Figure 1-1.
The Local Policy Editor

Go to Computer Configuration→Administrative Templates→Control Panel→Personalization. Double-click the "Do not display the lock screen" entry, select Enabled, then press Enter or click OK (Figure 1-2). Exit the Local Policy Editor, then reboot.

The new setting should take effect immediately. The next turn you reboot or wake your PC, you won't see the Lock screen. Instead, you'll go straight into logging into Windows 8.

Hacking the Hack

The Local Policy Editor comes only with Windows 8 Pro and Windows 8 Enterprise. But you can still turn off the Lock screen in any version of Windows 8 by using a Registry hack. (See Chapter 11 for details on the Registry.) In the Registry Editor, go to *HKEY_LOCAL_MACHINE\SOFTWARE\Policies\Microsoft\Windows\Personalization* and create a DWORD called *NoLockScreen*. Change its value from 0 to 1, exit the Registry Editor, and exit and restart Windows 8. (Note: If you don't find the Personalization key, you'll have to create it before creating the *NoLockScreen* DWORD.)

Figure 1-2.
Turning off the Lock screen

See Also

• Hack #02, "Hack Your Way Through the Lock Screen"

HACK 02   Hack Your Way Through the Lock Screen

Want to bend the Lock screen to your will? Here's how to do it.

There's a lot more to the Start screen than meets the eye. It's more than just a passing-through location, because the screen can also keep you updated with information grabbed from the Internet. In this hack, you'll learn about plenty of ways to customize it.

Note: In corporate environments, an IT department may have locked down some of these options. In this case, you'll be notified with the message, "Some settings on this page have been disabled by group policy."

Change the Lock Screen Image

The Lock screen is mostly controlled via a single settings screen. To get there, press Windows key+C to display the Charms bar, and select Settings→Change PC Settings→Personalize→Lock Screen. A screen appears, shown in Figure 1-3, that displays your Lock screen image at the top. Just beneath it are other Lock screen images you can use. Click any one of them to make it the new Lock screen image. To find other images you can use for the Lock screen, click the Browse button and browse through your pictures. Select the one you want to use, click Choose Picture, and you'll make it your new Lock screen image.

Figure 1-3.
Select a new Lock screen image here

Lock Down the Lock Screen Image

If you share your PC with someone, they have the same access to fiddling with it that you do. If you don't want anyone changing your Lock screen image, you can tell Windows 8 not to let it be changed.

Launch the Local Policy Editor by pressing Windows key+R to open the Run bar, type **gpedit.msc**, and press Enter or click OK. The Local Policy Editor launches.

Go to Computer Configuration→Administrative Templates→Control Panel→Personal-ization. Double-click the "Prevent changing lock screen image" entry, select Enabled, then press Enter or click OK. Exit the Local Policy Editor.

Note: As described at the end of the previous hack, if you don't have Windows 8 Pro and Windows 8 Enterprise, you can change the Lock screen by using a Registry hack. In the Registry Editor (Chapter 11), go to HKEY_LOCAL_MACHINE\SOFT WARE\Policies\Microsoft\Windows\Personalization and create a DWORD called NoChangingLockScreen. Change its value from 0 to 1, exit the Registry Editor, and exit and restart Windows 8. If you don't see the Personalization key, you'll have to create it before creating the NoChangingLockScreen DWORD.

If you decide you want to change the Lock screen, repeat these steps, except select Disabled, press Enter or click OK, then exit the Local Policy Editor. The setting takes effect the next time you reboot.

Customize Which Apps Show their Notifications on the Lock Screen

One of Windows 8's niftier features is that it displays notifications on the Lock screen from certain apps—email, social networking, calendar, and more. That way, if you want a quick rundown of what you need to know, it's right there for you. You don't even have to log into Windows 8; just check out the Lock screen.

Maybe you don't want to see updates from your social networking sites, but do want to see the current weather, or information from another app. Customizing exactly what shows up on your Start screen is a breeze.

Press Windows key+I, and then select Change PC Settings at the bottom of the Set-tings pane. From the right side of the screen that appears (Figure 1-4), select Lock Screen.

Down at the bottom-right of the screen, you'll see icons of the apps that automatically display notifications, with some plus signs to the right (Figure 1-5). Click a plus sign to reveal a list of apps that can display notifications. Simply pick one and it will display alerts and other information on the Start screen.

Note: When you click a plus sign, you'll see both the apps that already display notifications, as well as those that don't. If you choose one that already displays its notifications on the Start screen, nothing new happens—the app still displays notifications, with no change.

Lock screen   Start screen   Account picture

4.30
Friday, August 3

Browse

Lock screen apps

Choose apps to run in the background and show quick status and notifications, even when
your screen is locked

Choose an app to display detailed status

Figure 1-4.
Customizing what apps display information on the Lock screen

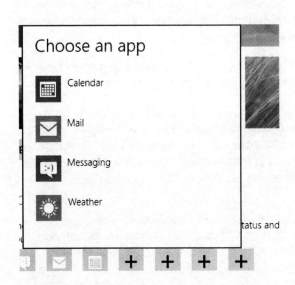

Choose an app

Calendar

Mail

Messaging

Weather

Figure 1-5.
The plus signs let you add notifications to the Lock screen

See Also

- Hack #01, "Disable Windows 8's Lock Screen"

HACK 03 Speed Up Boot Time

> Shorten the time it takes for your desktop to appear when you turn on your PC.

No matter how fast your PC boots, it's not fast enough. Here are several hacks to get you right to your desktop as quickly as possible after startup.

Hack Your BIOS for Faster Startups

When you turn on your PC, it goes through a set of startup procedures in its BIOS before it gets around to starting Windows. So, if you speed up those initial startup procedures, you'll make your system start faster.

You can speed up your startup procedures by changing the BIOS with the built-in setup utility. How you run this utility varies from PC to PC, but you typically get to it by pressing either the Delete, F1, F2, or F10 key during startup. You'll come to a menu with a variety of choices. Here are the choices to make for faster system startups:

Quick Power On Self Test (POST)

When you choose this option, your system runs an abbreviated POST rather than the normal, lengthy one.

Change Your Boot Order

If you change the boot order so that your BIOS checks the hard disk first for booting, it won't check any other devices, and will speed up your startup time.

Boot Up Floppy Seek

Disable this option. When it's enabled, your system spends a few extra seconds looking for your floppy drive—a relatively pointless procedure, especially considering how infrequently you use your floppy drive.

Boot Delay

Some systems let you delay booting after you turn on your PC so that your hard drive gets a chance to start spinning before bootup. Most likely, you don't need to have this boot delay, so turn it off. If you run into problems, however, you can turn it back on.

See Also

- Hack #04, "Speed Up Startup by Halting Startup Programs and Services"

HACK 04 # Speed Up Startup by Halting Startup Programs and Services

> Increase your PC's performance and speed up startup times by shutting off applications and services that you don't need.

One of the best ways to speed up your PC without having to spend money on extra RAM is to stop unnecessary programs and services from running whenever you start your PC. When too many programs and services run automatically every time you start up your system, startup itself takes a long time—and too many programs and services running simultaneously can bog down your CPU and hog your memory.

Some programs, such as anti-malware software, should run automatically at startup and always run on your computer. But many other programs, such as instant messenger software, serve no purpose by being run at startup. And while you need a variety of background services running on your PC for Windows to function, many services that run on startup are unnecessary.

Eliminating Programs that Run at Startup

The task of stopping programs from running at startup is particularly daunting because there's no single place you can go to stop them all. Some run because they live in the *Startup* folder, others because they're part of logon scripts, still others because of Registry settings, and so on. But with a little bit of perseverance, you should be able to stop them from running.

Cleaning Out the Startup Folder

Start by cleaning out your *Startup* folder. It's in *C:\Users\<User Name>\\AppData \Roaming\Microsoft\Windows\Start Menu\Programs\Startup*, where *<User Name>* is your Windows logon name. Delete the shortcuts of any programs you don't want to run on startup. As with any shortcuts, when you delete them, you're deleting only the shortcut, not the program itself.

Using the Task Manager

Taking the previous steps will stop the obvious programs from running at startup, but it won't kill them all. The best tool for disabling hidden programs that run on startup is the Task Manager's Startup tab, shown in shown in Figure 1-6. To run it, press Ctrl +Alt+Del and select Task Manager, then click the Startup tab. You can also run Task Manager by typing `Task Manager` on the Start screen and clicking the Task Manager icon that appears, or by pressing Ctrl+Alt+Esc.

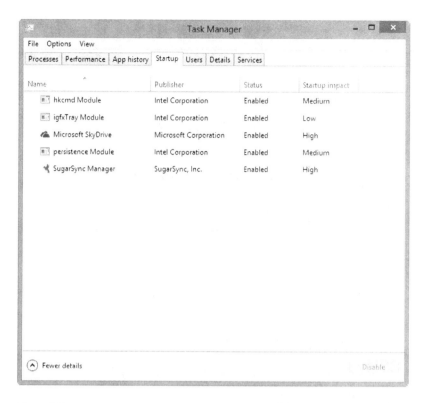

Figure 1-6.
The Startup tab of the Task Manager

You'll find the Startup tab exceptionally useful for deciding which programs and serv-ices should run at startup, and which can be safely disabled. Over on the right side, you'll see a "Startup impact" column. For each service and app listed, the column tells you whether the impact on startup is Low, Medium, or High. That lets you concentrate on disabling the Low impact items.

Sometimes the name of the app makes clear what it does. For example, Microsoft SkyDrive obviously runs Microsoft's SkyDrive client. But often, you'll have no clue what an app does. What to make of the "hkcmd Module" shown in Figure 1-6, for example. You can see in the Publisher column it's from Intel. But what is it, and what does it do? You'll need information like that to decide whether to disable it or not.

To gather information about a startup item, right-click it and select "Search online." That launches an Internet search using your default browser and default search en-gine. The results usually give you links to many sites with details about the service or app. In the instance of "hkcmd Module," for example, I was able to discover that it's an app that lets you get access to customizing an Intel chipset's graphics properties. See Figure 1-7 for an example of this.

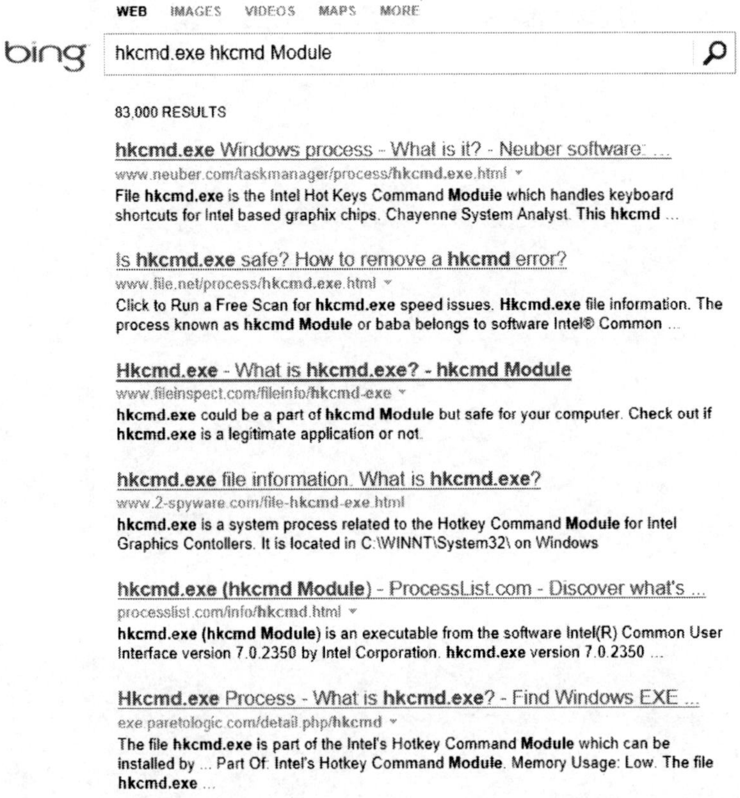

bing   hkcmd.exe hkcmd Module   🔍

83,000 RESULTS

hkcmd.exe Windows process - What is it? - Neuber software: ...
www.neuber.com/taskmanager/process/hkcmd.exe.html ▾
File **hkcmd.exe** is the Intel Hot Keys Command **Module** which handles keyboard
shortcuts for Intel based graphix chips. Chayenne System Analyst. This **hkcmd** ...

Is **hkcmd.exe** safe? How to remove a **hkcmd** error?
www.file.net/process/hkcmd.exe.html ▾
Click to Run a Free Scan for **hkcmd.exe** speed issues. **Hkcmd.exe** file information. The
process known as **hkcmd Module** or baba belongs to software Intel® Common ...

Hkcmd.exe - What is **hkcmd.exe**? - **hkcmd Module**
www.fileinspect.com/fileinfo/hkcmd-exe ▾
hkcmd.exe could be a part of **hkcmd Module** but safe for your computer. Check out if
hkcmd.exe is a legitimate application or not.

hkcmd.exe file information. What is **hkcmd.exe**?
www.2-spyware.com/file-hkcmd-exe.html
hkcmd.exe is a system process related to the Hotkey Command **Module** for Intel
Graphics Contollers. It is located in C:\WINNT\System32\ on Windows

hkcmd.exe (hkcmd Module) - ProcessList.com - Discover what's ...
processlist.com/info/hkcmd.html ▾
hkcmd.exe (hkcmd Module) is an executable from the software Intel(R) Common User
Interface version 7.0.2350 by Intel Corporation. **hkcmd.exe** version 7.0.2350 ...

Hkcmd.exe Process - What is **hkcmd.exe**? - Find Windows EXE ...
exe.paretologic.com/detail.php/hkcmd ▾
The file **hkcmd.exe** is part of the Intel's Hotkey Command **Module** which can be
installed by ... Part Of: Intel's Hotkey Command **Module**. Memory Usage: Low. The file
hkcmd.exe ...

Figure 1-7.
Mystery solved: details about "hkcmd Module"

To stop an app from running at startup, right-click it and select Disable. This prevents
it from running, although the app will still be on your hard disk.

When you stop programs from running at startup, it's best to stop them one at a time
rather than in groups. That way, you can make sure that you're not causing any system
problems. So, stop one and restart your PC. If it runs fine, stop another and restart.
Continue doing this until you've cleared all the programs you don't want to run
automatically.

After you've used the Task Manager to identify programs that run upon startup, you
may want to try disabling them from within the programs themselves. Run each program that starts automatically, and see if you can find a setting that allows you to
prevent it from running on startup.

Using the Registry to Halt Programs Running on Startup

Even the Task Manager won't necessarily let you identify and turn off all programs that run on startup. You might also need to hack the Registry to disable them. To do so, launch the Registry Editor by pressing Windows key+R, typing **regedit** in the box that appears or at a command prompt (see Chapter 11 for details) and go to HKEY_CUR RENT_USER\Software\Microsoft\Windows\CurrentVersion\Run. In the right pane, you will see a list of some of the programs that run automatically at startup. The Data field tells you the path and name of the executable so that you can determine what each program is. Right-click any program you don't want to run, and choose Delete. That will kill any programs that run and are specific to your account. To turn off programs that run for every user of the system, go to HKEY_LOCAL_MACHINE\SOFTWARE\Microsoft \Windows\CurrentVersion\Run and follow the same instructions for deleting other programs that you don't want to run at startup.

Shutting Off Services That Run at Startup

Constantly running in the background of Windows are *services*—processes that help the operating system run, or that provide support to applications. Many of these services launch automatically at startup. Although you need many of them, many aren't required and can slow down your system when they run in the background.

You can prevent services from running at startup using the Services Computer Management Console snap-in, shown in Figure 1-8. Run it by typing **services.msc** at the Start screen and clicking the icon that appears. You can also type **services.msc** into the Run box or command prompt box. The Services Computer Management Console snap-in includes a description of all services, so you can know ahead of time whether a particular service is one you want to turn off. It also lets you pause the service so you can test out your machine with the service off to see whether it's needed.

After you run the console, click the Extended tab. This view shows you a description of each service in the left pane when you highlight the service. The Startup Type column shows you which services launch upon startup—any services with "Automatic" in that column. Click the top of that column to sort together all the services that automatically launch on startup. Then highlight each service and read its description.

When you find a service that you want to turn off, right-click it and choose Properties. In the Properties dialog box that appears (Figure 1-9), choose Manual from the "Startup type" drop-down list. The service won't start automatically from now on (unless another service requires it in order to start), but you can start it manually via the console. If you want the service disabled so that it can't be run, choose Disabled. (If you disable a service that a critical Windows service depends on, that service won't be able to start either, which could cause problems.) If the service is necessary, but

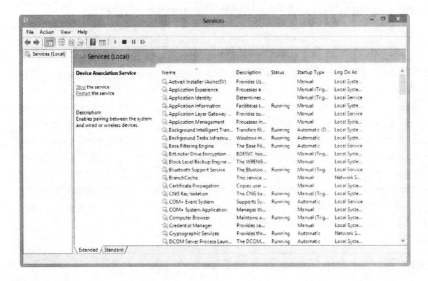

Figure 1-8.
The Services Computer Management Console

you'd still like your PC to start more quickly, you can choose Automatic (Delayed Start). When you choose this, the service won't launch immediately on startup, so your PC will start more quickly, but will wait a little bit, and load once you're using your PC. That way, the service will still be available to you, but it won't slow down startup.

To test the effects of turning off the service, turn off any services you don't want to run by clicking "Stop the service" in the left pane, or by right-clicking the service and choosing Stop. Note that some services can't be stopped while the system is running. You'll have to set them to "manual" and reboot to see the effect of turning them off.

Table 1-1 lists some common services you might want to halt from running at startup. (Some, such as Remote Registry, are disabled by default, but might have somehow been turned on.)

Table 1-1. Services you may want to turn off

SERVICE	WHAT IT DOES
Remote Registry	Allows remote users to modify Registry settings on the computer.
Windows Error Reporting Service	Turns on error reporting and delivery of solutions if your system crashes or hangs.

Figure 1-9.
The Properties dialog box of a service

Hacking the Hack

There's a new mode in Windows 8 called Fast Startup, that starts up your PC much more quickly after you've shut it down. With Fast Startup, when you turn off your PC, the kernel is saved to disk, and that kernel is then used to start Windows back up, significantly decreasing startup time.

Note that this feature only works when you shut your system down and then start it again. If you instead choose Restart rather than shutting your system down, Fast Startup doesn't come into play. By default, Fast Start is enabled, but it's a good idea to make sure it hasn't been turned off on your system. On the Start screen, press Windows key+W, type **Power**, and then click the Power Options icon that appears on the left side of the screen. Click "Choose what the power buttons do," and, on the screen that appears, in the Shutdown settings area (Figure 1-10), make sure the "Turn on fast startup" checkbox is turned on.

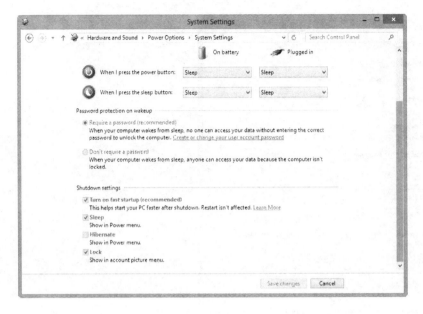

Figure 1-10.
Making sure Fast Startup is turned on

See Also

- Hack #03, "Speed Up Boot Time"

HACK 05 # Reset and Refresh Your PC Instead of Doing a Complete Reinstall

---

Have so many issues with Windows 8 that you need to reinstall it? There's a simpler way: Use Windows 8's Reset or Refresh options instead.

You know the moment, that moment when you realize that your operating system has such problems that there's only one solution: wipe it out and start from scratch by reinstalling it.

A full reinstall is a tremendous, time-consuming headache, because you have to copy all your data somewhere, wipe your hard disk, reinstall Windows, and then restore your data. It's rare that you'll get it exactly right. And that assumes that you even remember where your Windows installation disc is.

Windows 8, for the first time in Windows history, gives you a much better way. It introduces two related new features that let you essentially reset Windows 8 to the state it was in when you first installed it. The two new features are called Reset and Refresh. Here's what they do, and the differences between them:

Reset

This option puts your PC in the condition it was in to either when you first started it —if it came with Windows 8 on it—or when you first installed Windows 8. It wipes out your data and any apps you installed and puts your PC back into its original, pure Windows 8 state. It's a much simpler option than doing all that yourself manually. You won't even need your Windows install disc. (More on that later in this hack.) It's the PC equivalent of the "Restore to Factory Default" feature you'll find on many smartphones. Think of Reset as the nuclear option. Windows 8 erases and formats your hard drives, installs a fresh copy of Windows, and then starts into that new copy of Windows. There's even an option when you do a Reset for not just reformatting your hard disk before reinstalling Windows, but writing random patterns to every sector on the hard drive so that data, such as personal data, can't be recovered. You might use this alternative if you're giving away, selling, or recycling your PC.

Refresh

This feature reinstalls Windows, but doesn't wipe out your data, settings, or any Windows 8 native apps you've installed. (It does wipe out your Desktop apps, but there's a way to tell Refresh not to wipe them out, as you'll see later in this hack.) Your hard disks aren't erased or formatted. When you sign into the reinstalled Windows, your data will be there waiting for you, as will your settings and Windows 8 native apps.

To Reset or Refresh your PC, press Windows key+C and select Settings→Change PC Settings→General. Scroll toward the bottom of the screen (Figure 1-11) and on the right side, you'll see separate sections for Refresh and Reset. The Refresh section reads "Refresh your PC without affecting your files," and the Reset section reads "Remove everything and reinstall Windows." Click "Get started" in the appropriate section. Then just follow the simple prompts.

Note: When you perform a Refresh, you won't have to go through the normal initial Windows 8 Welcome and setup screens that walk you through to configure your settings and user account. That information is included already as part of the Refresh. With a Reset, however, you'll go through all those screens.

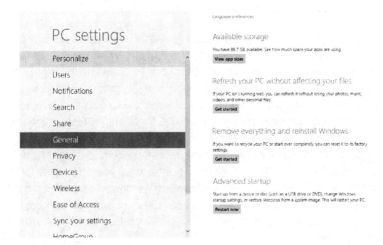

Figure 1-11.
Refresh or Reset your PC from this screen

Create a Custom Refresh Point

Mostly, you'll use the Refresh option, because you want to continue to use your files and apps. But there's a problem with Refresh: although it keeps all your data and your Windows 8 native apps, it wipes out your Desktop apps. If, like most people, you mainly use Desktop apps, this is not a good thing.

You can, however, create a custom refresh point that takes a snapshot of your system, and then uses that snapshot to refresh your PC. Part of that snapshot includes your Desktop apps, so when you refresh your system after creating one of these custom refresh points, your Desktop apps will be back waiting for you.

How does it do that? First, a little bit of background. When Windows 8 is first installed, the system creates and stores a refresh point. When you refresh your system, it uses that refresh point as the baseline for the refresh. But because that refresh point was created before you installed Desktop apps, it doesn't include information about them. When you create a custom refresh point, information about those apps is included, so they'll be on your system.

To create a custom refresh point, first create a new directory where you want to store it. The refresh point will be named *CustomRefresh.wim*. After that, run an elevated command prompt—that is, a command prompt with Administrator rights. To do it, right-click the lower-left edge of the screen and select Command Prompt (Admin). Then type the following in the command prompt:

```
recimg /createimage <directory>
```

where <directory> is the name of the directory you've just created. When you do that, Refresh will use the image in that directory instead of the one created during Windows 8's initial installation to perform a Refresh.

The `recimg` command gives you quite a bit of flexibility in creating and using Refresh points. What if you decide you want to create a new custom Refresh point because you've installed new apps, and want them as part of the Refresh? Simply create a new directory, and run the `recimg` command using it as the place to store the Refresh point.

But `recimg` can do more as well. If you have multiple directories with Refresh points, you can tell Windows 8 which is the current one that it should use for doing a Refresh. To do all that, and more, you'll need to know all of `recimg` command line options. Table 1-2 shows them all:

Table 1-2. The recimg commands and what they do

COMMAND	WHAT IT DOES
`/createimage <directory>`	Creates a custom Refresh point in a specified directory and tells Windows 8 to use that Refresh point in that directory when performing a Refresh.
`/setcurrent <directory>`	Tells Windows 8 to use the custom Refresh point in the specified directory when performing a Refresh. (You must first create a Refresh point in the directory.)
`/deregister <directory>`	Tells Windows 8 not to use the custom Refresh point in the specified directory when you perform a Refresh. When you deregister a Refresh point in a directory, Windows 8 will use the initial Refresh point it created during installation.
`/showcurrent`	Displays the location of the directory which contains the current custom Refresh point that will be used when performing a Refresh.
`/help or /?`	Shows help text for `recimg`.

See Also

- For more details about Reset and Refresh, see the Microsoft blog "Refresh and Reset Your PC" (*http://bit.ly/RRNOYW*).

HACK 06 Installing and Running Windows 8 on a Mac

Got a Mac and want to Run Windows 8 on it? Here's how.

More and more, people have not just PCs, but Macs as well. Some people like Macs so much, in fact, that they like to run Windows on their Mac. That way, they get the best of both worlds—Mac OS X *and* Windows on the same machine.

There are several ways you can do this. One is to use the Apple program called Boot Camp. This lets you run a dual-boot system; that is, you can boot into either Mac OS X *or* Windows 8. Apple has ample documentation for Boot Camp, so if you're interested in it, follow Apple's instructions—they're generally well done and straightforward.

> Note: *As I write this, Boot Camp doesn't formally support Windows 8. But, by the time you read this, it most likely will.*

Also, Boot Camp requires you to boot into either Mac OS X or Windows. When you want to switch between the operating systems, you'll have to reboot.

> Note: *You need a registered version of Windows 8 to run it on Mac OS X. It can't have the same registration code as the version you run on your PC, unless you have the right to run it on multiple devices. You can also use a trial version of Windows 8.*

There's another type of solution, that lets you run Windows 8 inside Mac OS X. In this case, you run your Mac as you would normally, and Windows 8 runs inside a Mac window. To do that, you use software to create a *virtual machine* (VM), and then run that virtual Windows 8 machine. Three popular programs let you do this: Parallels Desktop, VMWare Fusion, and VirtualBox. In this hack, I'll show how to use all three.

Installing and Running Windows 8 Using Parallels Desktop

Get a copy of Parallels (*http://www.parallels.com*). It costs $79.99. You'll also need a copy of Windows 8, either on DVD or other media or as an *.iso* file. Before you install Windows 8, you must install Parallels Desktop, which is the same simple process as installing any Mac program.

Now you're ready to install Windows 8. But since you're installing Windows 8 as a virtual machine, you have to install it from within Parallels Desktop. Run Parallels and select File→New. A screen like the one shown in Figure 1-12 appears.

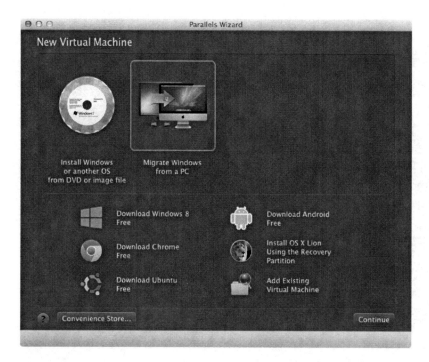

Figure 1-12.
Getting started to create a virtual machine for Windows 8 on a Mac using Parallels

On this screen, you have the choice of migrating Windows from an existing PC (which makes sense if you already have a Windows 8 PC) or installing Windows from either a DVD or an *.iso* file. Down toward the bottom of the screen, there's also an option for downloading Windows 8 for free. Keep in mind that this will be a trial version of Windows 8, not a fully paid one, so you can only use it for 90 days. It will likely be the Enterprise edition of Windows 8. You'll download it as an *.iso* file.

When you migrate, you'll choose the method you want to use for the migration: over a network, from an external storage device, or using a USB cable you can buy from Parallels in the company's "Switch to Mac" kit. From there, follow the wizard's instructions.

If you're instead installing a fresh copy of Windows 8, select the "Install Windows or another OS from DVD or image file," and click that option. On the next screen (Figure 1-13), choose whether you're going to install from a DVD or *.iso* file (Parallels calls it an *image file*). If you're installing from an *.iso* file, browse to the location of the file and choose it. Then click Continue.

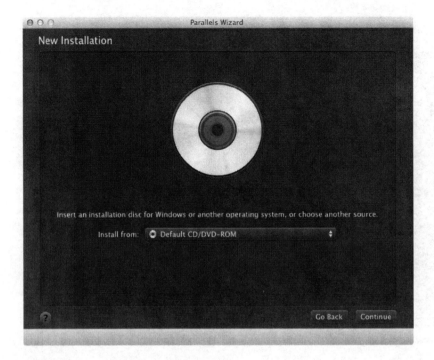

Figure 1-13.
Choosing where to install from

On the next screen (Figure 1-14), you'll need to enter your Windows 8 product key. If you're using a trial version of Windows 8, turn off the "This version requires a product key" checkbox. Also, if you're using the trial version, also turn off the "Express installation" option. (If you don't uncheck that box, your trial version may not install.)

If you keep "Express installation" checked and click Continue, your installation will be straightforward. Just follow the prompts and you're good to go. If you uncheck the box, the process will require a few more steps, so read on for the details.

Whether you use the express installation or not, on the next screen you come to (Figure 1-15), you'll be asked to choose between two different ways that Windows 8 can run:

Like a Mac

If you choose this option, you won't see the familiar Windows 8 interface, including the Start screen, Desktop, and so on. Instead, you'll only use applications that you install onto Windows, such as Office. Each of these applications will run in their own windows on Mac OS X, like a Mac OS X app. Unless you're only installing Windows 8 to run specific Windows programs, this isn't a good choice.

Figure 1-14.
Putting in the product key

Like a PC

Choose this alternative, and Windows 8 runs like normal in its own Mac window, with the Start screen, Desktop, and so on. This setup is the best choice for most people.

Make a choice and click Continue (the rest of this section assumes that you've chosen Like a PC). On the next screen, you'll see details of the virtual Windows 8 machine you're creating, including its name location, and similar options. Make any changes, or leave them as is, then click Continue.

At this point, Windows 8 starts installing on your Mac in the same way that it installs on a PC. You'll see the same prompts, choose the same options, and so on. You can see it in action in Figure 1-16. When you come to a screen asking whether to install as an Upgrade or Custom, select Custom. Then select the Mac's hard disk as the place to install Windows and continue. After the usual restarts, Windows 8 will be installed on your Mac as a virtual machine. You'll be able to run it every time you start Parallels (Figure 1-17).

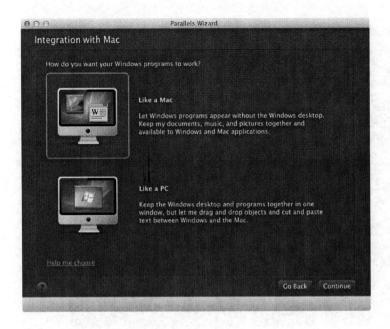

Figure 1-15.
Choosing how your Windows 8 programs will run

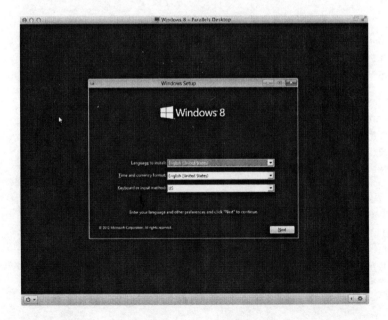

Figure 1-16.
Just like a PC: from here on in, the installation looks like a normal installation on a PC

Tip: It's a good idea to use the same Microsoft ID on Windows 8 on your Mac as you normally use on your PC. That way, all your settings, apps, and other information will automatically sync.

Figure 1-17.
Here it is—Windows 8 running on Parallels

Installing and Running Windows 8 Using VMWare Fusion

You can instead run Windows 8 on a Mac using VMWare Fusion (*http://www.vmware.com*); $49.99. The setup is much the same as with Parallels, so I won't go into quite as much detail here: the concepts are very much the same.

As with Parallels, you can either install Windows 8 from a DVD or .*iso* file, or you can migrate Windows 8 from an existing PC. To migrate, both the Mac and PC must be on the same network. Select File→Migrate Your PC, and then follow the prompts.

To install using a DVD or .*iso* file, select File→New, put your DVD in the drive and click Continue. If you're using an .*iso* file, click "Continue without disc." Select your installation media (in the case of the .*iso* file, you'll navigate to its location) and click Continue, as you can see in Figure 1-18.

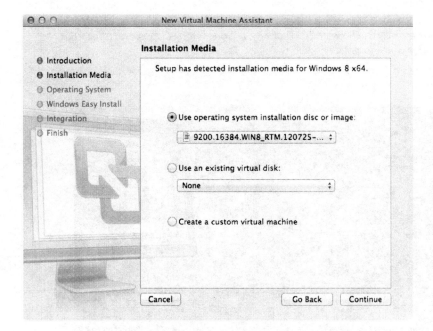

Figure 1-18.
Starting the installation of Windows 8 using VMWare Fusion

On the next series of screens, choose the operating system, account name, password, and Windows product key, if you have one. If you're installing a trial version of Windows 8, turn off the "Use Easy Install" option. You'll be sent to a screen describing the virtual machine you're setting up, including the memory you'll devote to it, maximum size of disk space it will use, and so on (Figure 1-19). Your best bet is to accept them and click Finish. On the next screen, give your machine a name or accept the one VMware Fusion gives you, click Save, and sit back while installation starts (Figure 1-20).

As with Parallels, select Custom when asked for the type of Windows 8 installation you want to perform and select the Mac's hard drive.

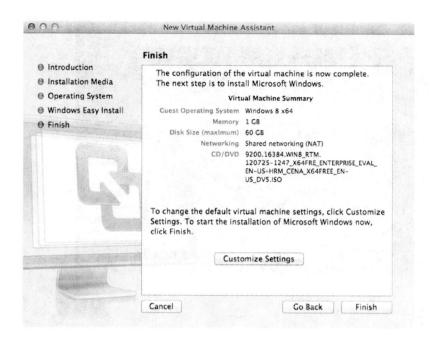

Figure 1-19.
Getting towards the end of getting VMWare Fusion ready to install Windows 8

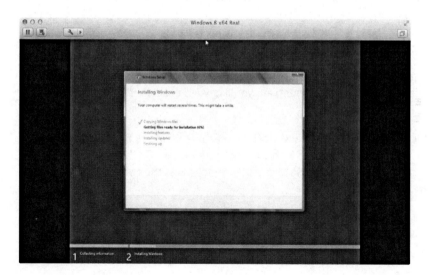

Figure 1-20.
VMWare Fusion installing Windows 8

After the usual Windows setup routine, you'll be running a copy of Windows 8 on your Mac, as you can see in Figure 1-21.

Figure 1-21.
Windows 8 running on VMWare Fusion

Running Windows 8 Using VirtualBox

Your final choice for running Windows 8 in a virtual machine is to use the free Virtual-Box software (*http://www.virtualbox.org*). The concepts for installing Windows 8 on it are identical to those for Parallels Desktop and VMWare Fusion, so this section is going to move pretty quickly. Refer back to the earlier sections if you need to.

One thing to keep in mind is that with VirtualBox, you can't migrate Windows 8 from a PC to your Mac, so if that's your plan, you'll have to use either Parallels Desktop or VMWare Fusion.

Install VirtualBox on your Mac and start it up. Grab a Windows 8 DVD disc, or an *.iso* file ready for installing Windows 8. In VirtualBox, click New. On the next screen, name your virtual machine, and choose Microsoft Windows 8 as the operating system. Click Continue.

On the next screen you're asked how much RAM to devote to Windows 8 (Figure 1-22). The default is 2 GB, but some people have reported being able to use only 1 GB. I suggest going with the default.

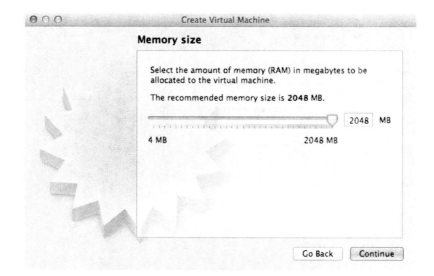

Figure 1-22.
Choosing how much RAM to devote to Windows 8 in VirtualBox

Next, you're asked to create a virtual hard drive. You've got several other options here. Go with the default size of 25GB and click Create. For the type of hard drive to create, you've got half a dozen choices. For example, one of them is to create an HDD (Parallels Hard Disk), in which case you'll also be able to use it with Parallels Desktop if the sun and stars align. But your best bet here is to go with the default, VDI (VirtualBox Disk Image).

After that, you're asked whether the hard drive should be of a fixed size or one that dynamically changes according to how much space it requires. The default is to choose a dynamically allocated drive, and I've found that to be a good choice. If you prefer, you can instead choose "Fixed size." That partition will take longer to create than a dynamically allocated one; however, it might lead to faster performance.

After all that, you come to a screen summarizing the name of the virtual drive and the size you've told it to be. You can make final changes here. Otherwise, click Create and the hard drive is created (Figure 1-23).

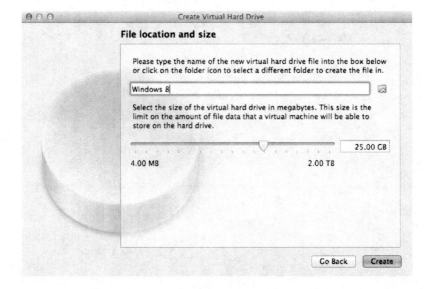

Figure 1-23.
Creating the virtual hard drive in VirtualBox where you'll install Windows 8

At that point, you've created a virtual hard drive and machine where you'll install Windows 8. You'll be sent to a screen, shown in Figure 1-24, that summarizes all of the settings you've chosen for when you install Windows 8. The screen lists all of your virtual machines. Click Windows 8. If you're adventurous, you can try fiddling around with these settings, such as for how much video memory to use, and so on. But keep in mind that they've been pre-chosen to work well with Windows 8, so my suggestion is to stay with the defaults.

Now you're ready to install Windows 8. Select the Windows 8 machine you've just created and click Start. On the next screen, select either the disc where you have the Windows 8 installation DVD, or else the *.iso* file you're going to use. Then click Start. From here on, it's just like a normal Windows 8 installation.

See Also

- Hack #07, "Use Hyper-V to Install and Run Other Operating Systems Inside Windows 8"

HACK 07 # Use Hyper-V to Install and Run Other Operating Systems Inside Windows 8

Have the need to run other versions of Windows—or even Linux—inside Windows 8? Here's how to do it.

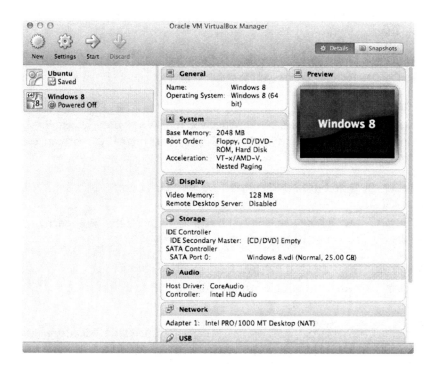

Figure 1-24.
The VirtualBox manager

Some people need to run multiple versions of Windows, including Windows Vista and Windows 7, either for testing purposes, for development, or just because they're enthusiasts. That used to mean buying and maintaining multiple computers.

If you've got Window 8 Pro or Windows 8 Enterprise, though, there's a much better way—Hyper-V. This software lets you run virtual machines in Windows 8, each running their own operating system. Hyper-V works in much the same way as other virtualized environments (see Hack #06, "Installing and Running Windows 8 on a Mac"). For each instance of an operating system you want to test, you create a virtual machine into which you install the operating system, using either a physical disc or an *.iso* file.

Note: If you don't have Windows 8 Pro or Windows 8 Enterprise, there's still a way to run other operating systems inside Windows 8. Get the free VirtualBox software (http://www.virtualbox.org). For details about using it, see the VirtualBox section of Hack #06, "Installing and Running Windows 8 on a Mac".

Hyper-V has some specific hardware requirements, so before getting started, get familiar with them:

Hyper-V only works on 64-bit versions of Windows 8

So if you've got a 32-bit version, you're out of luck.

You need at least 4 GB of RAM

Also, keep in mind that more is better. When you run a VM, it uses system RAM, and Windows 8 is using system RAM as well. If you have more RAM, you can run more VMs simultaneously.

Your hardware must be 64-bit and support Second Level Address Translation (SLAT)

If you've got a relatively new machine, it probably supports this. But machines with older dual-core processors probably won't cut it.

You won't be able to connect to hardware attached to your PC

So you won't, for example, be able to make use of a USB flash drive or other USB device.

If you're not sure whether Hyper-V will work on your system, don't fret, because when you try to install and use Hyper-V, it will tell you if it won't work.

By default, Hyper-V isn't enabled on Windows 8, so you've got to turn it on. Go to the Control Panel and select Programs→"Turn Windows features on or off." You'll see a screen like the one shown in Figure 1-25. Scroll to the Hyper-V section and turn on the checkbox next to it. Expand the category and make sure that all of the boxes underneath it are turned on as well. Then click OK.

Note: If the box next to Hyper-V is grayed out, that means that your Windows 8 PC can't run it.

Windows will spend a little while finding the files. You'll be prompted to reboot Windows 8 in order to complete the installation. After you reboot, click the Hyper-V Manager tile that's been added to the Start screen.

To create a new virtual machine, click the name of your Windows 8 device on the left side of the screen. Then, in the Actions panel on the right, select New→Virtual Machine, as shown in Figure 1-26.

Figure 1-25.
Enabling Hyper-V

Figure 1-26.
Starting to create a Virtual Machine

A wizard launches. Click Next. You're asked to give your new VM a name (Figure 1-27). Be as clear and descriptive as possible, because you might create multiple VMs and want to easily distinguish among them. At a minimum, it's a good idea to include the version of the operating system, such as Windows 7.

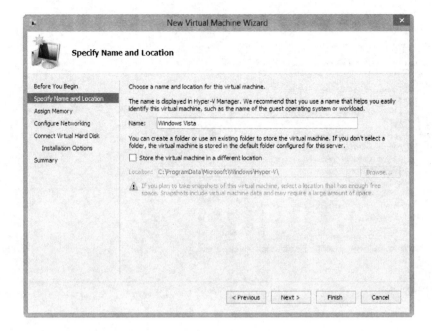

Figure 1-27.
Naming your Virtual Machine

You're also asked whether to use the default location for storing the VM's file, which is *C:\Program Data\Microsoft\Windows\Hyper-V*. Generally, using the default is a good idea. However, if you've got a relatively small hard disk, you should consider storing the files on a different physical hard disk than your main one, because each VM uses a substantial amount of hard disk space, generally more than 25 GB.

Click Next after making your choice. On the next screen, you're asked how much startup memory to use, and whether to use dynamic memory for the virtual machine. Consider the requirements of the operating system you're going to install, and use that amount. If you've got a lot of memory on your computer, turn on the box next to "Use Dynamic Memory for this virtual machine." Doing so allows Hyper-V to grow and shrink the amount of memory the VM uses. It's an especially useful option if you're going to run more than one VM at a time. Click Next.

Now you'll come to a screen that lets you configure networking for the VM. At first it appears there's no way to do this, because in the Connection drop-down box, there's only one choice: Not Connected. You'll need to create a virtual switch in order to connect to a network and the Internet. Back on the Hyper-V Manager main screen, click Virtual Switch Manager at right. On the next screen, select External, and then click Create Virtual Switch. On the screen that appears, give it a name if you want (Figure 1-28). If you've got more than one network adapter, select it from the drop-down list. Click OK when you're done.

Figure 1-28.
Creating a virtual switch to enable networking

Once you've done that, go back to the wizard, select the new network connection from the drop-down list, and then click Next. On the screen that appears, you'll create a virtual hard disk in which to run your operating system. Again, check the operating system you're installing to find out installation requirements. Generally, if you're going to install Windows 7, you'll do fine with the default size of 127 GB. Click Next.

> *Note: You'll need to have a registered version of Windows to run it on Hyper-V. It can't have the same registration code as the version you run on your PC, unless you have the rights to run it on multiple devices.*

On the next screen, you tell the wizard where to find the installation media for the operating system, such as a disc or *.iso* file. Make your selection, and you're ready to run your new VM. You'll go through the normal operating system installation process the first time you run it, but after then, you won't need to run the installation process each time.

To run a VM, launch the Hyper-V Manager and run it from there.

Hacking the Hack

If you want to give Linux a whirl, install it as a VM in Hyper-V Manager. Head to *http://www.ubuntu.com/download/desktop* and download the file you find there. It will be an *.iso* file. Go through the installation procedure I outlined in this hack, and use that *.iso* file as the Linux installation medium.

See Also

- Hack #06, "Installing and Running Windows 8 on a Mac"

2

Hacking the Start Screen, the Windows 8 Interface, and Apps

The new Windows 8 main interface—once called Metro, and now simply called Windows 8—is one of the biggest changes to Windows in several generations. Its Start screen sports big tiles, many of which are live and supply you with information without your doing anything. Windows 8 apps (which were once called Metro apps and which I call Windows 8 native apps) are specifically written for this new interface and also look different from anything you've seen in Windows before. For example, they lack menus and controls in their main interfaces and run full-screen.

This new Windows 8 interface and its apps may not seem hackable, but there's plenty you can get at, and you'll find out how to do that in this chapter. Whether you want to hack your way through the new Start screen, force Windows 8 apps to run side by side, or more, you'll find it here.

HACK 08   Create an Application Folder for Quick Launches on the Start Screen and the Desktop

Looking for a quick way to launch Desktop apps from the Windows 8 Start screen or from anywhere, for that matter? Here's how to do it, using the hidden Application Folder.

Once upon a time, in earlier versions of Windows, if you wanted to run an application but didn't see its icon anywhere, there was a quick and simple solution: Head to the Application folder, look for the proper subfolder, and find the *.exe* file that launches the program.

That's all well and good for earlier versions of Windows. But you won't find the Applications Folder visible in Windows 8.

It may not be visible, but it's still there, and you can use it for a nifty hack: quickly launching any app—including Windows 8 and Desktop apps—from either the Windows 8 Start screen or the desktop.

First, run File Explorer (previously known as Windows Explorer). Navigate to the Desktop, and create a new folder. After you create it, rename it:

`Applications.{4234d49b-0245-4df3-b780-3893943456e1}`

On the Desktop and in File Explorer, you'll see only its name—Applications. Double-click it, and you'll see a list of your applications: Windows 8 apps, Desktop apps, and many system apps, such as Control Panel (Figure 2-1). Windows 8 apps, oddly enough, don't appear at first to have any icons associated with them, but Desktop apps and system apps do. To run an app—including Windows 8 native apps—double-click it. (If you look closely enough in a folder, you can see the icons for Windows 8 native apps. They have white symbols on a white background.)

Figure 2-1.
The Applications folder includes Windows 8 native apps as well as Desktop apps

That takes care of the Application Folder on the Desktop. But the folder doesn't show up anywhere on the Windows 8 Start screen. Not yet, that is. Right-click it and select "Pin to Start." It's now pinned to the Start screen. To find it, scroll all the way over to the right. Double-click it, and the folder opens, with all your apps only a double-click away.

If you like, move it to a more prominent location on the Start screen by dragging it.

See Also

- Hack #09, "Put a Tile to Computer on the Start Screen"
- Hack #10, "Force Desktop Apps to Show up on the Start Screen"
- Hack #12, "Add Folders and Other Objects to the Start Screen"

HACK 09 Put a Tile to Computer on the Start Screen

Do you miss having one-click access to the Computer folder in Windows 8? Here's how to put a tile to it on the Start screen.

Here's a hack for everyone who longs to get to the Computer folder in Windows 8 quickly. It's simple to do.

Open File Explorer and go to *C:\Users\User Name\AppData\Roaming\Microsoft\Windows\Start Menu* where User Name is your account in Windows. You should see the *\Programs* folder. Right-click the folder and select Create Shortcut. The shortcut created will be called *Programs – Shortcut*. Right-click it and select Properties. Click the Shortcut tab, and in the Target box, delete what's there, and instead type this:

```
C:\Windows\explorer.exe explorer.exe /root,,::{20D04FE0-3AEA-1069-A2D8-
08002B30309D}
```

Go to the General Tab and rename the shortcut Computer. Then click OK (Figure 2-2).

A tile to launch Computer then appears on the Start screen (Figure 2-3).

Hacking the Hack

If you'd like, you can change the tiles icon on the Start screen. Using File Explorer, right-click the shortcut you've created on the Desktop, select Properties, and go to the Shortcut tab. Click Change Icon, and select an icon (Figure 2-4). That becomes the picture on the tile (Figure 2-5).

See Also

- Hack #08, "Create an Application Folder for Quick Launches on the Start Screen and the Desktop"
- Hack #10, "Force Desktop Apps to Show up on the Start Screen"
- Hack #12, "Add Folders and Other Objects to the Start Screen"

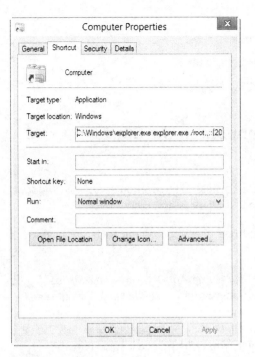

Figure 2-2.
Creating a shortcut to Computer

Figure 2-3.
The Computer tile on the Start screen

Figure 2-4.
Selecting an icon to appear on the tile

Figure 2-5.
The new icon on the tile on the Start screen

`HACK 10` Force Desktop Apps to Show up on the Start Screen

> Sometimes when you install a Desktop app it doesn't show up on the Start screen. Here's a way to make sure it appears.

When you install a Desktop app, its tile is supposed to show up on the Start screen, so you can run the app even from the Start screen by clicking it. I say "supposed to," because I've noticed that's not always the case. In fact, on one of my Windows 8 machines, when I installed Microsoft Office 2010, *none* of those apps showed up on the Start screen.

Tip: When you install a new Desktop App, its tile typically shows up all the way on the right of the Start screen, so you'll have to do some scrolling to find it.

There's a simple way to make the tiles appear, though. When you're on the Start screen, type the name of the app (Figure 2-6).

Figure 2-6.
The first step in adding a Desktop app to the Start screen

The app will appear on the left side of the screen. Right-click it or, on a touchscreen, slide it down a quarter of an inch. A checkmark appears next to it (Figure 2-7). At the bottom of the screen, you'll find a series of actions you can take. Click "Pin to Start," and the app's tile will be pinned to the Start screen.

You can now run the app from the Start screen by clicking its tile. To unpin it, right-click the tile and select "Unpin from Start." (On a touchscreen, you can slide the tile down a quarter of an inch until the checkmark appears, and then select "Unpin from Start" from the App Bar.)

See Also

- Hack #08, "Create an Application Folder for Quick Launches on the Start Screen and the Desktop"
- Hack #09, "Put a Tile to Computer on the Start Screen"
- Hack #12, "Add Folders and Other Objects to the Start Screen"

HACK 11 Hack the Windows 8 All Apps Screen

Didn't know that Window 8 had an Apps screen? You're not alone. Here's how to get to it, and how to hack it

Switching to Windows 8 from an earlier version of Windows can be a disconcerting experience, notably because it's so difficult to figure out which Desktop apps you've got installed. It's easy to find your Windows 8 native apps, because they're front and center on the Start screen. But that's not the case for Desktop apps, since they mostly don't show up on the Start screen. In earlier versions of Windows, you could always click the Start button and browse through them that way. But in Windows 8, the Start button has been sent into the Great Beyond. What to do?

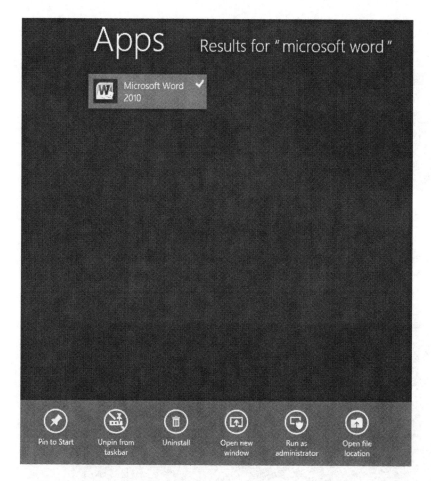

Figure 2-7.
The first step in adding a Desktop app to the Start screen

Although it's not immediately apparent, there is a way to browse through all your Desktop apps, using the "All apps" option that shows all of your Desktop apps (in addition to all of your Windows 8 native apps).

On the Start screen, either right-click an empty space, or else press Windows key+Z. That opens the App Bar. There's only one thing you can do here: click the "All apps" button at the lower right (Figure 2-8). (On a touch screen, slide in from the bottom of the touchscreen to open the App Bar.)

Figure 2-8.
Click here to see all of the apps installed in Windows 8

When you do that, you'll come to the "All apps" screen. It does exactly what it says: it shows you all the apps on your system. On the left, you'll find all the Windows 8 native apps, and to the right, the Desktop apps (Figure 2-9). Click any one to run it.

Figure 2-9.
The "All apps" screen

Notice that the Desktop apps on the righthand side are organized into groups— Windows Accessories, Windows Ease of Access, Windows System, and so on. If you've installed software, you'll notice that those apps may be in their own groups as well.

How does this mysterious organization happen? Very simply, as it turns out. It mimics the structure of two folders on your device. Any subfolders in those folders show up as groups on this screen—for example, the Windows Accessories group. Also, all the shortcuts in those folders show up as apps inside the group on this screen.

WINDOWS 8 HACKS

To change the organization of Desktop groups and apps on the "All apps" screen, you only need to change the shortcut and folder structure in those two folders.

The two folders are:

- *C: ProgramData\Microsoft\Windows\Start Menu\Programs*
- *C:\Users\UserName\AppData\Roaming\Microsoft\Windows\Start Menu\Programs*

UserName is your Windows 8 account name. *C: ProgramData\Microsoft\Windows \Start Menu\Programs* has all the apps that all users of the system will see, and *C:\Users\UserName\AppData\Roaming\Microsoft\Windows\Start Menu\Programs* has those that show up for an individual user.

Tip: You don't have to spend time in File Explorer navigating to these two folders. There's a quicker way to get to each. Press Windows key+R to get to the run box, type **Shell:common programs,** *and press Enter. That sends you to C:ProgramData \Microsoft\Windows\Start Menu\Programs. If you instead type* **Shell:programs** *and press Enter, you'll go to C:\Users\UserName\AppData\Roaming\Microsoft \Windows\Start Menu\Programs.*

Go into those folders, and add any folders that you want to show up as groups on the "All apps" screen. In those folders, add shortcuts to any apps you want to show up as part of those groups. Delete any folders and shortcuts that you don't want to appear.

See Also

- Hack #14, "Hack Your Way Through the Start Screen"

HACK 12 Add Folders and Other Objects to the Start Screen

Want to access a folder, file, or other object directly from the Start screen without using the Desktop or run File Explorer? Here's how to do it.

One of the nice things about older versions of Windows is the way you could access just about anything straight from the Desktop, like folders that you either put there directly or created shortcuts to. At first glance, it doesn't appear that it's possible to do the same thing with the Start screen.

In fact, though, it's not that tough to do. You simply open File Explorer, right-click the folder or file you want to put on the Start screen, and select "Pin to Start" (Figure 2-10).

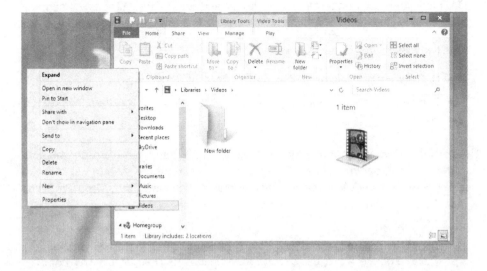

Figure 2-10.
The first step in adding a folder to the Start screen

When you do that, a new tile appears on the Start screen. Click to open it. That's all it takes. You may want to put the Libraries and Documents folders there, as well as any other folders you frequently access.

Don't stop with local folders, though. You can also put network locations on the Start screen. To do it, open File Explorer, and in the Network Location area, right-click any location and select "Pin to Start." In fact, you can even pin entire remote computers to the Start screen. In File Explorer, look in the Homegroup and Network folders on the left part of the screen, right-click the PC you'd like to access from the Start screen, and select "Pin to Start."

You can even pin various Windows resources and accessories as well. Go to *C:\ProgramData\Microsoft\Windows\Start Menu\Programs\Windows Accessories*, and you know the drill. Right-click any accessory and select "Pin to Start."

Note: You can't pin Desktop-based applications to the Start screen, aside from various Windows accessories and services, using this technique. To pin Desktop applications to the Start menu, see Hack #10, "Force Desktop Apps to Show up on the Start Screen".

Hacking the Hack

You can even pin websites to the Start screen. To do it, run the Windows 8 native version of Internet Explorer, and when you're on a website you want pinned, click the Pin icon to the right of the address bar at the bottom of the screen. If you want, rename the website in the screen that pops up, or leave it as is. Either way, click "Pin to Start" from the screen that appears, and it will be done.

See Also

- Hack #08, "Create an Application Folder for Quick Launches on the Start Screen and the Desktop"
- Hack #09, "Put a Tile to Computer on the Start Screen"
- Hack #10, "Force Desktop Apps to Show up on the Start Screen"

HACK 13 Run Windows 8 Native Apps Side by Side

> Windows 8 native apps run only full-screen, all by their lonesome, right? Not if you use this hack.

Windows 8 native apps are designed to take up your computer's full screen all by themselves—they're what Microsoft calls *immersive* applications. Unlike Desktop apps, you can't resize them so you can see multiple apps on your screen.

Well, not quite. There is a way to run Windows 8 native apps side by side on your screen, as you'll see in this hack, using a feature that Microsoft calls Snap.

First, make sure you're running two or more Windows 8 native apps. What you do next depends on whether you're using a tablet (or other touchscreen device), or a PC or laptop. If you're using a PC or laptop, move your mouse cursor to the top-left corner of the screen, then move it down, and you'll see all of your currently running apps (Figure 2-11). Drag and drop an app's thumbnail onto the screen (Figure 2-12).

Tip: When you drag and drop the thumbnail, don't drag it too far to the right. If you do, the app you just dragged will take up the full screen by itself.

When you do that, the second app runs in a sidebar along the lefthand side of the screen. You can interact with one app at a time by clicking it (Figure 2-13).

Figure 2-11.
The first step in running two Windows 8 native apps side by side: showing all your currently running apps

Figure 2-12.
Drag and drop the app you want to run side by side with the currently running app

WINDOWS 8 HACKS

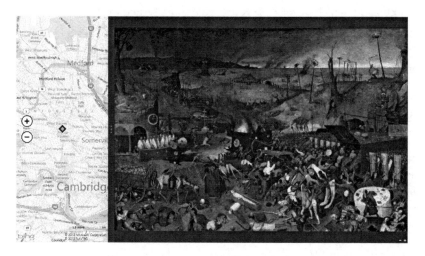

Figure 2-13.
Two Windows 8 native apps running side by side

If you look closely, you'll see that there's a border on the right side of the app running in the sidebar, with three dots on it. Use that to resize the app in the sidebar by making it take up more or less of the screen—drag it to the right or the left.

If you're using a tablet or other touchscreen device, to display your current running apps, swipe slowly from the left and then pull back your finger. That gesture displays the apps. Now drag and drop the app you want to run side by side with the currently running app. Control the size by dragging the border of the app running in the sidebar, just as you would with a mouse.

Note: Running apps side by side makes use of Windows 8's semantic zoom capabilities. Instead of zooming out to levels where you can no longer distinguish individual characters, Windows 8 uses semantic zoom to display the data as clearly as possible.

HACK 14 Hack Your Way Through the Start Screen

The Windows 8 Start screen is eminently hackable. Here's how to bend it to your will.

The Start screen is the most important location in all of Windows 8. Even if you mainly use Desktop apps like Office, you'll still spend plenty of time there. It's command central, and also the place you're automatically sent to when you log into Windows. (Unless you use Hack #18, "Bring Back the Windows Start Menu to Windows 8", which lets you head directly to the Desktop instead.)

Here's a handful of hacks that will help you get the Start screen working exactly the way you want it to.

Add and Remove Tiles

The apps you see when you log into the Start screen are probably not the apps you want to see there. No worries: It's a breeze to add and remove tiles from the Start screen.

First a little background about which apps show up on the Start screen. Not every app appears there; there are plenty of others buried on your computer that don't show up. Exactly why some apps show up and others don't is a bit of a mystery, but in general, the apps there are the ones you use frequently, or that Microsoft *thinks* you'll use frequently, or, more likely, *wants* you to use frequently.

Say there's an app whose tile you want to remove from the Start screen. Simply right-click an app and select "Unpin from Start" from the menu that appears at the bottom of the screen. You can select multiple apps this way and remove them in one fell swoop.

> *Tip: You can also use a keyboard to select an app to remove (Figure 2-14). Get to it by using the arrow keys, and when you're there, press the space bar. If you're using a tablet, drag down on the tile to select it.*

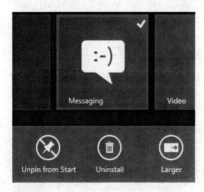

Figure 2-14.
Selecting an app to remove from the Start screen

Adding tiles takes a little more work, but it's still quite easy. If you know the name of the app you want to add, when you're on the Start screen, type its name. You're sent to the search screen, with the app on the left part of the screen. Right-click it, and from the menu that appears at the bottom of the screen, select "Pin To Start."

If you're not sure which app you want to pin and want to see what's available, you can see a list of every app you have (Figure 2-15). Press Windows key+Z, select the "All apps" button, and you'll see every app on your PC. Then select it and add it as outlined in this hack.

Figure 2-15.
The whole shebang: seeing all the apps on your computer

Customize Tiles

When you right-click an app to pin it to the Start screen, you'll notice you have many more choices than just pinning it. The choices you get vary according to the app you select. Here's the list and what each does:

- **Pin to Start**. You already know all about this one.
- **Unpin from Start**. If the tile's pinned to the Start screen, you can unpin it.
- **Pin to Taskbar**. You know this one from the tip earlier in this hack.
- **Unpin from Taskbar**. Simple and straightforward: it does what it says.
- **Uninstall**. Uninstalls the app.

- **Larger/Smaller**. Tiles in the Start screen are either large or small; this selection makes a small tile larger, or a large tile smaller.
- **Turn live tile on/off**. Live tiles grab information from the Internet and display that information right on the tile. For example, the Mail app displays the number of email messages in your inbox, and also displays the sender and basic information from each. If you don't want that tile to be live like that, turn it off. If you come across a live tile that isn't on, you can turn it on from here.
- **Clear selection**. If you choose more than one tile, the Clear selection option appears, and most other options go away. Selecting this clears every app you've selected, not just the last one.

Create and Customize Tile Groups

The apps on your Start screen are roughly organized into groups—ten grouped into their own large rectangle, for example. There doesn't seem to be much rhyme or reason to these groups. Why is Maps grouped with Store and Mail, for example?

You can easily customize the existing groups and create groups of your own. And you can also more logically organize which apps go into which groups as well.

Creating a new group is easy. Drag a tile away from an existing group. When you drag it far enough away from the group, and it's also far enough away from other groups, a vertical bar appears (Figure 2-16). When you see the bar, you can drop the tile, and a new group is formed. Now just drag other tiles into the group, or add them using the techniques described in this hack, and you're done.

That's just the start, though. You can do more with the group as well, like giving it a name (Figure 2-17). Hover your mouse over the bottom right corner of the Start screen and click the – icon. All of your groups and tiles will minimize to small thumbnails. Right-click a group and a Name Group icon appears at the bottom of the screen. Click the icon, type the group's name, and you're done. You can also move the group to a different location on the Start screen. Just drag it where you want it to be and drop it.

Change Your Theme

Your Windows 8 theme is really nothing more than a combination of two colors— a background color and a foreground color. You can change it when you want, although Microsoft plays design police, letting you choose only from certain pre-built combinations.

To change the theme colors, press Windows key+I, then select Change PC Settings at the bottom of the Settings pane. From the right section of the screen, select Start

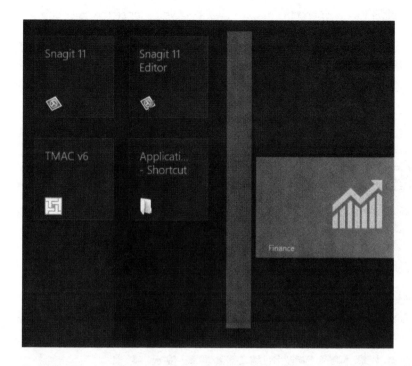

Figure 2-16.
Creating a new group

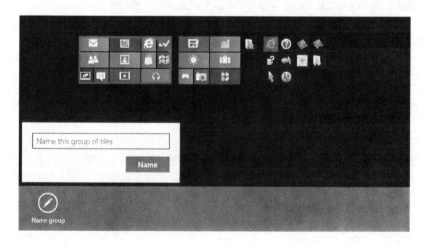

Figure 2-17.
Naming a new group

Screen and select the color combination you want. As you choose the color combination, you see it reflected in the preview screen above it. You can also choose the kind of background patterns you want from the choices just above the color strip and below the preview (Figure 2-18).

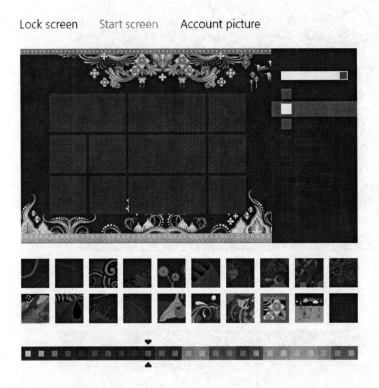

Figure 2-18.
Changing the Start screen's colors

Note: Changing the theme affects only the Start screen, not the Desktop.

Controlling Live Tile Behavior

Windows 8 gives you some control over how Live tiles behave. To do it, display the Charms bar by pressing Windows key+C, and then clicking Settings→Tiles. If you'd like to clear all information currently displayed on your tiles, click Clear (Figure 2-19). The old information vanishes, and only new information will show up.

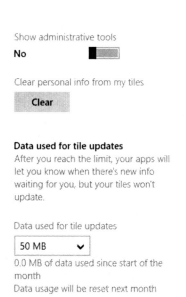

Show administrative tools

No

Clear personal info from my tiles

Clear

Data used for tile updates
After you reach the limit, your apps will
let you know when there's new info
waiting for you, but your tiles won't
update.

Data used for tile updates

50 MB ⌄

0.0 MB of data used since start of the
month
Data usage will be reset next month

Figure 2-19.
Among other things, you can wipe your Live tiles clean and start fresh

If your service provider charges you for bandwidth or has a bandwidth limit, you can
save on bandwidth by limiting the amount of data Live tiles use. Go to the "Data used
for tile updates" section, and from the drop-down menu, choose how much data you
want to allow for updating your tiles with new information. You can choose from 50
MB, 100 MB, 200 MB, 300 MB, 400 MB, and unlimited. Those numbers refer to the
amount of data use in a given month. Once you reach the limit for Live tiles you've set
for that month—100 MB, for example—the tiles will tell you that there's new information, but won't display it.

> *Tip: On the top of the Tiles Settings screen you'll notice an odd option: "Show
> administrative tools." Normally it's turned off. If you turn it on, a whole host of
> Windows 8 administrative tools show up as tiles on the Windows 8 Start screen—
> Disk Cleanup, Device Manager, and many others. And if install you the Remote
> Server Administration Tools to use Windows 8 as a management workstation for
> your networking environment, this folder gets filled with even more tools.*

See Also

- Hack #11, "Hack the Windows 8 All Apps Screen"

There's a lot more to Windows 8 Search than you think. Here's how to get the most out of it.

The basic Windows 8 search is straightforward: press Windows key+Q, highlight what you want to search (Apps, Settings, Files, and so on) and Windows 8 does your bidding. Simple, but not particularly powerful.

There's a lot more to Search than meets the eye, though. You can use it to search for financial information, sports, information, maps, and even through your email—without having to go through the relevant app. So if you're in the middle of using Word or Internet Explorer, say, and you want to search through your email or through maps, you can do it.

As always when doing a search, press Windows key+Q. Then highlight the app through which you want to search, for example, Maps or Mail. When you do that, the app itself launches on the left side of the screen, and your search box stays on the right side (Figure 2-20). Now type your search term.

Figure 2-20.
Searching through Maps

What happens next varies according to the app you're searching. When you do a search this way, you'll see results delivered however the app normally delivers results. So the results for Mail, for example, differ from the results for Maps.

You also need to understand the various types of search parameters you can use for the various Windows 8 apps. Most are self-explanatory—type in your search term, what else? But for others, some guidance is in order. Here's what you need to know.

Mail

Type a search term, and you search through subject, sender, email address, and body. If you'd like, though, you can launch a specialized search, for example, searching for specific senders, for specific subject lines, and so on. So to search for all the email messages that have the word "tennis" in the subject line, you'd type this:

```
Subject: Tennis
```

You can also search using From: and To: And you can search by date, like this:

```
Date: 7/20/2012
```

Finance

You can do normal searches here, and also search using a company's stock ticker symbol, such as MSFT for Microsoft and AAPL for Apple.

Maps

This search uses Bing Maps. Obviously, you can search for locations here. But you can do more than that—you can also find stores, services, and other information as well. So if you want to find restaurants in Cambridge, MA, simply type that into the search box, and that's what you'll find (Figure 2-21).

Figure 2-21.
Finding restaurants using the Maps search

There's plenty of other information you can find this way. Try searching for a certain type of store, a park in an area, and so on.

Music

Search by artist, album, and song. You can search your own music collection as well as the new Microsoft Marketplace.

More Search Hacks

Windows 8 also gives you some control over overall search behavior, including which apps show up in search and whether Windows saves your searches so you can run them again (Figure 2-22).

To control this and more, press Windows key+I to get to Settings, then select Change PC Settings→Search. (On a touch screen, slide in from the right side of the screen and select Settings, then select Change PC Settings→Search.) The bottom part of the screen shows you all the apps you can search in. Turn off any you don't want to show up in Search, and turn on any that you want to show up but aren't showing up. (Keep in mind this setting controls only Windows 8-native apps, not Desktop apps.)

If you'd like Windows to show the apps you search most commonly at the top of the screen when you do a search, turn on "Show the apps I search most often at the top." If you turn that off, they'll display in alphabetical order. This screen also lets you delete your search history, and you can tell Windows whether it should save your searches, so when you type the first few letters, your previous searches pop up so you can select them. That way, you'll save keystrokes. On the other hand, it also lets other people who use the device know what you're searching for, so if that concerns you, turn off the setting.

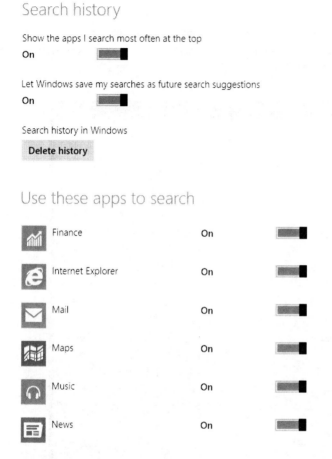

Search history

Show the apps I search most often at the top

On

Let Windows save my searches as future search suggestions

On

Search history in Windows

Delete history

Use these apps to search

Finance	On	
Internet Explorer	On	
Mail	On	
Maps	On	
Music	On	
News	On	

Figure 2-22.
Controlling the way Windows 8 searches

HACK 16 Use the Task Manager to Track App Use

Here's how to dig deep into the innards of your app use—and track down apps that aren't behaving well.

Which apps take up most of your CPU time or use the network most? Which Windows 8 native apps use the most bandwidth for updating their live tiles? Which apps are running right now? Which may be causing problems for your Windows 8 PC?

If you're the kind of person for whom these are burning questions (and if you're reading this book, they probably are), this hack is for you.

You can find all that and more using the Task Manager (Figure 2-23). This tool has been considerably tweaked and improved since previous versions of Windows, and it's particularly useful when you want to know everything there is to know about app use.

Run the Task Manager by pressing Ctrl+Alt+Delete and choosing Task Manager. If you're on the Windows 8 Start screen, you can also run it by typing `Task Manager` and then clicking its icon when it appears on the left portion of the screen.

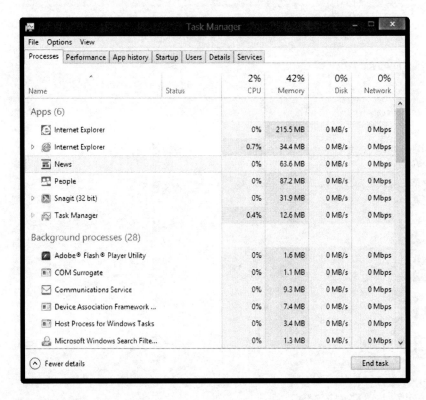

Figure 2-23.
Showing which apps are currently running, and what they're up to

Click the Processes tab. At the very top of the screen, you'll see the Apps section. It lists the number of apps currently running, and then beneath that, lists each app individually. You'll see four columns to the right of each app with this information:

CPU

Shows how much of the CPU any individual app is taking up. The number is listed as a percentage, so it shows you how much of your total CPU capacity each app takes up. If your PC is sluggish, it's a good idea to head here, because this is where you'll be able to track down any CPU hogs. Simply sort on this column and you'll find your culprit easily.

Memory

Lists the total amount of memory each app uses. If you've got a sluggish PC, sort on this column to see whether you've got a memory hog running.

Disk

Shows whether any app is currently writing to disk, and if it is, shows you its speed in megabytes per second. If your PC seems to be slow, and you notice that its disk light is flashing frequently, you may have a rogue app that's spending a lot of time accessing the disk and slowing things down. That's when you'd go here.

Network

Shows you the network use of any individual app.

Tip: The Task Manager is particularly useful for tracking down which Windows 8 native apps are running, because often you don't know which are running and which aren't. Unlike Desktop apps, Windows 8 native apps run only full-screen, so you can look at a glance and see which are currently running.

You may notice that some apps have small right-facing triangles next to them. If that's the case, it means the app has several tasks running simultaneously. For example, Internet Explorer may have a triangle next to it if you're currently downloading a file or have multiple tabs open (Figure 2-24).

Click the triangle to see all of the app's separate tasks. To switch to that task, simply double-click it.

Note: It's not uncommon that you'll see two separate icons for Internet Explorer in the Task Manager. That's because Windows 8 has two versions of Internet Explorer —the Windows 8 native app version, and the Desktop version. The Windows 8 native app version shows up as a solid blue square with the E icon knocked out in white. The Desktop app version has the E in blue against a white background. The two versions of Internet Explorer run separately, so that you can have one set of sites open in one version, and another set of sites open in the other version. The Windows 8 native app version doesn't show the tabs open in separate processes here on the Task Manager; only the Desktop version does.

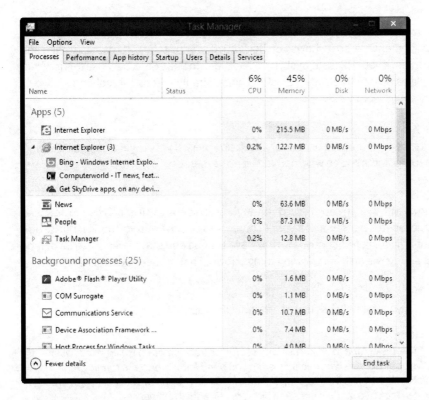

Figure 2-24.
Internet Explorer showing multiple tabs open

Delving into the App Innards

You can get plenty more information about each app, and do more as with it well, if you right-click (Figure 2-25). Right-click an app, and here's what you can do:

Switch to

Lets you jump straight to the app.

End task

Kills the app. This is a good choice when you find an app that's hogging your CPU or memory, and your PC is sluggish, or when an app is unresponsive for quite some time.

Resource values

Lets you change the way the Task Manager displays memory, disk, and network use. For each, you can have it display the usage either as a percent or an actual value—for example, 229.6 MB in the case of memory use.

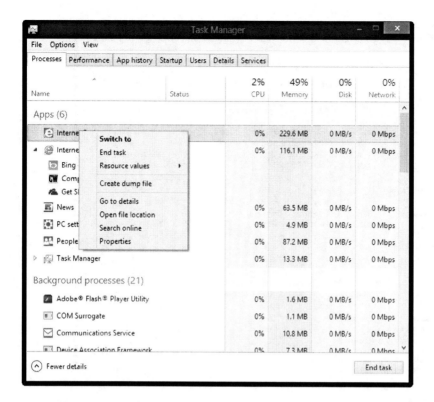

Figure 2-25.
Your choices when you right-click an app

Create dump file

This choice is for programmers, or it may come in handy for someone who's helping you with tech support. A dump file provides detailed information about the current state of an app, useful for debugging. For helpful information about dump files, see *http://support.microsoft.com/kb/315263*.

Go to details

Want more details about any individual app? Choose this option (Figure 2-26) and you'll see more than you can imagine. For each app, for example, you'll find out the name of the user running it (many are being run by the Windows 8 system, rather than a person, in which case they're labeled "SYSTEM.") You'll also get a description of the app, its status (running or suspended), and the file name. There's also the mysterious PID. That's shorthand for Process Identifier, and it identifies the order in which the app was spawned from the Windows kernel. It's mainly useful for techie troubleshooting.

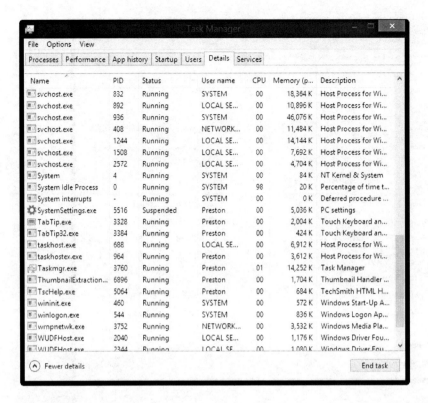

Figure 2-26.
Getting even more details about any app

Open file location

Select this to open the folder in which the app's executable file lives. Then you can use the file's icon for tasks such as creating Desktop shortcuts. Right-click the file and select Create Shortcut. You can pin it to the Taskbar that way as well.

Search online

Search for information about the executable file online in Internet Explorer (or your default browser). For example, if you notice an unfamiliar app and you're worried that it's dangerous, doing an online search usually turns up any reports of malicious behavior.

Properties

Here's where you can get even more information about an app, including its size, the location and name of its executable file, the day it was created, when it was last accessed, and so on (Figure 2-27).

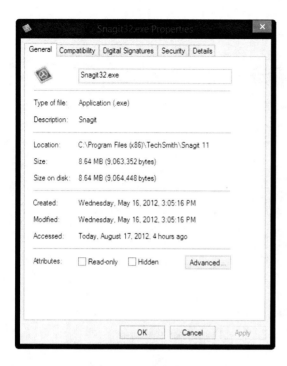

Figure 2-27.
Yes, here's even more details about an app

Checking out an App's Usage History

So far, everything in this hack shows you the current state of your app. But the Task Manager can tell you something about the app's usage history as well, and in some detail. In the Task Manager, click the "App history" tab, which reports on each app's usage history for a specific time period (Figure 2-28). To see the time period, look toward the upper-left portion of the screen, just below the tabs. It tells the usage time period it's measuring. Here's what you'll find out:

CPU time

Shows the total amount of CPU time the app has used.

Network

Shows how much bandwidth the app has used.

Metered network

Shows how much bandwidth on a metered network the app has used. When you're using a metered network, you pay if you exceed a certain bandwidth in a given month, so this can be a very important number for you. (See Hack #72, "Hack Windows 8 Wi-Fi, Wireless, and Network Settings" for more details about metered networks.)

Tile updates

Shows how data the app's live tile has consumed.

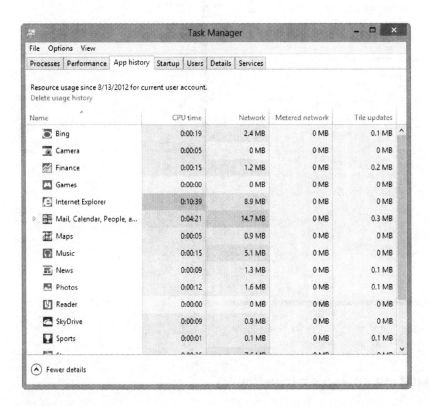

Figure 2-28.
The "App history" tab lets you trace what an app's been up to

---

Tip: Worried that a live tile is consuming too much data? Tell Windows 8 to stop the tile from grabbing live data. For details, see Hack #14, "Hack Your Way Through the Start Screen".

Hacking the Hack

Right-clicking an app and selecting Properties opens up a whole world of app and file management. You'll come to a dialog box (Figure 2-29) that lets you control many aspects of the app's executable file. It's a four-tabbed dialog box, bristling with options, so this section can't cover every possible option. Spend some time clicking around, and you'll discover plenty on your own.

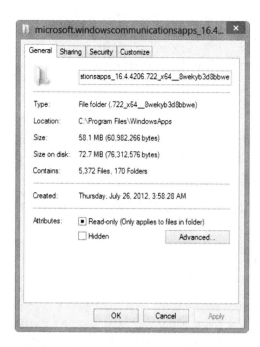

Figure 2-29.
The Properties dialog box: your entrée into a world of tweaking

On the General tab, in addition to getting information about the file such as its size and location, you can also choose to hide a file or make it read-only. Click the Advanced button, and you can tweak the folder that holds the file (Figure 2-30). Among other options, you can compress or encrypt the folder.

Figure 2-30.
Changing an app's folder settings

The Sharing tab lets you customize your sharing options. Click Advanced Sharing to get at even more options. Security lets you set permissions for who has access to the folder, and what kind of access they have; click the Edit and Advanced buttons to change those options. And the Customize tab lets you change the folder in a wide variety of ways.

See Also

- Hack #73, "Use Task Manager to Track Bandwidth Use of Individual Apps and Overall Network Use"

HACK 17 Use Your Own Graphic for Your User Account

You're not stuck with Windows 8's choices of picture for your user account. Here's a way to use any picture you desire.

The Windows graphic for your user account on the Start menu may not be to your taste. Worry not. You can put any picture there you want, as long as it's in the *gif*, *.jpg*, *.png*, or *.bmp* format. (Keep in mind, though, that *.bmp* files may cause your system to load more slowly because *.bmp* files tend to be very large.)

On the Windows Start screen, click your user account name and select "Change account picture" from the drop-down menu (Figure 2-31).

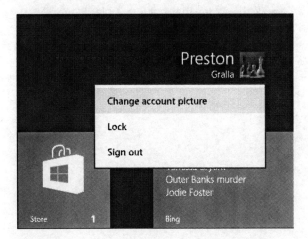

Figure 2-31.
The first step in changing your account picture

You're sent to the Personalize section of the PC settings area; specifically, to the "Account picture" setting screen (Figure 2-32).

Figure 2-32.
Command Central for changing your account picture

If you're using a device with a camera, at the bottom of the screen under "Create an account picture," you'll see a camera icon. Click the camera, and the Windows 8 Camera app launches. Look at the camera, smile, say "cheese", and click your mouse. A square appears on your screen (Figure 2-33). Reposition the square and resize it, and if you've got the picture you want, click OK. If you're not happy with it, click Retake.

Figure 2-33.
Smile and say "cheese!"

When you click OK, you're sent back to the PC Settings screen for setting your account picture. The photo shows up as your new account picture, and your old picture shows up below it (Figure 2-34). If you'd like to revert to your old account picture (not a bad idea if you've taken a photo like I did), click it. Otherwise, keep it (Figure 2-35).

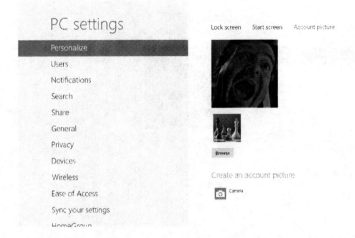

Figure 2-34.
The new account picture in the Settings area

Figure 2-35.
The new account picture onscreen

Your photo now shows up as your account picture. It is also used on the Login screen, the Start screen, and indeed any place that consumes Microsoft Account information.

Maybe you're not feeling particularly photogenic, or you have some pictures you'd prefer to use for your account. You can instead use a picture or photo on your computer, on SkyDrive, or on your network. On the "Account picture setting" screen, click Browse; your local Pictures folder opens. You can choose a picture from there, or keep browsing for more. Click "Go up" to navigate to the folder above that folder, which is the Libraries folder. From here, you can navigate to other folders.

Instead of choosing "Go up," you can click Files to see even more folders to navigate to. If you're looking for photos in SkyDrive, scroll down and click the SkyDrive icon. You can even navigate to folders on other computers on your network by using these navigational tools. Your best bet for finding pictures is in the Photos folder (Figure 2-36), because this shows photos from multiple locations—on your PC, on SkyDrive, on other devices on your network, and on Facebook.

Figure 2-36.
Browsing through your network for pictures to use for your account picture

Click the image you want to use as an account picture, then select "Choose image." You'll be back on the Account Picture setting screen, and that photo will be your new account picture. Below it, you'll see other account pictures you've used (Figure 2-37). Click any of those images to use it instead.

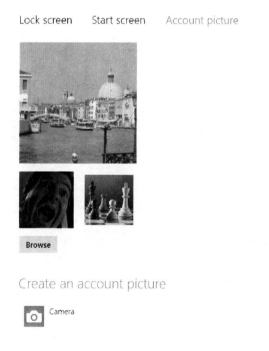

Figure 2-37.
Browsing through your network for pictures to use for your account picture

If you want to get rid of all the pictures other than your current account picture, right-click any picture just above the Browse button and select Clear History. All of the pictures in this window will go away, along with their cropping settings. (They won't be deleted from wherever you grabbed them, just cleared from this screen.)

3

Hacking the Desktop

Ah, the Desktop. Remember it? That's where, in previous versions of Windows, you were immediately sent when you logged into Windows.

With Windows 8, those days are gone. Instead, you head straight to the Start screen. It's as if Microsoft has become embarrassed by the Desktop and wishes you'd stay away. And in some ways, the Windows 8 Desktop isn't the same as in previous versions of Windows, notably because the Start button has been removed.

However, the truth is, if you use a traditional PC rather than a tablet, you'll be spending plenty of time on the Desktop and using Desktop apps, possibly even more time than you do on the Start screen. (After all, the Start screen and Windows 8 native apps are geared toward tablet users.)

That's where this chapter comes in. In it, I'll show you how to hack the Desktop and its apps to make the Desktop a true power user's tool again. Want to boot directly to the Desktop rather than the Start screen? I'll show you how to do that. Want to get back some of the features of the old Start screen? That's here as well. So are command-line hacks, getting back the Quick Launch toolbar, hacking File Explorer (previously called Windows Explorer) and more. As the saying goes, everything old is new again.

HACK 18   Bring Back the Windows Start Menu to Windows 8

> Are you a fan of the Start Menu that Microsoft banished from Windows 8? Fear not—there's a simple way to bring it back in all its glory.

Of the many decisions Microsoft made in designing Windows 8, eliminating the Start Menu was clearly the most controversial. In previous versions of Windows, the Start Menu was a kind of universal cockpit for Windows. It let you quickly find and launch applications, do searches, restart and shut down Windows, and much more.

Microsoft spent a fair amount of time not only taking away the Start Menu, but digging through Windows code to get rid of hand-done hacks that could bring it back. So many of the hacks for bringing it to Windows 8 that were available for preview versions of the operating system don't work on the final version.

However, there are two ways to bring it back, and to do much more as well—download and use Start8 from Stardock or StartFinity from WinAbility Software. They both bring back the Start Menu, and offer a kind of hacker's heaven of other hacks, including one that lets you boot directly to the Desktop, bypassing the Windows 8 Start screen.

Start8

To use Start 8, first head to the Stardock Win8 page (*http://www.stardock.com/products/start8/*). Click the "Get It Now" button and from the page that appears, click "Get it Now" again to buy it for $4.99, or click "Try it Free" for a thirty-day trial. If you click the button for a trial, you'll have to enter your email address. You'll then be sent an email that includes a link that you can click to download the application.

Install it, and you can configure how it works by clicking the appropriate button on the lefthand side of the screen, such as for the Start button's visual style, what items should be on it, and much more (Figure 3-1). Here's what each of the buttons control:

Style

This controls its visual style, such as its visual theme, whether it should be translucent, what the button should look like (including an image on your PC), and so on.

Configure

You've got plenty of options here, such as whether to show recently used applications, what shortcuts you want on the menu, whether to open submenus when you pause on them with the mouse pointer, how many icons the menu should have, and what the power button should do.

Control

This gives you a dizzying array of options, including going directly to the Desktop when you sign into Windows 8, controlling how Window 8 native app navigation works, disabling the Charms bar when you're on the Desktop...and much, much more.

Whatever you decide, don't worry—you can change the options later.

Once you've configured it, you're ready to go. Tap the Windows key on your keyboard, and up pops an old friend—the Start button (Figure 3-2). It looks and works much like the one you've come to know.

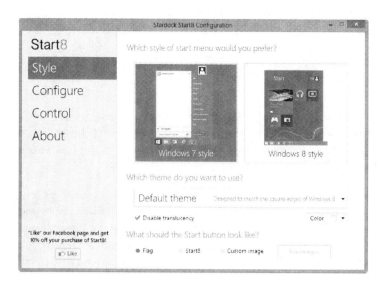

Figure 3-1.
Configuring Start8

Figure 3-2.
What's that shiny thing in the bottom-left corner of the Desktop? Oh, now I remember—it's my old friend, the Start button.

Take some time getting used to it, because even though it works much like the old Start button, it also includes some Windows 8 features. To change how it works, right-click it and select Configure Start8 and hack away.

StartFinity

There are two versions of StartFinity—a $14.95 version that lets you customize how it works, and the free Starter Edition that doesn't let you customize it. Other than that, the versions are essentially the same. Note that you can only use the free Starter Edition on non-business computers for non-business tasks.

Get the free version at *www.winability.com/startfinity-free/* and the for-pay version at *www.winability.com/startfinity/*. Note that for the free version, you'll have to enter your email address, and you'll be sent an email with a link to download the free software. Keep in mind that when you do that, you'll also have to agree to get sent email from WinAbility, the maker of StartFinity, although the company says that you'll be able to unsubscribe.

Install it, and it brings back the Start button and menu (Figure 3-3). It's simple and straightforward. Click the Start button and get to work.

See Also

- Hack #19, "Use the Built-In Mini Start Menu"
- Hack #21, "Hack a Quick-and-Dirty Start Menu for the Desktop"

HACK 19   Use the Built-In Mini Start Menu

Windows 8's main interface doesn't include the Start Menu. But there's a hidden mini one, and here's how to get to it.

Windows 8's tile-based interface and its Desktop are noticeably missing a Start menu. As you know from Hack #18, "Bring Back the Windows Start Menu to Windows 8", there's a way to add one back. But you may not need to do that, since there's already a mini start menu built right into the operating system, and you can get there whether you're on the main tiled interface or on the Desktop.

There are two ways to do it: Either right-click the bottom-left corner of the screen or press Windows key+X. Either way, the mini-menu pops up (Figure 3-4; its formal name is the Power User menu) with plenty of choices.

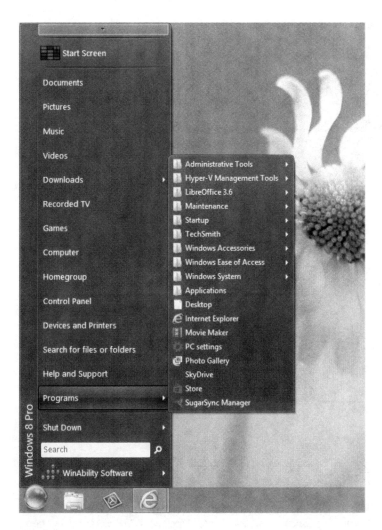

Figure 3-3.
The Start button, courtesy of StartFinity

The choices are generally self-explanatory, although some of them don't necessarily lead you where you may think. "Programs and Features," for example, sends you to a Control Panel applet that lets you uninstall Desktop programs, look at Windows updates you've installed, and turn certain Windows features on or off. The Mobility Center sends you to an applet that lets you do things such as change your display brightness, change your screen orientation, change presentation settings, and similar options—and the truth is, it's not particularly useful, so you might want to stay away.

Figure 3-4.
Windows 8's mini start menu

Hacking the Hack

You can edit the apps that show up on the Power User menu. In Windows Explorer, go to *C:\Users\User Name\AppData\Local\Microsoft\Windows\WinX*, where User Name is your account name. (First, make sure that you can view hidden files in Windows Explorer—in the Windows 8 Desktop, launch File Explorer, click the View tab on the toolbar, and turn on the "Hidden items" checkbox. That displays folders and files that are normally hidden from view.) When you do that, you'll see three folders: Group1, Group2, and Group3. Each of these groups contains shortcuts to one of the apps that show up on the Power User menu. Group1 contains the Desktop; Group2 contains the Control Panel, Run, Search, Task Manager, and Windows Explorer; and Group3 (Figure 3-5) contains two for the Command Prompt (one of which is an Admin command prompt), Computer Management, Device Manager, Disk Management, Event Viewer, Power Options, Programs and Features, System, and Windows Mobility Center.

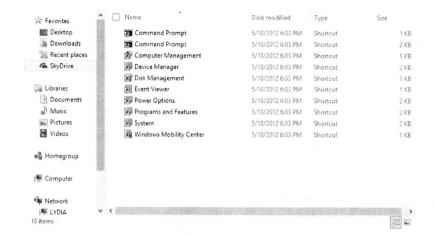

Figure 3-5.
The Group3 folder and its shortcuts

If you look closely at the Power User menu, you'll notice that these groups correspond to three groups on it, separated by faint lines. Group1 is at the bottom, Group2 just above that, and Group3 at the top.

To edit the Power User menu, you simply make changes to these folders. If you delete a shortcut, for example, it no longer appears on the Power User menu. If you add a shortcut to another folder, it appears on the menu wherever you place it—for example, if you put it in Group1, it appears at the bottom. And you can also add new folders called Group4 and so on, to add other groups to the mini Start menu, ready for you to add shortcuts.

Sign out of Windows and then sign in again, and the changes will take effect.

See Also

- Hack #18, "Bring Back the Windows Start Menu to Windows 8"
- Hack #21, "Hack a Quick-and-Dirty Start Menu for the Desktop"

HACK 20 Bring the Quick Launch Toolbar Back to the Desktop

In Windows 8, the Quick Launch Toolbar seems to be a thing of the past. But with this quick hack, you can easily bring it back.

The Windows 8 Desktop is missing more than just the Start button. You also won't find the Quick Launch toolbar—that useful toolbar containing your frequently accessed programs that lived to the right of the Start menu. You could have several programs there, and see them all just by clicking a small double-arrow icon.

It's easy to bring it back to the Windows 8 Desktop. Launch File Explorer, click the View tab on the toolbar, and turn on the "Hidden items" checkbox. That displays folders and files that are normally hidden from view.

Now head to the Desktop, right-click the Taskbar, and select Toolbars→New Toolbar (Figure 3-6).

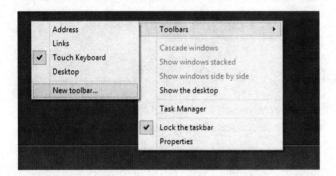

Figure 3-6.
Adding a new toolbar to the Taskbar

On the screen that appears, type **%appdata%\Microsoft\Internet Explorer\Quick Launch**. That places a Quick Launch toolbar at the far right of the taskbar. It also includes the Show Desktop button that is missing from the Windows 8 Desktop. If you want to move the Quick Launch toolbar to the left, right-click the taskbar, uncheck "Lock the Taskbar," and drag to the right. Lock it when you have it where you want. You can now use the Quick Launch toolbar by clicking the double-headed arrow (Figure 3-7). It works just like previous versions of Windows.

Figure 3-7.
An old friend: the Quick Launch toolbar, now in Windows 8

See Also

- Hack #18, "Bring Back the Windows Start Menu to Windows 8"

HACK 21 # Hack a Quick-and-Dirty Start Menu for the Desktop

> Here's one more way to add a Start menu to the Desktop. It's not quite a full-blown one, but it still does the trick.

Looking to add the Start menu back to the Desktop, but don't want to use third-party software? You can add a quick-and-dirty one in a few minutes. It's not the full Start menu, but it does let you browse through Start items and launch them.

In the Windows 8 Desktop, launch File Explorer, click the View tab on the toolbar, and turn on the "Hidden items" checkbox. That displays folders and files that are normally hidden from view.

Then, right-click the Desktop's taskbar and select Toolbars→New Toolbar. On the screen that appears, navigate to *C:\Program Data\Microsoft\Windows\Start Menu* and select it. That places a Start Menu toolbar at the far right of the taskbar. If you want to move the Start Menu toolbar to the left, right-click the taskbar, uncheck "Lock the Taskbar," and drag to the left. Lock it when you have it where you want. You can now use the Start Menu by clicking the double-headed arrow (Figure 3-8). It works just as in previous versions of Windows.

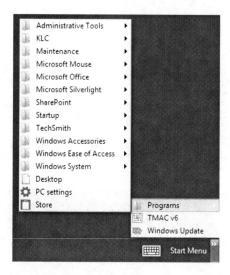

Figure 3-8.
Adding a quick-and-dirty Start menu to the Desktop

Hacking the Hack

You can add other toolbars to the Desktop using a similar technique. Right-click the taskbar and choose Toolbars, and you can add the following ones by checking them:

Address

> Adds a box into which you can type URLs. Press Enter after adding one, and you'll go to the site in Internet Explorer (or your default browser).

Links

> Displays your Internet Explorer favorites.

Touch keyboard

> Shows a keyboard icon. Click it, and an onscreen keyboard appears for typing.

Desktop

> Lists all the icons on your Desktop for easy navigation (Figure 3-9). It even displays some items that aren't visible on the Desktop, such as Homegroup. If any item has subfolders underneath it (such as Homegroup and Network), you'll see an arrow next to it. Move your cursor to the arrow to see all of the subfolders.

Figure 3-9.
The Desktop toolbar

To turn off any toolbar, right-click the taskbar and choose Toolbars, then take away the check next to the toolbar.

See Also

- Hack #18, "Bring Back the Windows Start Menu to Windows 8"
- Hack #19, "Use the Built-In Mini Start Menu"

Turn on Windows "God Mode" on the Desktop

Here's how to get access to all of the most important Windows 8 settings from a single Desktop location, using the so-called "God Mode."

Windows 8 has countless settings you can hack, tweak, and customize. Many of them are accessible via the Control Panel and other scattered locations throughout Windows. It can be time-consuming to find them all, and the likelihood is that you'll never remember where they all live. That means that many tweaks and hacks are far away, and some you'll never even find.

There's a simple solution: Use what some people call "God Mode." Despite its name, it's not really a separate mode. Instead, it's a hidden folder that gives you fast access to all those settings. All you have to do is bring it out of hiding and place it on the Desktop.

To do it, right-click the Desktop and select New→Folder (Figure 3-10). Rename the folder `GodMode.{ED7BA470-8E54-465E-825C-99712043E01C}`.

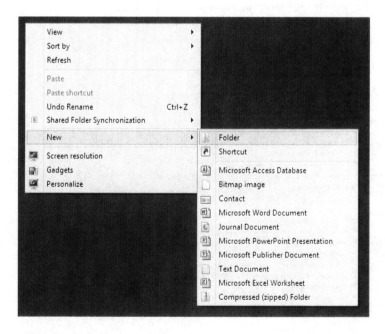

Figure 3-10.
Creating a new folder on the desktop

The folder icon changes, and it has the name GodMode (Figure 3-11).

Figure 3-11.
The God Mode folder on the Desktop

Note: The "God.Mode" text isn't what turns the folder into a special folder—it's the {ED7BA470-8E54-465E-825C-99712043E01C}.You can use any text before the curly brackets you want. So if you wanted the folder to be called Fred.Folder, you could do that as well by renaming it like this: Fred.Folder{ED7BA470-8E54-465E-825C-99712043E01C}. It would show up as FredFolder on the Desktop, but still have the same features.

Double-click the icon, and you'll come to a folder that has many dozens of tweaks, settings, and hacks (Figure 3-12). They're organized by category, and you can expand or shrink each category by clicking the small triangle next to each. Each category displays a number next to it, showing how many settings there are.

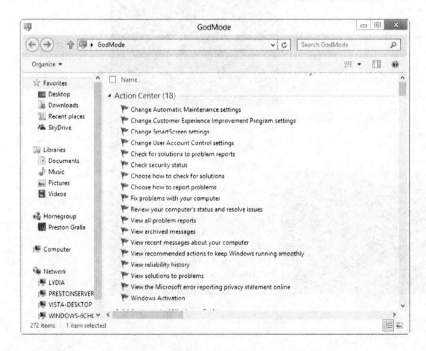

Figure 3-12.
Some of the settings available in God Mode

To make a tweak or use any hack, double-click it. In some cases you'll follow a wizard, in other cases you'll need to fill in dialog boxes, and in yet other cases you'll be sent to the Control Panel or other Windows location to do the work.

Hacking the Hack

In the God Mode folder, you can create shortcuts to any of the items in the Quick Launch folder, in the Start Menu folder, and in the Power User Menu folder. That way they're always within easy reach.

HACK 23   Run the Desktop and Window 8 Native Apps Side by Side

Windows 8 apps and the Desktop and its apps are mutually exclusive, right? Wrong. With this hack, you can run Windows 8 apps and the Desktop and its apps side by side.

Windows 8 is essentially a hybrid operating system: the old-style Desktop, and the newer-style Windows 8 environment, including the Start screen and apps written specifically for Windows 8. These apps are "immersive" and meant to take up the entire screen. You can't resize them, as you can with Desktop apps, to see multiple ones onscreen.

You may think that the Desktop is the Desktop, and Windows 8 native apps are Windows 8 native apps, and never the twain shall meet.

But that's not quite the case. Using a feature that Microsoft calls Snap, you can run a Windows 8 native app and the Desktop or a Desktop application side by side on the same screen.

Note: Snap requires a minimum screen resolution of 1366 × 768.

To begin with, make sure that you're running a Windows 8 app. Now let's say that you want to run the Desktop (or a Desktop application) side by side. Go back to the Desktop (or a Desktop application), move your mouse cursor to the left side of the screen, and you'll see all of your currently running apps, including Windows 8 native apps (Figure 3-13). Drag and drop its thumbnail onto the screen (Figure 3-14).

Warning: Make sure not to drag the thumbnail too far to the right before you drop it. If you do, the app you just dragged will take up the full screen by itself.

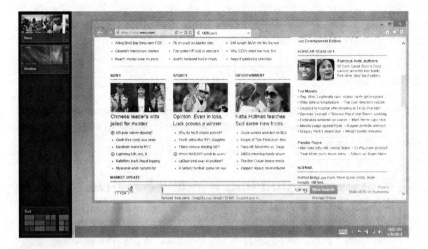

Figure 3-13.
Showing your currently running apps while you're in the Desktop

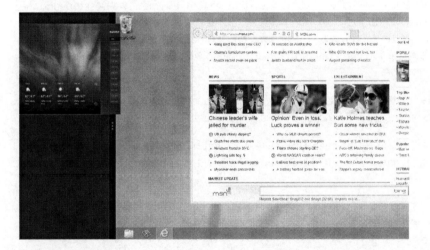

Figure 3-14.
Drag and drop the Windows 8 app

Now Windows 8 native apps run in a sidebar along the lefthand side of the screen (Figure 3-15). Each app displays its information in the most convenient way for you, instead of just zooming it to bits. For instance, when you snap the Desktop to the side, it shows the Smart Previews of running applications. This feature is called semantic zoom. You can use each app as you would normally.

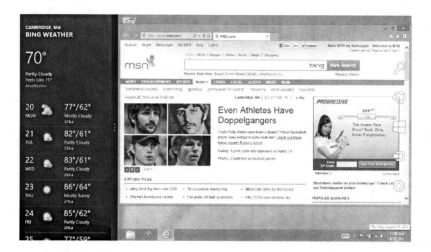

Figure 3-15.
A Windows 8 native app running side by side with a Desktop app

There's a border with three dots on it running on the right side of the app running in the sidebar, separating the apps. Drag it to the left or right to resize the app by making it take up more or less of the screen.

Note: If you're running a Windows 8 native app and want to run a Desktop app side by side with it, follow this same technique.

What if you're using a device with a touchscreen? You can still run apps side by side. First, to display your currently running apps, swipe slowly from the left and then pull back your finger. That displays the apps. Now drag and drop the app you want to run side by side with the currently running app. Control the size by dragging the border of the app running in the sidebar, just as you would with a mouse.

See Also

- Hack #13, "Run Windows 8 Native Apps Side by Side"

HACK 24 # Put Helpful Navigation Icons on the Desktop

The Windows 8 Desktop is a bare thing. Here's how to place useful navigation icons on it to make life easier.

Once upon a time, Windows had a variety of useful navigation icons on the Desktop—icons that would send you straight to your user account folder, for example. Those days are long gone. But if you'd like, you can put them all back.

To do it, right-click the Desktop and choose Personalize→"Change desktop icons." The Desktop Icon Settings screen appears (Figure 3-16).

Figure 3-16.
Adding icons to the Desktop

Here's what you can display, and what each one does:

Computer

Opens the Computer folder (Figure 3-17), which shows all your hard drives, Network Locations, Favorites, Libraries, and more.

User's Files

Opens the folder that contains folders with your personal files—Favorites, Downloads, My Documents, My Music, My Pictures, SkyDrive, and many others.

Tip: On the Desktop Icon Settings screen, the checkbox reads "User's Files," but on the Desktop, the folder has your user account name—"Fred Jones," for example.

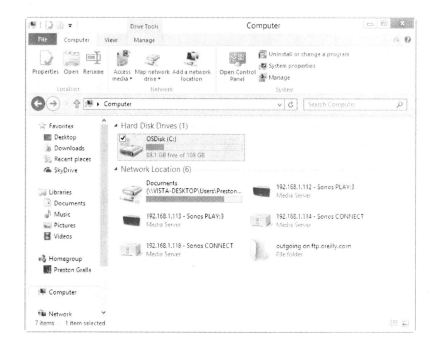

Figure 3-17.
The Computer folder

Network

Displays all the computers and devices on your home network (Figure 3-18). If you have any media devices on your network, such as Sonos streaming media players or Windows Media Connect devices, they show up here as well. So will any servers and your network router. Windows show up, but not smartphones or any other tablets.

Note: The Homegroup won't show up in the Network folder, even if you're a member of a Homegroup.

Recycle Bin

By default, this is the only navigational icon to show up.

Control Panel

Launches the Windows 8 Control Panel.

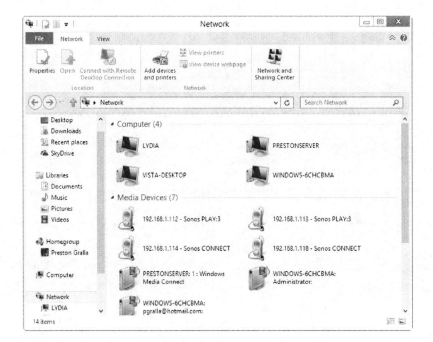

Figure 3-18.
The Network folder

Checkmark the boxes next to the icons you'd like placed on the Desktop, then click OK. They'll all appear down the left side of your screen (Figure 3-19). If you prefer them to be in different locations, just drag them. Be aware, though, that this arrangement might get lost when you change screen resolution or if the display driver unexpectedly shuts down.

Hacking the Hack

You're not stuck with the default icons for each of the folders that you've just put on your Desktop. You can change any that you'd like. On the Desktop Icon Setting screen, highlight any icon you want to change, select Change Icon, and from the screen that appears, click the new icon you want to use, and then click OK (Figure 3-20).

Figure 3-19.
The new navigational items, now on the Desktop

Figure 3-20.
Selecting a new icon for a Desktop folder

HACK 25 # Make the Desktop More Tablet-Friendly

> Windows 8 tablets are built primarily for the Start screen and Windows
> 8-specific apps. But you may have times when you want to use the Desk-
> top. Here's how to make the Desktop more tablet-friendly.

Try using the Desktop on a Windows 8 tablet. I dare you—go ahead and give it a shot.
Not easy or much fun, is it? It simply wasn't built for touch. Icons and various options
boxes and buttons are so small that you'll find yourself making the wrong choice simply because there's no way to be that precise when everything is so small.

You can, though, make the Desktop more tablet-friendly by making everything larger.

Make Everything Larger

The simplest way to make the Desktop more tablet-friendly is to make text and icons
on it larger.

Press and hold your finger on the Desktop until the circle turns to a square, then release
your finger. From the menu that appears, select "Screen resolution." Tap "Make text
and other items larger or smaller." On the screen that appears, select "Medium –
125%" and tap Apply (Figure 3-21). You'll be logged out of Windows 8 and must log
back in to make the changes take effect.

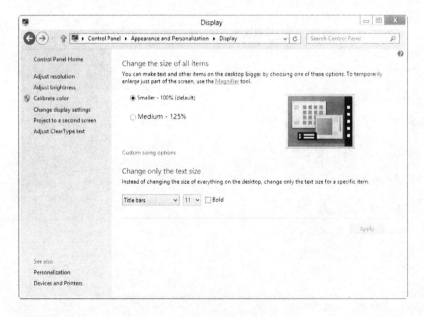

Figure 3-21.
Changing the screen resolution to make Desktop items larger

When you get to the Desktop, you'll see that not only has the text been made larger, but so has everything else, including the icons, dialog boxes, and so on (Figure 3-23, in comparison to Figure 3-22). This makes it much easier to tap on precisely what you want to choose. And it's not just the items on the Desktop that are larger—so are any Desktop applications that you run.

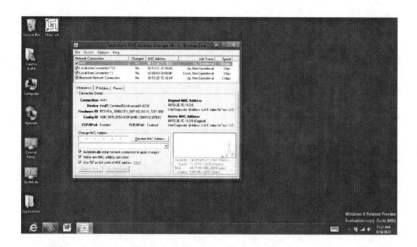

Figure 3-22.
Using the default size for text on the Desktop

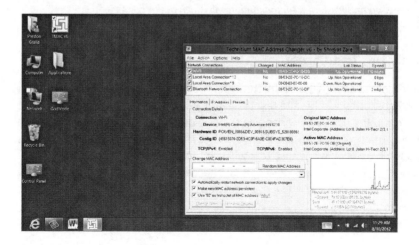

Figure 3-23.
Using larger-sized text

What if the Medium setting doesn't do the trick for you—what if it's too large or too small? No problem. You can fine-tune the size of Desktop items and text. On the screen that lets you change item sizes, tap "Custom sizing options." In the "Scale to this percentage of normal size" box, type a number that matches how much larger you want items and text to be. You can also drag the ruler to do the same thing (Figure 3-24). You'll see the sample text change as you make your selection. Fine-tune the size, click OK, then click Apply. You'll be logged out and have to log in again for the changes to take effect.

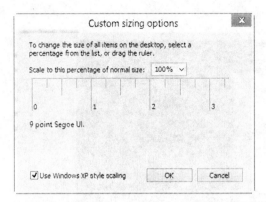

Figure 3-24.
Using larger-sized text

Note: Making the text and other items larger and smaller on the Desktop and its applications doesn't affect the Windows 8 Start screen or apps written specifically for Windows 8 rather than the Desktop. Their sizes won't be changed, with one exception—the arrow selector will get larger. Also, if you're on the Start screen and run a Desktop application, that application will run in the larger size.

Make Only the Text Larger

Maybe you're satisfied with the size of the icons and other objects on the Desktop and in Desktop apps, but you'd like the text to be larger. In that case, you can change just the text size. On the screen for changing the size of text and other items, go to the "Change only the text size" option (Figure 3-25). There's a drop-down box that lets you select the type of object whose text you want to make larger—title bars, menus, message boxes, and so on. Select one, then choose a new text size and whether to make it bold. Click Apply. You'll be logged out and have to log back in for the changes to take effect.

Figure 3-25.
Changing only the text size

HACK 26   Hack the Notification Area Using the Registry Editor

Use Registry hacks to control the Notification area.

The system tray, also called the Notification area, is the small area on the far-right side of the taskbar, in which utilities and programs that run in the background, such as antivirus software, display their icons.

I don't find it a particularly intelligent use of screen real estate, so I prefer not to see the icons there. To hide them, run the Registry Editor (Figure 3-26; Hack #118, "Hack Away at the Registry") and go to :`HKEY_CURRENT_USER\Software\Microsoft\Windows\Cur rentVersion \Policies\Explorer`. You may need to create the Explorer key if it doesn't already exist. Among other things, this key controls the display of objects throughout Windows. Create a new `DWORD` called `NoTrayItemsDisplay`. Assign it a value of 1. (A value of 0 keeps the icons displayed.)

Exit the Registry, log out, and log back in again, to make the change take effect.

Hide Only Certain Icons in the Notification Area

You may want to display some icons in the Notification area but not others; luckily, you can hide icons on a case-by-case basis. You do it by delving through menus,

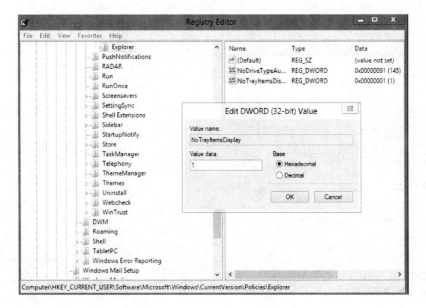

Figure 3-26.
Using the Registry Editor to hide icons in the Notification area

though, not by hacking the Registry. Right-click the taskbar and choose Proper-
ties→Taskbar. The Taskbar and Start Menu Properties dialog box appears. This dialog
box, as the name implies, lets you control how the taskbar and Start Menu look and
function.

In the Notification area tab, click Customize; the Customize Notifications dialog box
appears as shown in Figure 3-27.

In the Behaviors column, click the program's listing, and then choose from the drop-
down menu either to always show notifications and icons, to hide notifications and
icons, or to only show notifications. Click OK twice. Your changes will take effect immediately.

See Also

- Hack #20, "Bring the Quick Launch Toolbar Back to the Desktop"

HACK 27 Change Folders in the Open Dialog Box

Change the folders that appear in the Open and Save As dialog boxes in
Windows 8 apps.

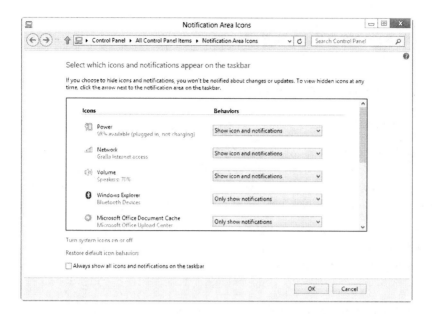

Figure 3-27.
Hiding specific icons in the Notification area

When you use certain Windows applications (such as Notepad) to open or save a file, on the left side of the Open dialog box are a group of icons and folders (such as Documents, Music, Pictures, Videos, Homegroup, Desktop, and more) to which you can navigate to open files.

That's useful. More useful, though, would be the ability to list only those folders you use, and to put any folder there, not just ones Windows decides you need.

In fact, it's simple to do. The Open dialog box lets you put just the folders of your choosing on the left side. Note that when you do this, it will affect Windows applications such as Notepad and Paint that use the Open and Save common dialog boxes. However, it won't affect Microsoft Office applications or other applications that don't use the common dialog boxes.

The locations of the Open and Save As dialog boxes mirror the locations on the left side of the screen in File Explorer. In fact, that's where they get them from. So if you add or take away locations from that area of File Explorer, they'll be added or taken away in the dialog boxes.

To remove a location, right-click it and select Remove. To add a folder location, add a shortcut to the folder. In File Explorer, go to the folder you want to add. Right-click it and select "Create shortcut." Then drag the shortcut to the location on the left side of File Explorer. It will then show up in common dialog boxes.

HACK 28   Control the Control Panel

Hide Control Panel applets from appearing.

The Control Panel: love it or hate it, it's a very simple way to organize all the applets and features of Windows. But the Control Panel's multilayered organization forces you to click far too many times to get to the applet you want. And its clutter of applets that you may use rarely, if ever, makes navigation even more difficult.

The solution? Start by cleaning up the Control Panel, hiding applets that you rarely use. Note that when you hide the applets, you can still use them; you just won't see their icons displayed in the Control Panel. You can, however, search for them in the Control Panel, and they'll show up. They simply won't appear when you browse.

I'll show you two ways to Control the Windows 8 Control Panel: one using the Registry, and the other using the local Group Policy Editor. In this hack, you'll not only find out ways you can control the Control Panel, but you'll also see how you can apply that knowledge to create different customized Control Panels.

Hide Unused Applets with the Registry

To hide unused applets using the Registry, start by typing **regedit** at the Run box or a command prompt. Go to `HKEY_LOCAL_MACHINE\SOFTWARE\Microsoft\Windows\Current Version\ Control Panel\don't load`.

The key, as its name implies, determines which Control Panel applet icons are not loaded into the Control Panel. You can still run those applets from the command line, and they may also appear in other places. And you can still search for them in the Control Panel and then use them. You just won't see their icons in the Control Panel when you browse through.

To hide an applet, create a new `String` value whose name is the filename of the applet you want to hide. For example, to hide the Mouse Control dialog box, the `String` value would be *main.cpl*. See Table 3-1 for a list of Control Panel applets and their filenames.

Note: By default, there are a fair number of applets that Windows 8 doesn't display, and you'll see their String values in the Registry. If you want them displayed, delete the String value.

Table 3-1. Control Panel applets and their filenames

APPLET	FILENAME
Accessibility Options	access.cpl
Add Hardware Wizard	hdwwiz.cpl
Add or Remove Programs	appwiz.cpl
Display Properties	desk.cpl
Game Controllers	joy.cpl
Internet Properties	inetcpl.cpl
Mouse Properties	main.cpl
Network Connections	ncpa.cpl
ODBC Data Source Administrator	odbccp32.cpl
Phone and Modem Options	telephon.cpl
Power Options Properties	powercfg.cpl
Region and Language Options	intl.cpl
Sound and Audio Devices	mmsys.cpl
Speech Properties	sapi.cpl
System Properties	sysdm.cpl
Time and Date Properties	timedate.cpl
User Accounts	nusrmgr.cpl

Create separate String values for each applet you want to hide, then exit the Registry. The applets will vanish from the Control Panel. To make a hidden applet appear again, delete its string value from this same Registry key.

Hide Unused Applets with the Group Policy Editor

If you have Windows 8 Professional or Windows 8 Enterprise, you don't need to get your hands dirty with the Registry to hide unused applets; instead, you can use the Group Policy Editor to accomplish the same task. (See Chapter 11 for more details about how to use the Group Policy Editor.) The Group Policy Editor is primarily used for setting network and multiuser policies and rights, but it can also be used to customize the way Windows looks and works. Run the Group Policy Editor by typing **gpedit.msc** at the Run prompt or the command line.

Once you've run it, go to *Administrative Templates\Control Panel*, double-click "Hide specified Control Panel applets" and choose Enabled. After you click Enabled, choose Show→Add and type the canonical name of each Control Panel applet you want to hide. (Find them in Table 3-2.)

Table 3-2. Selected Control Panel applets and their canonical names

APPLET	FILENAME
Action Center	*Microsoft.Action.Center*
Administrative Tools	*Microsoft.AdministrativeTools*
AutoPlay	*Microsoft.AutoPlay*
Backup and Restore	*Microsoft.BackupAndRestore*
BitLocker Drive Encryption	*Microsoft.BitLockerDriveEncryption*
Color Management	*Microsoft.ColorManagement*
Date and Time	*Microsoft.DateAndTime*
Device Manager	*Microsoft.DeviceManager*
Devices and Printers	*Microsoft.DevicesAndPrinters*
Display	*Microsoft.Display*
Ease of Access Center	*Microsoft.EaseOfAccessCenter*
Folder Options	*Microsoft.FolderOptions*
Game Controllers	*Microsoft.GameControllers*
HomeGroup	*Microsoft.HomeGroup*
Internet Options	*Microsoft.InternetOptions*
Keyboard	*Microsoft.Keyboard*
Mouse	*Microsoft.Mouse*
Network and Sharing Center	*Microsoft.NetworkAndSharingCenter*
Notification Area Icons	*Microsoft.NotificationAreaIcons*
Parental Controls	*Microsoft.ParentalControls*
Pen and Touch	*Microsoft.PenAndTouch*

APPLET	FILENAME
Performance Information and Tools	Microsoft.PerformanceInformationAndTools
Personalization	Microsoft.Personalization
Power Options	Microsoft.PowerOptions
Programs and Features	Microsoft.ProgramsAndFeatures
RemoteApp and Desktop Connections	Microsoft.RemoteAppAndDesktopConnections
Scanners and Cameras	Microsoft.ScannersAndCameras
Sound	Microsoft.Sound
System	Microsoft.System
Tablet PC Settings	Microsoft.TabletPCSettings
Taskbar and Start Menu	Microsoft.TaskbarAndStartMenu
Troubleshooting	Microsoft.Troubleshooting
User Accounts	Microsoft.UserAccounts
Windows Defender	Microsoft.WindowsDefender
Windows Firewall	Microsoft.WindowsFirewall
Windows Mobility Center	Microsoft.MobilityCenter

Click OK in each dialog box that appears. When you exit the Group Policy Editor, the specified applets will no longer appear in the Control Panel. (Note that it can take up to 90 minutes for the change to appear. If you want it to it appear right away, reboot your machine.)

This technique is best for when you want to hide only a few applets. If you want to hide most of the applets and just display a few, there's another method you might want to try. Run the Group Policy Editor and go to `User Configuration\Administrative Tem plates\Control Panel`, the section that handles the Control Panel. As you can see when you get there, you can do a lot more than hide the Control Panel's unused applets in this section of the Group Policy Editor; you can also control many other aspects of how the Control Panel looks and functions.

Now double-click "Show only specified Control Panel applets" (Figure 3-28). Get ready for a bit of counterintuitive selecting. To disable Control Panel applets, you must choose the Enabled radio button, because you're enabling the feature to show only certain Control Panel applets. Strange, but true.

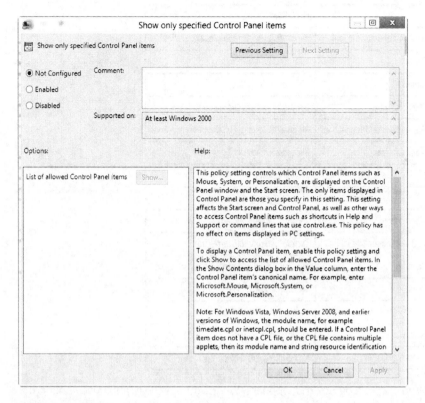

Figure 3-28.
Hiding Control Panel applets using the Group Policy Editor

To decide which applets to show, click the Show button. The Show Contents screen appears. Click Add, and you're ready to list all the Control Panel applets that you want to appear. For each item that you want to appear, type its Control Panel canonical name, which you can find in Table 3-2. For example, if you want Network and Sharing Time applet to appear, type `Microsoft.NetworkAndSharingCenter`.

When you've listed all the Control Panel applets that you want to appear, click OK and exit the Group Policy Editor. Only the applets you've chosen to display now appear in the Control Panel.

To customize other aspects of how the Control Panel works, follow the same instructions as outlined previously—double-click the item you want to change and pick your options.

The Group Policy Editor gives you instant access to changing dozens of interface settings. Here's how to use it to create your own personalized taskbar.

The Group Policy Editor does more than just customize the Control Panel (Hack #28, "Control the Control Panel"); it gives you control over many aspects of the Windows 8 Desktop as well—in particular, the taskbar.

Run the Group Policy Editor by typing **gpedit.msc** and then go to User Configuration \Administrative Templates\Start Menu and Taskbar. As you can see in Figure 3-29, the right pane displays all the settings you can change. If you click the Extended tab at the bottom of the screen, you'll see a description of the setting that you've high-lighted, along with an explanation of each option. To change a setting, double-click it and choose your options from the menu that pops up.

Note: Do you notice something odd about this Group Policy setting? It's titled "Start Menu and Taskbar," even though the Start Menu has been taken away in Windows 8. So you can safely ignore the various Start Menu settings, because the Start Menu no longer exists.

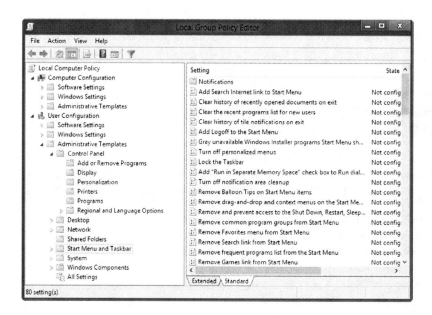

Figure 3-29.
Customizing the taskbar in the Group Policy Editor

There's not room in this hack to go into detail about each setting you can change, so I'll tell you about some of my favorites. There's a way to resize the taskbar and make it larger, but I find that to be immensely ugly. So "Prevent users from resizing the taskbar" is high on the list of options I turn on. If you share your PC with other people, the Group Policy Editor is a great way to make sure no one can change the taskbar except you. So, when you have the Start Menu and Taskbar working the way you want, they'll stay that way until you want to change them. Enable "Lock all taskbar settings" and no one will be able to change their settings except you (or another user who has administrator privileges and knows how to work with Group Policies).

HACK 30   A Power User's Hidden Weapon: Improve File Explorer's Context Menu

> File Explorer's context menu is an underused tool. But with these four additions and edits to the menu, it'll turn into a powerhouse that you'll use every day.

File Explorer's right-click context menu is one of the most basic of all Windows tools. It provides many shortcuts for whenever you want to take action on a file or a folder. But the right-click menu is missing several basic options, such as the ability to choose the folder where you want to move or copy the chosen file. And when you install new applications, they have a nasty habit of adding their own context-menu options that you'll rarely use.

The end result: a right-click menu cluttered with unwanted options and lacking several useful ones. But you can extend the power of the menu with the four hacks in this section.

Add "Copy To Folder" and "Move To Folder" Context Menu Options

I spend a lot of time copying and moving files between folders. More often than not, when I click a file in File Explorer, I want to copy or move it to another folder. That means I spend a good deal of time dragging files around or copying and pasting them.

But with a Registry hack, you can save yourself time: you can add Copy To Folder and Move To Folder options to the context menu. When you choose one of those right-click options, you can browse to any place on your hard disk to copy or move the file to, and then send the file there. To add this option, run the Registry Editor (Hack #117, "Don't Fear the Registry"). Then go to `HKEY_CLASSES_ROOT\AllFilesystemObjects\shellex\Con textMenuHandlers`.

The shellex name tells you that it's a shell extension key that lets you customize the user shell or the interface. Create a new key called `Copy To`. Set the value to

{C2FBB630-2971-11d1-A18C-00C04FD75D13}. Create another new key called Move To. Set the value to {C2FBB631-2971-11d1-A18C-00C04FD75D13}. Exit the Registry. The changes should take effect immediately. The Copy To Folder and Move To Folder options will appear. When you right-click a file and choose one of the options, you can move or copy the file, using a dialog box like the one shown in Figure 3-30.

Figure 3-30.
Specifying a destination using the Copy To Folder option

Add and Remove Destinations for the "Send To" Option

The right-click context menu does have one useful option, Send To, which lets you send the file to any one of a list of programs or locations—for example, to a drive, program, or folder.

It would be nice to edit that list, adding new locations and programs and taking away existing ones that you never use. How locations and programs show up on the menu at first appears to be somewhat of a mystery, but in fact it's easy to hack.

Go to *C:\Users\User Name\AppData\Roaming\Microsoft\Windows\SendTo*. The folder is filled with shortcuts to all the locations you find on your Send To context menu. To remove an item from the Send To menu, delete the shortcut from the folder. To add an item to the menu, add a shortcut to the folder by highlighting the folder, and on the Ribbon, choose File→New Item→Shortcut and following the instructions for creating a shortcut. The new setting takes effect immediately; you don't have to exit File Explorer for it to go into effect.

Open the Command Prompt from the Right-Click Menu

I began computing in the days of DOS, and I still can't give up the command prompt. When it comes to doing down-and-dirty tasks such as mass deleting or renaming of files, nothing beats it. I find myself frequently switching back and forth between File Explorer and the command prompt.

Often, when using File Explorer, I want to open the command prompt at the folder that's my current location. That takes too many steps: opening a command prompt and then navigating to my current folder. However, there's a quicker way; you can add an option to the context menu that opens a command prompt at your current folder. For example, if you were to right-click the C:\My Stuff folder, you could then choose to open a command prompt at C:\My Stuff.

To add the option, run the Registry Editor (Hack #117, "Don't Fear the Registry"), then go to `HKEY_LOCAL_MACHINE\Software\Classes\Folder\Shell`. Create a new key called `Command Prompt`. For the default value, enter whatever text you want to appear when you right-click a folder—for example, **Open Command Prompt**. Create a new key beneath the `Command Prompt` key called `Command`. As shown in Figure 3-31, set the default value to `Cmd.exe /k pushd %L`. That value launches Cmd.exe, the command prompt. The /k switch executes the command that follows, but leaves the prompt running in interactive mode. That is, it lets you issue commands from the command prompt; the command prompt isn't being used to issue only a single command and then exit. The `pushd` command stores the name of the current directory, and `%L` uses that name to start the command prompt at it. Finally, exit the Registry. The new menu option shows up immediately. Note that it won't appear when you right-click a file; it shows up only when you right-click a folder.

Clean Up the "Open With" Option

When you right-click a file, one of the menu options is Open With, which provides a list of programs for you to open the file with. This list changes according to the type of file you're clicking. Depending on the file type, the list can get long, because programs frequently add themselves to this list when you install them. To make things worse, there are times when the listed programs aren't applicable. For example, do you really want to open a .jpg bitmap graphics file with Microsoft Word? I think not.

You can clean up the Open With list using a Registry hack. Run the Registry Editor, and go to `HKEY_CURRENT_USER\Software\Microsoft\Windows\CurrentVersion\Explorer\FileExts`.

Look for the file extension whose Open With list you want to edit, and find its `OpenWithList` subkey—`HKEY_CURRENT_USER\Software\Microsoft\Windows\CurrentVersion\Explorer\FileExts\.doc\OpenWithList`, for example. The subkey has an alphabetical list of String values. Open each value, and examine the value data. It is the name of one of

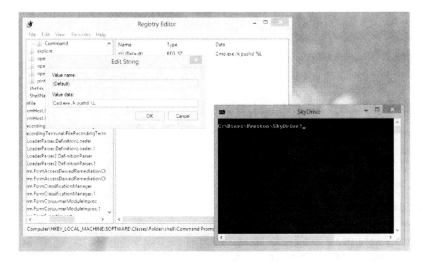

Figure 3-31.
The Registry code for creating the right-click command prompt (on the left), and the command prompt, opened (on the right)

the programs on the Open With list (e.g., `Winword.exe`). Delete any entry that you don't want to appear. Don't delete the value data; delete the `String` value listing. In other words, if the value data for the `String` value is `Winword.exe`, delete the entire string rather than just the value data. Exit the Registry.

> *Note: In some cases, you may see an entry for OpenWithProgIds instead of Open-WithList. These ProgIds are more obscure shorthand for the programs they are associated with. For example, the entry for .rtf includes two ProgIds: rtffile (the default handler for RTF files: WordPad) and Word.RTF.8 (Microsoft Word).*

Hacking the Hack

If you're a fan of the new Ribbon on the Windows 8 File Explorer, there's no need to edit the Registry in order to open a command prompt anywhere. Simply navigate to the folder where you want to open a command prompt and select File→Open Command Prompt.

Similarly, you don't need to edit the Registry to get to the "Move to" and "Copy to" features. They're also available on the Ribbon, on the Home tab.

See Also

- Hack #31, "Open an Administrator Command Prompt Anywhere in File Explorer"
- Hack #32, "Hack Your Way Through File Explorer"

HACK 31 Open an Administrator Command Prompt Anywhere in File Explorer

> Need to launch an administrator prompt on the fly when you're deep inside a folder? Here's an easy way to do it.

Command-line junkies can get frustrated in Windows 8 because some command-line tools require you to open an administrator command prompt. It's particularly frustrating when you're using File Explorer, and you realize that you need to launch an administrator command-line prompt at a particular folder, especially one that's nested several levels deep. You have to go through the annoying steps required to launch an administrator command prompt, and *then* go through the equally annoying steps of using the CD command to get to the right folder.

There's a simpler way. A command-line hack lets you add a right-click option to File Explorer called Open Administrator Command Prompt Here. That way, you can simply right-click in the folder in which you want to open an administrator prompt, make your selection, and the prompt...well, the prompt opens promptly.

First, launch the Registry Editor by typing **regedit** at the Start Search box or a command prompt (see Chapter 11 for details). Go to HKEY_CLASSES_ROOT\Directory\shell, and create a new key called runas. After you create the key, double-click the Default string, and give it the value Open Administrator Command Prompt Here.

Next, in that new key, create a new string value called NoWorkingDirectory. Leave the value data field blank. Your Registry should look like Figure 3-32. Underneath the key you just created, HKEY_CLASSES_ROOT\Directory\shell\runas, create a new key called command. Double-click the key's default value, enter the following text, and click OK:

```
cmd.exe /k "pushd %L && title Command Prompt"
```

Figure 3-33 shows the value being edited in the Registry Editor.

Next, go to HKEY_CLASSES_ROOT\Drive\shell and create a new key called runas. After you create the key, double-click the Default string, and give it the value Open Administrator Command Prompt Here.

Next, in that new key, create a new string value called NoWorkingDirectory. Leave the value data field blank. The new string name should be NoWorkingDirectory, and the value data field should be blank.

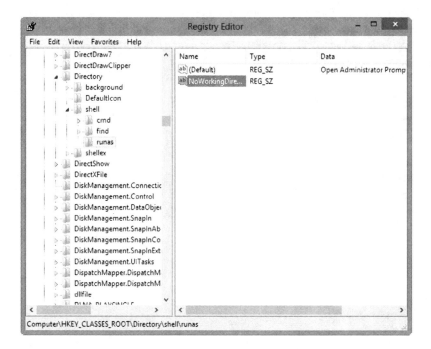

Figure 3-32.
Creating the Registry key for adding the administrator command prompt to the File Explorer context menu

Figure 3-33.
Creating the Registry key for adding the administrator command prompt to the File Explorer context menu

Underneath the key you just created, `HKEY_CLASSES_ROOT\Drive\shell\runas`, create a new key called `command`. Double-click the key's default value, enter this, and click OK:

```
cmd.exe /k "pushd %L && title Command Prompt"
```

Exit the Registry. Open Windows Explorer, and right-click any folder or drive. There will now be a new menu choice, Open Administrator Command Prompt Here, as you can see in Figure 3-34. Click it; an administrator command prompt will open, and you'll be at the folder you just right-clicked.

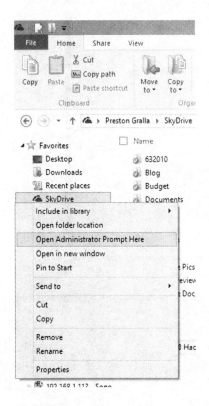

Figure 3-34.
The Registry editing has paid off.Here's the new prompt, in all of its glory.

Hacking the Hack

If you don't want to do all that editing to the Registry, you can create a *.reg* file that when double-clicked automatically creates all the proper Registry entries for you. Open Notepad, and type in the following:

```
Windows Registry Editor Version 5.00
[HKEY_CLASSES_ROOT\Directory\shell\runas]
@="Open Administrator Command Prompt Here"
"NoWorkingDirectory"=""
[HKEY_CLASSES_ROOT\Directory\shell\runas\command]
@="cmd.exe /k \"pushd %L && title Command Prompt\""
[HKEY_CLASSES_ROOT\Drive\shell\runas]
```

```
@="Open Administrator Command Prompt Here"
"NoWorkingDirectory"=""
[HKEY_CLASSES_ROOT\Drive\shell\runas\command]
@="cmd.exe /k \"pushd %L && title Command Prompt\""
```

Give the file a name with the extension *.reg*, such as *command prompt.reg*. Double-click it, and the changes will be applied to the Registry.

And if you don't like to use the Registry at all, you can use the new Ribbon on the Windows 8 File Explorer, to open an administrator command prompt anywhere. Simply navigate to the folder where you want to open a command prompt and select File→Open Command Prompt→Open command prompt as administrator.

See Also

- Hack #30, "A Power User's Hidden Weapon: Improve File Explorer's Context Menu"
- Hack #32, "Hack Your Way Through File Explorer"

HACK 32 Hack Your Way Through File Explorer

> The Windows 8 File Explorer offers far more options than did its predecessor in earlier Windows versions, Windows Explorer. Here's how to bend it to your will.

Windows 8 File Explorer looks very different than its previous incarnation, Windows Explorer, did in earlier versions of Windows. The biggest change is the addition of the Ribbon, which puts common (and not-so-common) tasks, features, and views within easy reach.

Most of those tasks, features, and views are straightforward and self-explanatory. But there are some that you might overlook or not quite understand—and that's a shame, because they can be quite useful. Here's how to hack through them and get the most out of File Explorer.

Turn Panes on and Off

File Explorer has several useful panes you can turn on and off. Click the View tab to find them. The Preview pane can be a big time saver: turn it on, and a new pane appears at right, showing you a preview of the file you've highlighted. Similarly, the Details pane is quite helpful. Click it to open it on the right side, where it shows you information about any file, such as size, date modified, and when it was created (Figure 3-35).

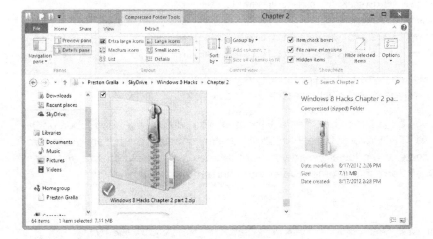

Figure 3-35.
File Explorer's Details Pane

Note: You can't have both the Details Pane and Preview Pane opened at the same time. They occupy the same screen real estate at the far right of File Explorer.

On the Ribbon, click the drop-down arrow at the bottom of the Navigation Pane icon, and you get some handy choices as well, notably to turn the Navigation Pane (the pane on the left side of the screen) on or off, show only the most important folders in the Navigation Pane, or show them all.

Change Icon Sizes

Want the icons next to folders larger or smaller? Want to make them disappear entirely, and display them only in a list? Want the list to show details about file size or not? On the view pane, just to the right of the options for turning panes on and off, you'll can make all these modifications (Figure 3-36).

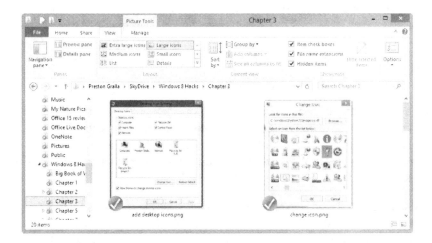

Figure 3-36.
You want big? File Explorer gives you big icons.

Add and Customize Columns

By default, File Explorer shows three columns of information about each file: date modified, type, and size. But you can add plenty more as well. On the View tab, click the down arrow next to Add columns (Figure 3-37), and you can add others as well, including the date created, authors, title, and more. Just click the down arrow next to "Add columns" on the View tab to add them.

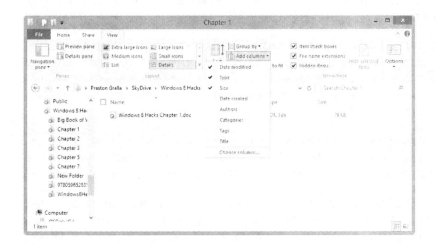

Figure 3-37.
Choosing new columns to add to File Explorer

Near the "Add columns" choice, you get a host of ways to change how those columns display, including how you sort them, group them, and make them all fit on a single screen.

Hidden Files and Folders...and More

Microsoft assumes that most people don't want to muck around in the plumbing of Windows, and so because of that, hides many system files and folders. However, given that you're reading this book, you clearly want to muck around as much as you can—and that means seeing every Windows file and folder there is, including system files and folders.

On the View tab, check the box next to "Hidden items" to display all those system files and folders. The same holds for file name extensions—by default, Windows 8 doesn't show them. If you'd like to see them, turn on the "File name extensions" checkbox.

Tip: For even more display options and other options, click the down arrow next to Options and select "Change folder and search options." You'll find the most useful options for fiddling with on the View tab, such as whether to show drive letters, whether to display file icons on thumbnails, and more.

Using the Invert Selection Feature

On the far-right side of the Home tab, there's a surprisingly useful option whose name, "Invert selection," makes no sense. Make it your friend; it'll help you in plenty of situations.

The options near it make plenty of sense. "Select all" will select all files in a folder, and "Select none," will deselect them. But let's say that you've hand-selected a number of files by holding down the Ctrl key while clicking files. Once you've selected them, you can now perform a task on them all—delete them or copy or move them somewhere else, for example.

For example, suppose you've got 30 files in a folder, and you want to delete 26 of them. Normally, you would either delete every one individually, or else go through the mind-numbingly boring process of selecting 26 of them by hand, and then deleting them.

That's where "Invert selection" comes in. Select the four by hand that you *don't* want to delete, and then click "Invert selection." Suddenly, all the files that you selected are no longer selected, and the other 26 *are* selected. You've just inverted the selection; that is, deselected those you had selected, and selected those you hadn't selected. You can now mass delete the 26 files.

See Also

- Hack #30, "A Power User's Hidden Weapon: Improve File Explorer's Context Menu"
- Hack #31, "Open an Administrator Command Prompt Anywhere in File Explorer"

4

Productivity and System Performance Hacks

Has a Windows PC ever seemed fast enough? One processor core, two processor cores, four processor cores, and more and more memory...no matter how powerful the hardware, you always want it to go faster.

In this chapter, you'll find plenty of ways to improve system performance and get more productive when using Windows 8. Whether using the Task Manager to rev up your PC, using the new File History tool for recovering old versions of files, or finding out about free alternatives to Microsoft Office and more, you'll find plenty of useful hacks.

HACK 33 Three Quick System and Performance Hacks

Want to get more out of Windows 8 fast? Use these three fast hacks.

Sometimes you want to delve deep into Windows 8, spending a good deal of time in order to wring out big performance gains.

Given that you're reading this hack, this isn't one of those times. Because I'm going to offer you three quick hacks that let you get more out of Windows by spending hardly any time at all. They'll let you schedule maintenance, display hidden administrative tools, and check your RAM for problems.

Schedule Windows 8 Maintenance

Windows 8 does a very good of maintaining your Windows 8 device in top shape behind the scenes—checking for software updates, performing system diagnostics, and performing security scans. It does this on a schedule of its own devising.

That schedule, though, might not be best for you. Maybe you'll be working while maintenance is going on, and Windows disrupts your work. Or maybe you'd like it to perform certain tasks more frequently or less frequently. But no matter what the reason, it's easy to change Windows 8's default maintenance schedule. To get started, launch Control Panel and then choose System and Security→Action Center→Maintenance.

To run any maintenance task manually, click "Start maintenance," and Windows 8 goes off and performs all of its normal maintenance tasks. It displays a small notification that "Maintenance is in progress."

To instead change the maintenance schedule, launch Control Panel and then choose System and Security→Action Center→Maintenance→"Change maintenance settings." From the screen that appears (Figure 4-1), choose the time of day you want the maintenance to be performed.

Figure 4-1.
Changing your automatic maintenance schedule

If you don't see the "Start maintenance" or "Change maintenance settings" options when you get to this screen, click the down arrow next to Maintenance.

Display Administrative Tools

Windows 8 has a whole host of very useful administrative tools, such as the Performance Monitor, Resource Monitor, memory diagnostics, and many more. But looking at the tiles on the Start screen, you wouldn't know that. That's a problem, because you can't even see what useful administrative tools Windows 8 has.

There's an easy fix. When you're on the Start screen, press Windows key+C, select Settings→Tiles, and turn on the "Show administrative tools" setting (Figure 4-2). When you do that, they'll all be within easy reach on the Start screen. You'll likely have to scroll all the way over to the right to see them, grouped together (Figure 4-3).

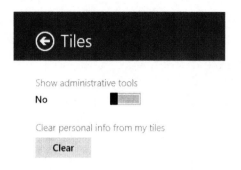

Figure 4-2.
The toggle switch for turning administrative tools on and off

Figure 4-3.
Turn on the display of administrative tools, and you'll get tile-based access to them

There's another way to get access to these tools. Right-click the lower-left corner of the screen, and a menu pops up with to several of them, as well as some tools not available as tiles, such as the elevated command prompt.

Perform a Memory Check

Now that you've turned on administrative tools, it's time to start using them. If you've found your system experiencing odd problems, you may have problems with your memory. Click the Windows Memory Diagnostics tile (you'll be reminded to save your work and close running programs if you haven't already), and then click "Restart now and check for problems" (Figure 4-4). Your computer will shut down, and Windows will check for memory problems. Be patient, because the test can take some time. You can watch a progress bar as the test digs into your computer's memory.

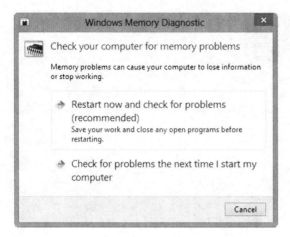

Figure 4-4.
Checking for memory problems

See Also

- Hack #34, "Troubleshoot Performance Issues Using the Resource Monitor"
- Hack #35, "Track Performance and Reliability with the Reliability Monitor"
- Hack #36, "Peer Deep into Your System with the Performance Monitor"
- Hack #37, "Speed Up System Performance with the Task Manager"

HACK 34 Troubleshoot Performance Issues Using the Resource Monitor

Got a sluggish PC? The System Monitor is one of the best ways you'll find in Windows 8 for tracking down the source of the problem.

At some point in the life of your Windows 8 device it may become sluggish, slow down, or otherwise have problems. Tracking down these problems can be exceedingly difficult. As you'll see in Hack #37, "Speed Up System Performance with the Task Manager", the Task Manager is one very good tool for finding them.

But there's also a very useful, lesser-known tool called the Resource Monitor (Figure 4-5) that helps as well. It's extremely useful for tracking down the cause of sluggish performance. It shows you what kind of resources your system uses, and which applications and services are making the most use of your system.

To run it, type *Resource Monitor* at the Start screen, click Files, and then click the Resource Monitor icon that appears. (If you're turned on the display of Administrative tools, as outlined in Hack #33, "Three Quick System and Performance Hacks", you can also click the Resource Monitor tile on the Start screen.)

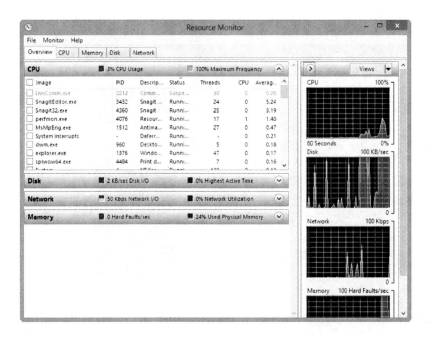

Figure 4-5.
The Windows 8 Resource Monitor is an excellent tool for tracking down the cause of sluggish performance

The Overview tab display a snapshot of your system—CPU use, disk use, network use, and memory use. On the righthand side, you see their use over time. On the lefthand side, you see details about their use. Click the down arrow next to CPU, Disk, Network, or Memory to display details. Or you can instead just look at the overview. The other tabs—CPU, Memory, Disk, and Network—show in-depth details.

The Resource Monitor is easy to interpret. If you see high usage on any of the tabs, you'll know you've got a problem there. Then, it's time to track down the cause. Each tab shows you which applications or services are making use of that particular re-source. For example, the CPU tab shows all the apps and services using the CPU. It shows a running average of CPU use for each app and service. Those that use the most

CPU are listed at the top; those that use it the least are listed at the bottom. So, for example, if you've got an over-taxed CPU, look at which apps or service overuse it. Close them to solve the immediate problem, and consider finding alternatives for the future.

The other tabs work the same way. The display in each tab varies according to what information is the most useful. For example, the Memory tab (Figure 4-6) shows, in addition to which programs and services are using memory, how much is currently used, cached, reserved for hardware, and so on.

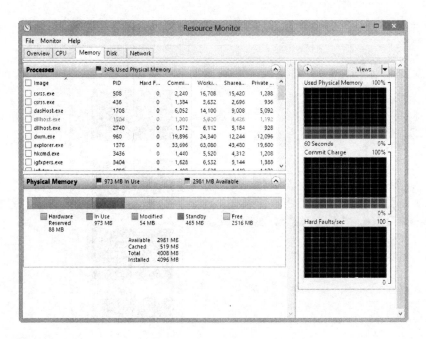

Figure 4-6.
The Windows 8 Resource Monitor is an excellent tool for tracking down the cause of sluggish performance

See Also

- Hack #33, "Three Quick System and Performance Hacks"
- Hack #35, "Track Performance and Reliability with the Reliability Monitor"
- Hack #36, "Peer Deep into Your System with the Performance Monitor"
- Hack #37, "Speed Up System Performance with the Task Manager"
- Hack #41, "Troubleshoot with the Action Center"
- Hack #42, "Track Down Windows 8 System Woes"

Track Performance and Reliability with the Reliability Monitor

Here's the single best place to go in Windows 8 for getting the inside info on system performance and reliability.

Windows 8 offers a great tool for checking your system's reliability and tracking down potential causes of problems. It's the Reliability Monitor, and it offers a real-time, live snapshot of system performance, as well as a historical view of overall reliability, complete with detailed information about system crashes.

To run it, type *Reliability* at the Start screen, click Files, and click the "view reliability history" icon that appears. It shows how reliable your PC has been over time, gives it a reliability rating, and offers details about system crashes (Figure 4-7).

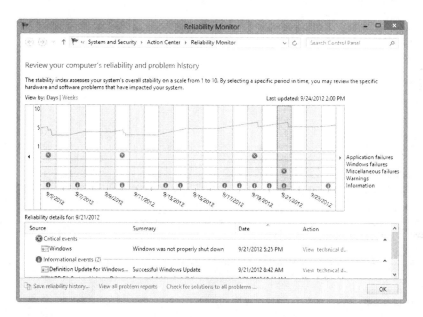

Figure 4-7.
Windows 8's Reliability Monitor

The blue line moving across the graph represents a number that Windows 8 calculates gauging your system's overall reliability on a scale from 1 to 10. Every time there's a system failure, application failure, and so on, the index drops—sometimes precipitously, especially if there has been more than one failure in a day. For example, on my Windows 8 PC, I had three failures in one day, and the reliability index dropped from over 5 to under 3.

For every day that your system doesn't have a failure, the index rises a little bit. But exactly how Windows 8 calculates the amount of drops and rises is rather mysterious.

Even more important than the overall reliability index are the details of each system crash. Go to each day that has a crash, and see the cause: an application, an overall system failure, and so on. Look for patterns, such as if a certain application frequently crashes. If so, uninstall it, or look for an update that fixes the problem.

Beneath the moving chart, issues are grouped into categories, including Application failures, Windows failures, Miscellaneous failures, Warnings, and Information, so you can see at a glance what kind of issues you have.

Down at the bottom of the screen, click "View all problem reports," and rather than seeing a moving chart over time, you instead see a list of all of your problems, including summaries, as in Figure 4-8.

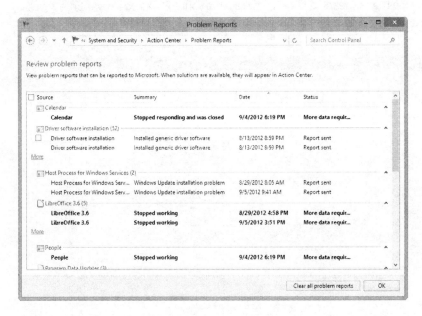

Figure 4-8.
Windows 8's Reliability Monitor's summary of problems

Hacking the Hack

If you want details about each crash and system problem—excruciating detail, in fact—double-click any of them. You'll see a screen like that shown in Figure 4-9. Details include the file name and path, and the kind of information that might be useful to programmers to track down the cause of the problem. Click the "Copy to clipboard" link at the bottom of the page, and all the details will be copied to the clipboard. From there, you can paste it into a file and send it to tech support, who might be able to use it to help with troubleshooting.

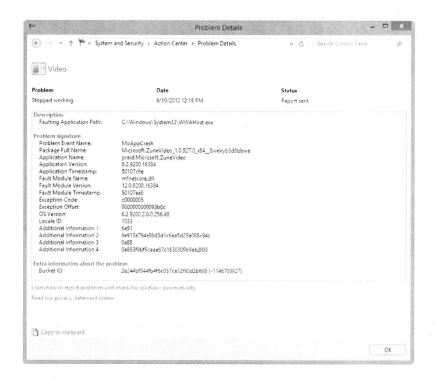

Figure 4-9.
Double-click an issue in the Reliability Monitor to get the full story

See Also

- Hack #33, "Three Quick System and Performance Hacks"

- Hack #34, "Troubleshoot Performance Issues Using the Resource Monitor"

- Hack #36, "Peer Deep into Your System with the Performance Monitor"

- Hack #37, "Speed Up System Performance with the Task Manager"

HACK 36 Peer Deep into Your System with the Performance Monitor

If you're looking for x-ray vision into your PC's performance, here's where to go. Just don't expect to understand what you see.

Sometimes you want to see something just because you want to see it. Not necessarily because it might help you accomplish something, but because... well, sometimes it's not that clear *why*, but you just do.

That's how I feel about the Performance Monitor. This tool shows you more details about the inner workings of your Windows 8 system, hardware, and software than you could possibly imagine. Whether you understand what you see is another thing entirely. But sometimes, it's fun just to see.

To launch the Performance Monitor, type *Performance Monitor* at the Start screen, click Files, and click the Performance Monitor icon that appears. (If you've turned on the display of Administrative tools, as outlined in Hack #33, "Three Quick System and Performance Hacks" you can also click the Performance Monitor tile on the Start screen.) You can see the Performance Monitor in action in Figure 4-10.

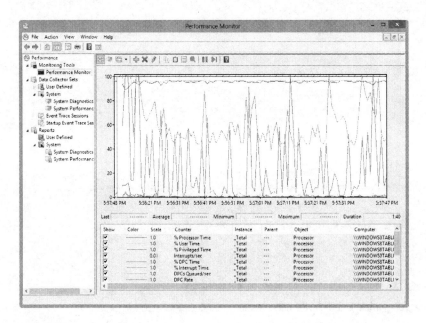

Figure 4-10.
Windows 8's Performance Monitor

What you see may or may not look exactly like what you see in the figure, because the Performance Monitor is extremely configurable. It shows a moving snapshot of system performance in exquisite detail over time. You can easily add those details, so you can monitor hard disk performance, processor performance, browser performance, and so on.

Performance Monitor works by using what it calls *counters*, which are modules that track your system's use. To add a counter, right-click in the graph area, select "Add counters" and then scroll through the available counters (Figure 4-11). Some are easy to figure out, such as Processor or Print Queue. Others, such as Pacer Pipe or NUMA Node Memory, will be baffling.

Each counter is made up of one or more subcounters, often many more. And here's where things can get confusing, even when you think you have a sense of what a counter does. In the Processors subcounters, for example, it's clear what %Processor Time does, but not DPC Rate.

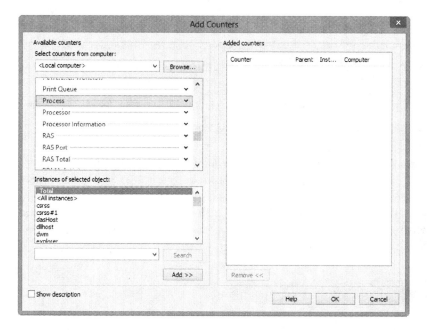

Figure 4-11.
Adding counters to the Performance Monitor

Add whichever you want, and then head to the graph to watch your system's performance.

See Also

- Hack #33, "Three Quick System and Performance Hacks"

- Hack #34, "Troubleshoot Performance Issues Using the Resource Monitor"

- Hack #35, "Track Performance and Reliability with the Reliability Monitor"

- Hack #37, "Speed Up System Performance with the Task Manager"

HACK 37
Speed Up System Performance with the Task Manager

This humble tool does more than show you which applications are running; it can help juice up your PC's performance as well.

As you may know, the Task Manager shows you all programs and processes running on your system and lets you shut down any you don't want to run any longer. But it can do much more than that; it can also help fine-tune system performance.

There are five common ways to run the Task Manager:

- Press Ctrl+Shift+Esc.
- Right-click the taskbar on the Desktop, and choose Task Manager.
- Type *Task Manager* at the Start screen, and then click the Task Manager icon that appears.
- Press Ctrl+Alt+Del, and then choose Task Manager from the screen that appears.
- Right-click the lower left portion of your screen and select Task Manager.

In Windows 8, unlike in previous versions of Windows, the Task Manager has two interfaces: A stripped-down simplified one, shown in Figure 4-12, and a much more detailed robust one, shown in Figure 4-13, which you use for troubleshooting and improving system performance. To switch between them, click the "More details" down arrow when you're in the simplified version, or click the "Fewer details" up arrow when you're in the more detailed version.

Figure 4-12.
The simplified interface of the Task Manager

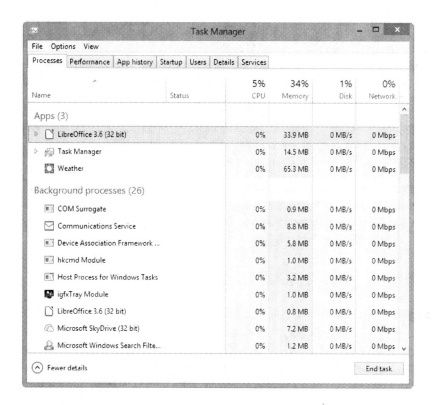

Figure 4-13.
The more robust Task Manager interface

The robust, detailed version of Task Manager has seven tabs, but you'll generally use the App History, Processes, and Performance tabs to help improve system performance. In this hack, I'll cover how to use the detailed version of the Task Manager.

> *Note: The Task Manager is also a great tool for speeding up system startup and stopping unnecessary programs from launching at startup. For details on how to use it, see* Hack #04, "Speed Up Startup by Halting Startup Programs and Services".

Before you can learn how to use the Task Manager to improve performance, you'll need some background about the tabs you'll use most: Processes, Performance, Users, and App history.

Processes Tab

The Processes tab (shown in Figure 4-14) reports on every process running on your computer, as well as a variety of services run by the operating system and currently running apps. It reports on the percentage of the CPU that each process uses, as well as how much memory, disk capacity, and network resources each process uses.

When you right-click any app, service, or process, you get a menu of choices that allow you to manage it in a variety of ways, including ending it along with any related processes (if there are any), as shown in Figure 4-14.

When you right-click an application, a menu of choices lets you manage the application in several ways; you can switch to it, move it to the front, minimize it, maximize it, or end it. The Go To Process option takes you to the application's process on the Processes tab. You can get more information about the application this way.

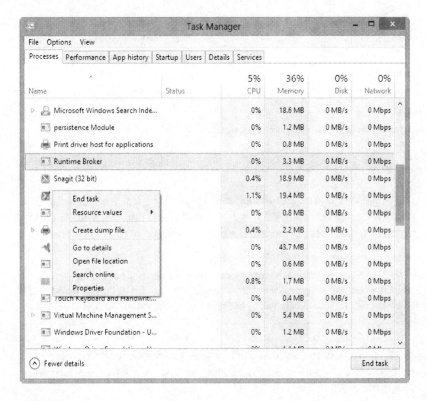

Figure 4-14.
Right-clicking a process on the Processes tab

Performance Tab

The Performance tab shows a variety of performance measurements, including CPU, Memory, Disk, Ethernet, Bluetooth, and Wi-Fi use, as shown in Figure 4-15.

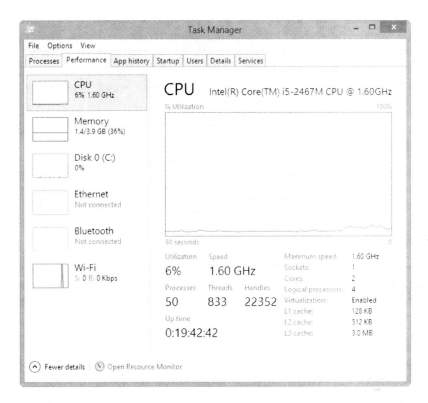

Figure 4-15.
The Performance tab lets you see how individual system elements are running

You'll use this tab more than any other when tracking system performance and un-stopping bottlenecks. The Performance tab has thumbnail graphs on the left showing high-level details about the performance of each measurement it tracks. Click any thumbnail, and the right-side portion of the screen shows a larger, more detailed graph and additional information. For example, click Memory, and you'll get information about your total memory, how much is in use, how much is available, how much is cached, and so on.

There are multiple ways to use this tab to help improve system performance. Look at the thumbnail graphs and see if utilization is too high on any of them. If you've got high CPU use of more than 80 percent or more, you might be experiencing system slowdowns. As I'll explain later in this hack, you can then track down which apps are using too much CPU and close them down. Similarly, if you see high memory use, you'll want to track down which apps are using too much memory, and close them down as well—and I'll show you how to do that later in this hack, too. And you can do the same thing with the other thumbnails. Wi-Fi shows you your bandwidth speed, among other details, for example, so that you can tell whether you've got connection problems.

Task Manager updates its data every two seconds, and each vertical line on the graphs represents a two-second interval. To change the update time, choose View→Update Speed, and select High or Low. When you select High, updates take place twice a second. When you select Low, updates take place once every four seconds. To stop updating altogether, select Pause. To do an immediate update, select "Refresh now" or press F5.

App History Tab

If you're familiar with the pre-Windows 8 Task Manager, you'll see a big difference between this tab and the old Applications tab in previous versions of the Task Manager. The old Applications tab displayed a list of every application currently running on your PC, like Word, Excel, Windows 8 native apps, or any other application. It also reported on the status of each application.

In the Windows 8 Task Manager, you check the Processes tab to get that kind of information. The Windows 8 App history tab serves a very different purpose—to provide information about Windows 8 native apps, and see the ways in which they've been used over time. It doesn't give information about Desktop apps.

For each app, the tab shows the total CPU time it's taken up, the total amount of network bandwidth it's used, the total metered bandwidth it's used (see Hack #72, "Hack Windows 8 Wi-Fi, Wireless, and Network Settings"), and the total amount of data used by the apps' tile updates.

How can this tab help you? Perhaps its greatest use is in tracking down network bandwidth hogs. Check the Network, "Metered network, "and "Tile updates" columns to see each app's bandwidth use. You'd expect a network-centric app like Internet Explorer to use a lot of bandwidth, so don't be surprised if it's your biggest bandwidth consumer. But if you see an app whose operation is not Internet-centric or network-centric taking up gobs of bandwidth, you might have a problem.

Similarly, if you notice that an app that you rarely run takes up what seems to be an inordinate amount of CPU time, you've probably found a CPU hog.

What to do in those cases? Consider uninstalling the app or finding an alternative to it.

Users Tab

This tab displays the currently logged-on users of your machine and shows how much CPU, memory, disk, and network resources the currently logged-on user is consuming (Figure 4-16). If you see any currently logged-on user taking up too many resources, consider switching to that account and logging the user off.

You can also see details about the apps, resources, and services for each user by clicking the triangle next to that user. From there, you can identify any apps, resources and services that take up too much CPU, memory, disk, or network resources. You may be able to close down those apps, resources, and services as a way to ease the stress on your system.

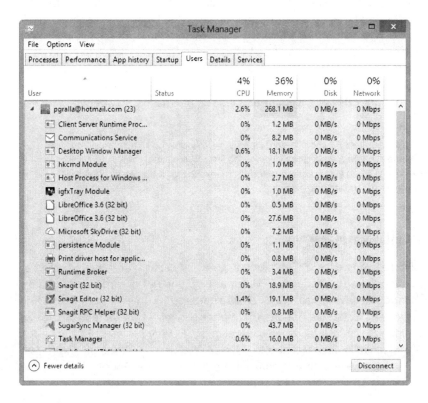

Figure 4-16.
The Task Manager's Users tab

Monitor CPU Use

Today's microprocessors can handle most tasks easily, but CPU-intensive software or tasks such as computer-aided design (CAD) programs, CD burning, and games can slow down a system significantly. So can multitasking many apps simultaneously. A common cause of CPU slowdown is that one or more programs or processes take up too much of the CPU's attention. You can use the Task Manager to monitor your CPU use and, based on what you find, take steps to help your system run faster.

Monitor your CPU usage using the Performance tab of the Task Manager. If you find a problem, head over to the Processes tab. On that tab, check the percentage of the CPU that any individual program uses. To make it easier, click the CPU column; it will show the apps, services, and processes that take up the most CPU time at the top. The topmost listed takes up the most, the second listed takes up the second most, and so on. Once you determine which one you want to close, right-click it, and select End Task. (For an app, though, you'll be better off if you instead switch to it and close it down from the app interface. That way, you won't lose any files or data associated with it.) Your system will get a quick performance boost. If you need to run that application, close any other applications that take up too much CPU attention.

> *Tip: It's probably not a good idea to close down Windows 8 native apps from the Task Manager. Windows 8 does a very good job of monitoring them, and closes or pauses them when you no longer need them, except for background tasks like updating its tile or fetching new mail.*

Tracking CPU usage in real time

If your CPU regularly uses a high percentage of its capacity, it means there's a bottleneck. You should upgrade the CPU, buy a new computer, or run fewer programs. But how can you know whether your CPU has a bottleneck? Check your CPU use. Run Task Manager, and make sure Options→Hide When Minimized is selected. Now, whenever you minimize the Task Manager, it will sit in the Taskbar's System Tray area. The first time you minimize Task Manager like this on Windows 8, you should drag it from that area and place it next to the icons for the Action Center, Power, Network, and Sound.

Now, minimize the Task Manager. It will appear as a small bar graph in the System Tray that lights up green as you use your CPU. To see your current CPU usage, hold your mouse cursor over the Task Manager's icon in the System Tray. Try running different combinations of programs, and monitor your CPU use with each combination. If you find your CPU is overburdened on a regular basis, it's time for an upgraded CPU or a new computer.

Give Program and Processes More of Your CPU's Attention

Windows gives a *base priority* to every program and process running on your PC; the base priority determines the relative amount of CPU power the program or process gets, compared to other programs. Here are the priorities Windows assigns:

- Low
- Below Normal
- Normal
- Above Normal
- High
- Real Time

Most programs and processes are assigned a Normal priority. But you might want to give a program like a CAD or graphics program more of your CPU's attention. That way, the program will get the CPU power it needs and run more smoothly and quickly. If there are programs or processes that normally run in the background or rarely need your CPU, you can give them less of your CPU's attention.

You can use the Task Manager to change the priorities assigned to any process or program. The Low, Below Normal, Normal, Above Normal, and High priorities are self-explanatory, but *Real Time* may be unfamiliar. Real Time devotes an exceedingly high number of CPU cycles to the given task—so much so that even the Task Manager might not be able to interrupt any program or process assigned that priority. So don't assign a Real Time priority to any program or task unless it will be the sole program or task running on the PC. Of course, if it's the only program or task running, you really don't need to give it a high priority, because it already has your CPU's complete attention.

To change the priority of a running program or process, use the Details tab. On that tab, right-click the program or process whose priority you want to change, highlight Set Priority, and choose a priority, as shown in Figure 4-17.

Be careful when using this feature, because it can have unintended consequences and lead to system instability. If you find it causes problems, stop using it.

Note: Keep in mind that when you assign a new priority to a process or program, that new priority sticks only as long as the program or process is running. Once the program or process ends and you restart it, it defaults to the priority assigned to it by Windows.

Figure 4-17.
Setting a priority using the Details tab

See Also

- Hack #33, "Three Quick System and Performance Hacks"

- Hack #34, "Troubleshoot Performance Issues Using the Resource Monitor"

- Hack #35, "Track Performance and Reliability with the Reliability Monitor"

- Hack #36, "Peer Deep into Your System with the Performance Monitor"

HACK 38   Windows 8 Keyboard Shortcuts

> Want to be more productive when using Windows 8? Use these keyboard
> shortcuts instead of mousing around.

Think of all the time you spend in Windows 8 using your mouse to accomplish simple
actions—opening the Charms bar, opening a new window in Internet Explorer, showing the Desktop. It's plenty of time and plenty of movement.

It doesn't have to be that way. You can get a lot done just using your keyboard. Use out the following tables for keyboard shortcuts, and you'll save miles of mouse movements, and plenty of time as well.

Windows Key Shortcuts

KEYBOARD COMBINATION	WHAT IT DOES
Windows key	Goes to Start screen or toggles between the Start screen and your current action
Windows key+C	Open Charms bar
Windows key+D	Show the Desktop
Windows key+E	Open Windows Explorer
Windows key+F	Go to Files in the Search charm
Windows key+H	Go to the Share charm
Windows key+I	Go to the Settings charm
Windows key+K	Go to the Devices charm
Windows key+L	Locks your PC
Windows key+M	Minimize all windows (only on the Desktop)
Windows key+O	Lock the screen orientation
Windows key+P	Open Projection Mode pane
Windows key+Q	Go to the Search charm
Windows key+R	Launch the Run box
Windows key+T	Put the focus on the Taskbar and cycle through your running Desktop apps
Windows key+U	Open the Ease of Access Center
Windows key+V	Cycle through your notifications
Windows key+W	Go to Settings in the Search charm
Windows key+X	Open the power user menu
Windows key+Z	Go to the app bar
Windows key+1 through 9	Go to the app on the corresponding position on the Taskbar (Desktop only)
Windows key++	Zoom in (when using Magnifier)
Windows key+−	Zoom out (when using Magnifier)
Windows key+,	Peek at the Desktop (on Desktop only)
Windows key+.	Snap a Windows 8 native app to the right (Windows key+Shift+. snaps it to the left)
Windows key+Enter	Opens the Narrator
Windows key+Spacebar	Switches the input language and keyboard layout

KEYBOARD COMBINATION	WHAT IT DOES
Windows key+Tab	Cycle through the Windows 8 native app history
Windows key+Esc	Exit the magnifier
Windows key+Home	Minimize non-active desktop windows
Windows key+Page Up	Move Start screen or any Windows 8 native app to left monitor
Windows key+Page Down	Move Start screen or any Windows 8 native app to right monitor
Windows key+Break	Open System Properties
Windows key+Left arrow	Snap desktop window to the left
Windows key+Right arrow	Snap desktop window to the right
Windows key+Up arrow	Maximize desktop window
Windows key+Down arrow	Restore/minimize desktop window
Windows key+F1	Run Windows Help and Support

Other Keyboard Shortcuts

KEYBOARD COMBINATION	WHAT IT DOES
Ctrl+A	Select all
Ctrl+C	Copy
Ctrl+E or F4	Select the Search box in Internet Explorer (Select Address Bar in Desktop version)
Ctrl+N	Open new window in Internet Explorer (Desktop version only)
Ctrl+R or F5	Refresh
Ctrl+V	Paste
Ctrl +X	Cut
Ctrl+Y	Redo
Ctrl+Z	Undo
Ctrl+Tab	Cycle through the Windows 8 native app history
Ctrl+Esc	Go to the Start screen
Ctrl+Ins	Copy
Ctrl+F4	Close the active document (closes the current tab in Internet Explorer)
Ctrl+click	Select multiple items in File Explorer
Ctrl+Shift	Select a group of contiguous items in File Explorer
Ctrl+W or Ctrl+F4	Close the current window in Internet Explorer (Desktop version)
Ctrl+Shift +Esc	Run the Task Manager

KEYBOARD COMBINATION	WHAT IT DOES
Ctrl+Shift+N	Create a new folder in Windows Explorer
Ctrl+Alt+D	Dock the Magnifier at the top of the screen
Ctrl+Alt+L	Put Magnifier into lens mode
Ctrl+Alt+I	Invert the Magnifier's colors
PrtScn	Take a screenshot and place it on the Clipboard

See Also

• Hack #39, "Using Windows 8 Gestures"

HACK 39 Using Windows 8 Gestures

> Got a tablet or touchscreen device? Here's the lowdown on gestures you can use.

Windows 8 is the first Microsoft operating system designed from the ground up to run using a touchscreen with a feature called multitouch, Obviously, this feature is mostly intended for tablets, but you'll find plenty of desktops and laptops with touchscreens as well.

But touchscreen gestures aren't always intuitive, and there are some you may not know about. So use the following table of touchscreen gestures to get up close and personal with your Windows 8 device.

Note: Not all of these gestures work in all places and apps on Windows 8, so you may need to test some. Typically, they don't work on Desktop apps.

Windows 8 Gestures

GESTURE	WHAT IT DOES
Tap	Opens an item. It's the equivalent of clicking with a mouse.
Tap and hold	Pops up a menu to display more information about the item.
Slide and drag	Tap and hold an item, then drag it to a new location. It's the equivalent of dragging an item with a mouse.
Pinch with two fingers	Zooms out. Used in apps such as Maps, where you commonly zoom in and out.
Spread with two fingers	Zooms in. Used in apps such as Maps, where you commonly zoom in and out.

GESTURE	WHAT IT DOES
Rotate with two fingers	Rotates the display in the direction you move your fingers. Very few apps use this gesture.
Swipe horizontally	Scroll sideways through a screen, such as through the Start screen to see apps off the side of the screen.
Swipe vertically	Scroll up or down.
Short downward swipe on an item	Selects an item and shows additional options, often in an app bar.
Swipe in from the upper edge or lower edge of the screen in a Windows 8 native app or the Start screen	Activates the app bar
Swipe in from the left edge of the screen to the right	Displays the Charms bar
Swipe in from left edge of the screen	Displays a thumbnail of the previously run app
Swipe slowly in from the left edge of the screen	Displays a second app side-by-side with the current app on your screen.
Swipe quickly in from the left edge of the screen, then swipe quickly back	Displays thumbnails of all your running apps.
Pull down from the top	Close an app
Swipe left or right in Internet Explorer (Windows 8 native app only)	Go forward or back

See Also

- Hack #38, "Windows 8 Keyboard Shortcuts"

HACK 40 Use File History to Recover Your Files

> Windows 8 has its own Wayback Machine called File History. Here's how to turn it on and use it so you'll never lose a version of a file again.

It happens to everybody: you've accidentally deleted a file and now can't find it. Or you've made changes to a file, only to realize that it was better before you made the changes. Or maybe you simply want to see a file's entire version history. Or, worst of all, your hard disk crashed, and you want to recover files.

Windows 8's File History brings that capability, much like that of Mac OS X's Time Machine, for the first time to Windows. Windows 7 had a feature similar to it, called Previous Versions. But Previous Versions was hard to find and even harder to use. It was, to be honest, something of a failure.

Not so File History. It's a great, though not perfect, feature of Windows 8. There's a good chance that you don't know about it, because it's not enabled by default and there's no app tile for it, so it's not that easy to find. But as you'll see in this hack, once you use it, you'll be glad you found it.

Before we get hacking, a few words about what File History does and how it works. It backs up whatever it finds in your Libraries, on your Desktop, in Contacts, and in Favorites, and then lets you restore what it's backed up, including interim versions of your files.

This all means backing up a lot of files, because your Libraries contain, at minimum, the following folders:

- My Documents
- Public Documents
- My Music
- Public Music
- My Pictures
- Public Pictures
- My Videos
- Public Videos
- SkyDrive (only if you've installed the local SkyDrive client and have local SkyDrive folders on your PC)

Tip: As you'll see later in this hack, there are ways to exclude folders from File History. So if you don't want to back up, for example, videos because they take up too much space, you can exclude folders that contain your videos.

In addition to that, you can add individual folders to File History as well.

With that as background, let's get started.

Turning on File History

By default, File History is turned off, and Windows 8 doesn't even tell you it's there. But it's not too hard to find. On the Start screen, type **File History**, click Settings, and then click the File History icon that appears on the left side of the screen. You'll come to a screen like the one in Figure 4-18.

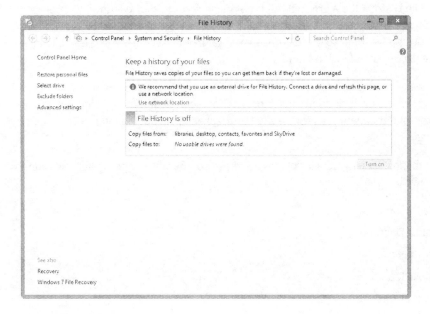

Figure 4-18.
Welcome to File History

You'll need to set where to save copies of your files. You can't choose the hard drive on which you have the files you want backed up, because that would defeat one of the main purposes of the feature—the ability to restore files from a crashed hard disk.

If you have more than one hard disk, you can use one of those disks as the location for storing the backed-up files. But it's a better idea to instead use a different disk or location; for example, a folder on another PC on your network, or USB-attached storage.

When you get to the screen, you'll be told that File History is turned off. You'll also see any additional hard drives beyond your primary one, as well as any removable storage connected to your device, such as a USB hard drive or USB flash drive. If you haven't connected them, now's the time to do it.

Select the disk you want to use for storing files for File History and then click "Turn on." If you instead want to use a network location, click "Use network location," then from the screen that appears click, "Add network location," and browse to and select the location you want to use. During that process, you can also create a new folder on your network to be your backup location (Figure 4-19). Click Select Folder when you've chosen the location.

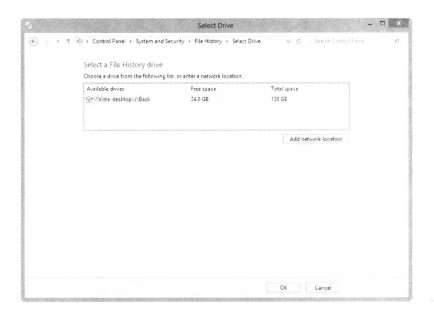

Figure 4-19.
Adding a network location where you'll back up files

Note: You can only add network locations on devices to which you have access.

Once you've chosen the location to backup your files, whether it's on a disk or network location, click "Turn on." When you do, a screen asks whether you want to tell other members of your Homegroup network about this location. In that way, everyone on the network can use a common backup location. Click Yes to notify them, and No not to. After that, you'll be sent back to the File History screen, shown in Figure 4-20. File History immediately sets to work, and begins backing up your files.

When you come back here again, you'll see a notification telling you when the last time File History backed up your files was. You can also tell File History to back up your files right then by clicking the Run Now link. If you want to exclude any folders, click the "Exclude folders" link, select the folders you want excluded, and File History won't back them up.

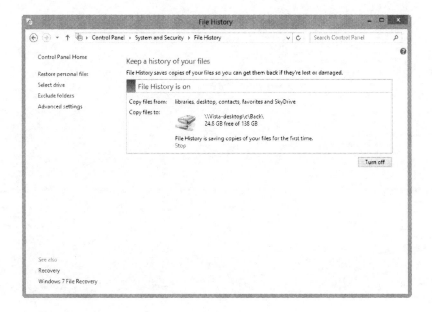

Figure 4-20.
Adding a network location where you'll back up files

Hacking File History

You've got plenty of options for changing the way that File History works (Figure 4-21). Click "Advanced settings" to change the following settings:

Save copies of files

Lets you set how frequently your files are saved. The default is every hour, but you can select any time between every ten minutes to daily.

Size of offline cache

File History uses a cache on your system disk to replicate your backups. This cache can be sizable, but this option lets you limit the size. The default size is 5% of the disk, but you can change that to be as low as 2% or as high as 20%.

Keep saved versions

How long do you want to save the versions of your files? The default is forever. That can take up a substantial amount of disk space, so you can also set limits on how long to keep them. Your choices are between one month and two years, and forever. You can also select "Until space is needed," as a way to balance your need for old files versus your need for disk space.

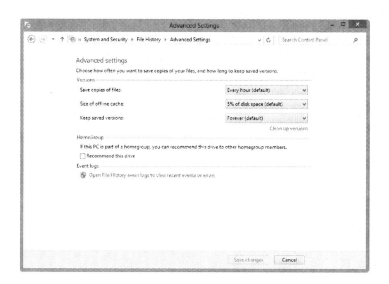

Figure 4-21.
Changing the way File History works

Also notable on this screen is the "Open File History events logs to view recent events or errors" link. Click it and you'll open the Windows 8 Event Viewer, which reports on any issues File History might have had. When File Viewer opens, you'll see some details about it. Click the event to see even more details, as shown in Figure 4-22.

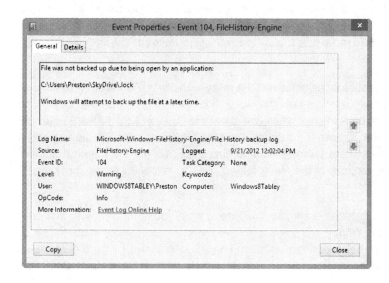

Figure 4-22.
Peering into a problem that File History encountered

Using File History to Recover Files

To recover files with File History, go to the File History screen and click "Restore personal files," or launch File Explorer and click History on the Home tab. It makes much more sense to use the File Explorer way to restore files, because you can first head right to the folder where you want to either recover deleted files or recover a previous version of an existing file. In Figure 4-23, you can see what File History looks like when accessed this way.

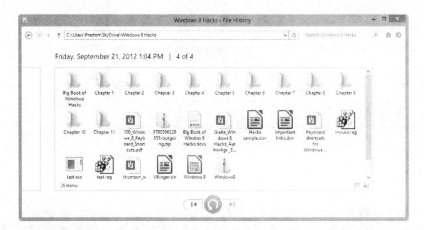

Figure 4-23.
Opening File History from File Explorer

You'll see the most recent versions of your files. You can navigate from here much the same way you do in File Explorer—double-click folders to drill down, click the up arrow at the address bar to move up a folder, and type an address into the address bar to go to a specific folder.

Much more interesting is the bottom of the screen. There, you'll find a way to go back in time to see previous versions of the files and folders—and restore them. Click the back button to go back in time; when you're back in time, click the forward button to go forward in time. You see the date and time the folder or file was backed up at the top of each screen. There's also a pair of numbers, like "4 of 4." That means that there are total of four versions of the file or folder, and you're looking at the most recent version.

Recovering a file or folder is simple. Navigate to what you want to recover and click the green button. What you'll see depends on whether you've highlighted a file or folder that's been deleted, or for which you have a later version. Figure 4-24 shows what happens when you're clicking an older version of an existing file. In that case, you can replace the newer file with the older one, skip the file and do nothing, or compare information about the two files to see which you want to keep. In that case, click "Compare info for both files" and a screen like the one in Figure 4-25 appears, showing basic details about each file. You can then decide which to keep.

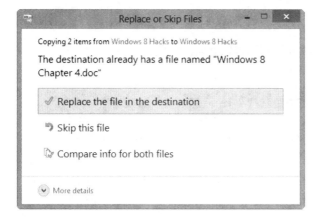

Figure 4-24.
Starting to restore a file

Figure 4-25.
Comparing two files to see which to keep

But what if you want to keep both files—the old and the new? Instead of clicking the green button, right-click the file (or folder), and from the screen that appears, select "Restore to." You can then restore the file to a different location than the current file; that way, you'll be able to have both files. In addition, when you right-click, you can instead preview the file by first selecting Preview.

See Also

- Hack #05, "Reset and Refresh Your PC Instead of Doing a Complete Reinstall"

HACK 41 Troubleshoot with the Action Center

This little-used tool can help fix problems with your Windows 8 device, including ones you never even knew you had.

As you can see in this chapter, Windows 8 includes plenty of tools for juicing performance and troubleshooting problems. You've likely overlooked one called the Action Center, but it's worth visiting; see Figure 4-26. To run it, type **Action** at the Start screen, highlight settings, and click the "Action Center" icon that appears.

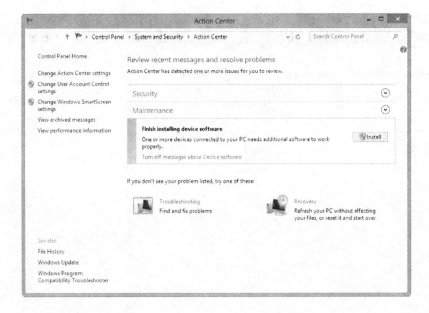

Figure 4-26.
The Windows 8 Action Center

Using the Action Center is exceptionally easy and intuitive. Click Troubleshooting to track down any problems with your PC, and click Recovery to refresh your PC with a quick reinstall of Windows (Hack #05, "Reset and Refresh Your PC Instead of Doing a Complete

Reinstall"). Pay attention to the Maintenance area, because it'll prod you to take actions you may have missed. For example, on my Windows 8 PC, I hadn't realized that a proper device driver wasn't installed, and the Maintenance section prompted me with a nice clear Install button. Click the down arrow next to it, and you'll find a variety of links to various maintenance tools, as you can see in Figure 4-27.

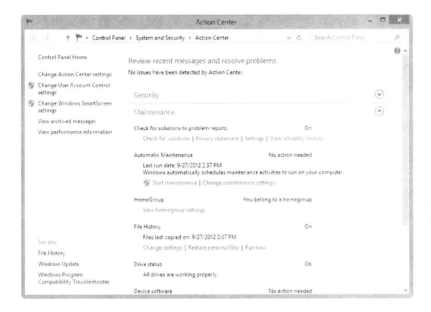

Figure 4-27.
The Windows 8 Action Center's maintenance area

There are also links for checking your security, looking at old messages from the Action Center, and more. Take a few minutes to check them out. Your PC will thank you.

See Also

- Hack #34, "Troubleshoot Performance Issues Using the Resource Monitor"
- Hack #36, "Peer Deep into Your System with the Performance Monitor"
- Hack #42, "Track Down Windows 8 System Woes"

HACK 42   Track Down Windows 8 System Woes

Here's a great, little-known tool for tracking down system performance issues and helping resolve them.

As you use your PC, Windows 8 records an astonishing amount of information. Memory usage, network usage, system startup, application crashes, system slowdowns: all that and far more is captured in mind-boggling detail.

A well hidden system tool, Event Viewer, lets you get at all that information so that you can see what caused any problems you're having. Based on that, you may be able to fix them.

Launch it by typing *Event Viewer* at the Start screen and clicking its icon. (You can also right-click the lower-left portion of your screen and select Event Viewer from the pop-up menu.) The Event Viewer (Figure 4-28) launches; it lets you read a wide variety of Windows 8 system logs and data.

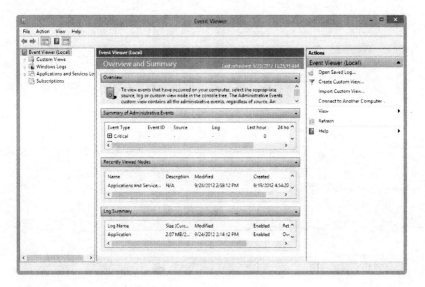

Figure 4-28.
Windows 8's Event Viewer

The Event Viewer is an exceedingly complex application with a wide variety of uses, and a full explanation of it is beyond the scope of this book. So what follows are some of the most important ways to use it to track system performance.

In the left pane, click Windows Logs. A variety of subfolders appear, including Applications, Security, Setup, System, and Forwarded Events. The most important of these from a performance point of view are Applications and System, so scroll through them.

When you click either subfolder, you'll see a list of events that happened on your PC—for example, an app crashed, files were backed up, and so on. Mostly, these are purely informational, and frequently, you won't be able to understand much about the event. Events that are normal, and in which no problems were recorded, have a blue icon of the letter *i*.

Problematic events have other icons, and as you scroll through the subfolders, look for these icons. A yellow warning icon indicates a problem of some sort, although not a severe one. A red warning, shown in Figure 4-29, indicates a more severe issue.

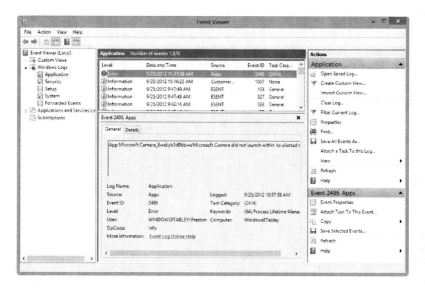

Figure 4-29.
A red warning icon indicates a serious problem

The Applications and Services Log's top-level folder is where most of the action is if you're interested in system performance. Beneath it, you'll find a variety of subfolders. The most important subfolder of all is the *Microsoft\Windows* subfolder, which has far, far more information than the main Windows Log. You'll find dozens of subfolders underneath *Microsoft\Windows*, and each of these has subfolders, often multiple ones.

Most of the subfolders are self-explanatory. Want to see how the Windows Defender anti-malware app is doing? Head to the Windows Defender subfolder. There are also subfolders for many other Windows services.

Most useful of all, from a performance standpoint, is the Diagnostics-Performance subfolder. Click to expand it, then click the Operational page (Figure 4-30). This page contains information about system performance, and reports on overall system problems and slowdowns. An event with a red exclamation point means there was a serious error; one with a red X means the error was a critical one.

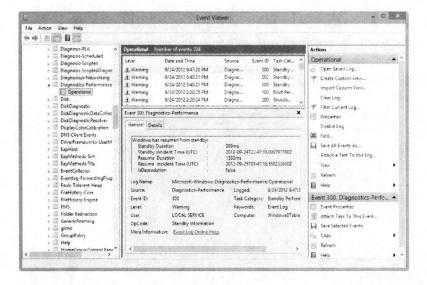

Figure 4-30.
This Windows Vista PC clearly has problems

Scroll through all the errors and warnings. For more detail about any one of them, double-click it, and an Event Properties screen like that shown in Figure 4-31 appears, showing you the details in an easier-to-read format.

As you scroll through the page, look for patterns among the problems. Does a particular application seem to cause issues frequently? If so, consider uninstalling it or upgrading to the latest version, if one is available. Does the problem happen at a certain time of the day? If so, think of what you do on your PC at that time; do you run too many programs at once then?

The Event Viewer won't actually be able to solve problems for you or speed up your system. But by viewing its logs, as outlined in this hack, it can help you see where you have performance issues, and you can take it from there.

See Also

- Hack #34, "Troubleshoot Performance Issues Using the Resource Monitor"
- Hack #36, "Peer Deep into Your System with the Performance Monitor"
- Hack #41, "Troubleshoot with the Action Center"

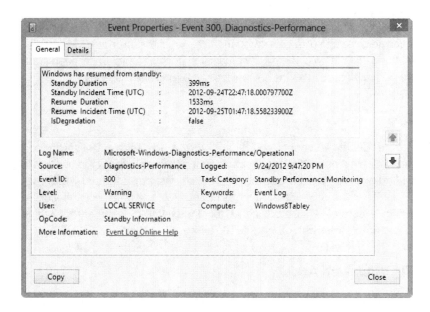

Windows has resumed from standby:
Standby Duration   :   399ms
Standby Incident Time (UTC)   :   2012-09-24T22:47:18.0007977000Z
Resume Duration   :   1533ms
Resume Incident Time (UTC)   :   2012-09-25T01:47:18.5582339000Z
IsDegradation   :   false

Log Name: Microsoft-Windows-Diagnostics-Performance/Operational
Source: Diagnostics-Performance   Logged: 9/24/2012 9:47:20 PM
Event ID: 300   Task Category: Standby Performance Monitoring
Level: Warning   Keywords: Event Log
User: LOCAL SERVICE   Computer: Windows8Tabley
OpCode: Standby Information
More Information: Event Log Online Help

Figure 4-31.
Details about a problematic system event

HACK 43 Save Money: Use These Free Alternatives to Microsoft Office

> Microsoft Office can cost a bundle. Here's how to find similar productivity suites for free.

The cost of a new computer can be misleading, because that price includes only the hardware. Generally, you'll have to pay for productivity software, notably Microsoft Office, and that can cost a bundle.

But you needn't spend that much money, or any money at all. You can instead use free, downloadable alternatives. They might not have all the bells and whistles of Microsoft Office, but they'll likely have everything you need. And they also will write and read files created with Microsoft Office, so you'll still be able to use the worldwide standards for files, such as *.docx*, *.doc*, *.xls*, and so on.

LibreOffice

This free open-source suite is my favorite of all alternatives to Microsoft Office. It does most things I need—and probably that you'll need. In fact, I used LibreOffice (*http://www.libreoffice.org*) to write significant portions of this book. It includes a word processor, spreadsheet, presentation program, drawing program, database, and math program.

Apache OpenOffice

This free, open source suite (*http://www.openoffice.org*) is the forerunner to LibreOffice—LibreOffice is based on it. It has the same set of apps as LibreOffice. I don't find it as useful as LibreOffice, but as the saying goes, your mileage may vary.

Google Docs

If you've got a Google account, you've got access to Google Docs (*https://docs.google.com*), a set of productivity apps designed to work in the cloud on Google Drive. You'll find apps for word processing, spreadsheets, presentations, drawings, and forms. I don't like the interface as much as LibreOffice, and find it doesn't include all of LibreOffice's features. Also, it's designed for cloud computing rather than offline work. But if you collaborate with others, it's the best suite for you.

Microsoft Office Web Apps

Yes, Microsoft does offer this free alternative to Microsoft Office. It's web-based, so you'll need to be connected to the Internet to use it. It has Web versions of Word, Excel, PowerPoint, and OneNote and connects to SkyDrive. It does have some drawbacks, including that not all apps can create documents, and sometimes can only edit them. Get to it via SkyDrive or here (*http://office.microsoft.com/en-us/web-apps*).

Zoho Office

Here's another Web-based office suite, with a word processor, presentation software, spreadsheet, calendar, online organizer, and plenty more. There are also a variety of higher-level business apps—some for free, some for pay. I prefer Google Docs or Microsoft Office Web apps, but if you need higher-level apps, this is a good place to turn. Get it here (*http://www.zoho.com*).

5

Cloud and Social Networking Hacks

Windows 8 is the first version of Windows written from the ground up to take advantage of the cloud and of social media like Facebook and Twitter. Unlike in previous versions of Windows, you don't have to retrofit those capabilities—they're built right in.

That's not to say that you can't hack them, because you can. You can especially juice up Windows 8's cloud features, especially the way it works with the cloud-based storage service SkyDrive. In this chapter, you'll learn how to do all that, plus get more out of Windows 8's other cloud capabilities and its social networking features.

HACK 44 Use SkyDrive to Sync Your Files Everywhere

> Microsoft claims that Windows 8 is built for the cloud, pointing to its SkyDrive cloud-based service. But there's a whole lot more SkyDrive can do for you than is first obvious.

Windows 8 is the first Microsoft operating system built with the cloud in mind, and there are plenty of cloud-based features built into its guts; for example, its integration with social media services like Facebook and Twitter, and the way it can sync your settings across Windows 8 devices.

Then, of course, there's SkyDrive, Microsoft's cloud-based storage service. It's got a big fat tile on the Start screen, so it's only a click (or, on tablets, a tap) away. But the SkyDrive built into Windows 8 isn't particularly useful. It's little more than a pretty interface to the SkyDrive service.

If you really want to get the most out of SkyDrive and the Microsoft cloud, you need to install a free Microsoft Desktop app, also called SkyDrive. This app turns SkyDrive from a moderately useful service into a must-have—it's a way to sync your local documents with documents in the SkyDrive cloud, and to keep documents in sync on all your devices, without you having to do a thing.

First, head to SkyDrive for Windows (*https://apps.live.com/skydrive*) and click the "Get the app" link under SkyDrive for Windows. Download and install it, and then sign in with your Windows Live ID—the same ID you used when you installed Windows 8. The drive installs to *C:\Users\YourAccount\SkyDrive* where YourAccount is your Windows 8 user name, and shows up as a separate folder.

If you've already used SkyDrive, it will automatically populate that folder with all of your SkyDrive documents. Whenever you add a document to it from your Windows 8 PC, it automatically syncs to the cloud (Figure 5-1). And whenever you directly add a document to the cloud from another computer or device, it syncs back down to your Windows 8 PC. That means that any document in SkyDrive you add or change on any device automatically syncs to every other device.

Note: As I write this, the iOS and Android versions of SkyDrive aren't as powerful as the PC and Mac versions. They'll let you access files from other devices, but won't let you sync files from an iOS device or Android device to SkyDrive. But that may have changed by the time you read this.

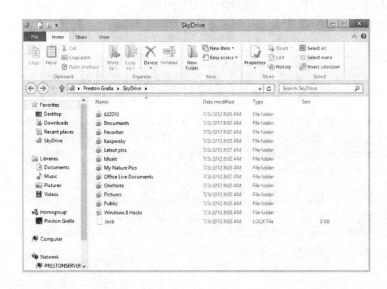

Figure 5-1.
SkyDrive on your Windows 8 PC automatically syncs to the cloud version of SkyDrive

To get to your local SkyDrive on your Windows 8 PC, open File Explorer. It will show up as a separate drive in the favorites area on the upper left, just below Desktop, Downloads, Recent Places, and any other favorites you've put there. You can also get to it from File Explorer by going to *C:\Users\YourAccount\SkyDrive* where, YourAccount is your Windows 8 user name. There's another way to get to it as well. Double-click the small SkyDrive icon that shows up in the Notification area after you install SkyDrive.

What's also nifty about the SkyDrive syncing app is that it's automatically recognized by all of your other Windows apps. So if you use Office, for example, all Office apps will be able to see your local SkyDrive files and save and open files from there.

Look for Colored Icons

Look closely at the SkyDrive files on your Windows 8 PC, and you'll notice small icons next to them. A green checkbox means that the file or folder has been fully synced with the cloud-based version of SkyDrive. A blue arrow means that a sync is in progress. Keep in mind that if you close the SkyDrive app in the Notification Area, when you add new files to SkyDrive, they won't sync to the cloud. To make them sync, simply launch the SkyDrive Desktop app.

Access to All of Your Files from Everywhere

There's a little known feature of SkyDrive that you might find immensely useful—the ability to access all of your computer's files from the cloud, not just those in SkyDrive. So if you're away from your main computer and need important files, you can get them even if they're not in SkyDrive.

You won't be able to do this using the Windows 8 native SkyDrive app, which, to be honest, is not much more than a pretty face. All that app does is let you access your files stored in the SkyDrive cloud.

Instead, use a browser and head to your cloud-based SkyDrive account (*https://skydrive.live.com*). On the lefthand side of the screen, you'll see a list of all of your devices that are connected to SkyDrive. Click the device whose files you want to access, and you'll see a list of all of the device's folders (Figure 5-2).

Figure 5-2.
Accessing a remote PC from SkyDrive on the Web

Navigate through the device's folders as you would normally; for example, clicking to the Documents folder. You'll see a listing of all the subfolders and files (Figure 5-3).

Figure 5-3.
A listing of all folders underneath Documents on a remote PC accessed via SkyDrive on the Web

WINDOWS 8 HACKS

Navigate to any file or folder you want to get access to, check the box next to it, and then click the Download link that appears on the upper right. You'll get a message asking if you want to open the file or save it. If you open the file, it will open in whatever app created it. If you save it, it will be copied to SkyDrive on the Web, and you can access the file from there. The file will also automatically sync with all the devices on which you've installed the SkyDrive app, so you'll get access to it everywhere.

Hacking the Hack

You can use SkyDrive not only on a Windows PC, but on other devices as well, including Macs and Android devices. Head to *https://apps.live.com/skydrive* and download and install the app appropriate for the device. If you use Outlook, you can also download an app called Xobni that lets you access your Web-based SkyDrive files from Outlook so you can send them as email attachments. If you've installed the SkyDrive app for syncing to your PC you won't need it, though, because you'll have those apps on your local PC, available to Outlook.

See Also

- Hack #45, "Make SkyDrive Play Nice with Other Windows Folders"
- Hack #46, "Recover Deleted Files on SkyDrive"
- Hack #47, "More SkyDrive Hacks"

HACK 45   Make SkyDrive Play Nice with Other Windows Folders

SkyDrive uses its own folder structure, outside of the normal Windows 8 Libraries folders. This causes big problems if you want to sync anything in your Libraries folders. Fear not, though—this hack solves the problem.

SkyDrive's biggest drawback is that it forces you to operate outside of Windows' and Office's normal folder structure. When you use Windows 8 (or earlier versions of Windows) and Office, you're constantly prompted to save your files in the Microsoft-approved folder structure, which in Windows 8 is under *C:\Users\YourName\Libraries \Documents\My Documents*, where YourName is your user name.

This is a big problem. It means that if you want to use SkyDrive to sync your folders, you can't sync any under My Documents, or in any other folder that's not in your SkyDrive folder, which is *C:\Users\YourName\SkyDrive*, where YourName is your user name. So if you've created an entire folder structure, you'll have to throw it out the window if you want to use SkyDrive to sync it.

Why did Microsoft choose to make the SkyDrive folder structure not work with your normal Windows structure? Who knows? But it's certainly a serious problem. However, there's a hack you can use so that any Windows 8 folder will automatically sync to SkyDrive. In this way, you'll be able to continue using your existing folder structure, and it'll also show up in SkyDrive and sync everywhere.

To do it, you're going to use a small utility built into Windows 8 called *mklink.exe*. The *mklink* utility lets you create what are called symbolic links, or directory junctions. That lets you, in essence, create a new mirror folder of an existing folder. That new mirror folder directs you to the original, already-existing directory. When used in concert with SkyDrive, though, it syncs that directory into your local SkyDrive, and that will then get synced out to all your other devices that use SkyDrive. So you'll have access to the files and folders everywhere.

To do it, you're going to have to use the command prompt. In our example, let's say that you have a folder called *C:\Users\YourName\Libraries\Documents\My Documents\Budget* and you'd like to get that folder to sync in SkyDrive. First, open File Explorer and go to the *C:\Windows\System32* folder. Right click *mklink.exe* and select "Run as Administrator" from the screen that appears.

A command prompt opens in the *C:\Windows\System32* folder. Type in a command using this syntax, and then press Enter:

```
mklink /D "C:\Users\YourName\SkyDrive\newfolder\" "C:\Existingfolder"
```

In place of `newfolder`, type the name of folder you want to create in SkyDrive, and in place of `Existingfolder`, type the folder you want synced. So in our example, you'd type:

```
mklink /D "c:\Users\YourName\SkyDrive\Budget\" "C:\Users\YourName\Libraries
\Documents\My Documents\Budget"
```

After a moment, you'll get a prompt that the symbolic link was created. Head over to your local SkyDrive folder, and you'll see the new folder there, with your files in it. After the local SkyDrive folder syncs to the cloud and other devices, you'll see that the folder and its files have been replicated everywhere.

Include SkyDrive in your Windows 8 Libraries

Want to bring SkyDrive and your Windows 8 folder libraries a little closer together? Easy—you can make your SkyDrive appear in your libraries. That way, you won't have to navigate to an entirely different location when an app defaults to Windows 8 Libraries.

Launch Windows Explorer, and right-click SkyDrive. From the menu that appears, select "Include in Library," and then choose in which library you want it to appear—Documents, for example, since that's where you're likely to save things (Figure 5-4). You can also create a new library and place it there.

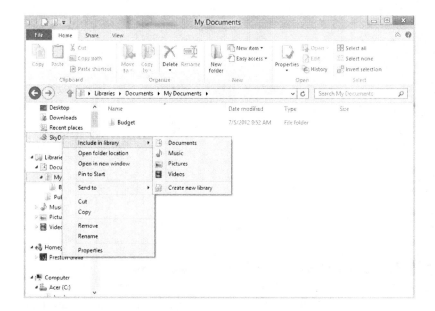

Figure 5-4.
Right-click the SkyDrive folder, then choose in which library to include your SkyDrive

When you're done, your SkyDrive will show up in the library you chose (Figure 5-5). Note that it's in essence a symbolic link. Your SkyDrive still lives in the same location; it only looks as if it's in the library as well. So you'll see it in two locations. If you'd like to remove it from the library, right-click it in the library and select "Remove location from library." You'll no longer see your SkyDrive in the library, but it still exists in its original location.

> *Tip: If you like, you can have SkyDrive subfolders show up in libraries, instead of the whole SkyDrive. Simply right-click the subfolder you want to appear in a library, and follow the same instructions from there.*

See Also

- Hack #44, "Use SkyDrive to Sync Your Files Everywhere"
- Hack #46, "Recover Deleted Files on SkyDrive"
- Hack #47, "More SkyDrive Hacks"

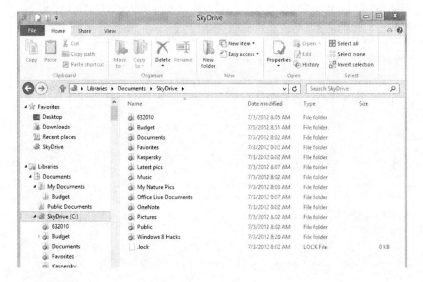

Figure 5-5.
SkyDrive, showing up in the Windows 8 Documents folder

HACK 46 Recover Deleted Files on SkyDrive

> Here's how you can turn back the past with SkyDrive and get back files
> you've deleted on it, as well as previous versions of files you've edited.

One of my favorite Windows 8 features is called File History, which lets you find old
versions of files or files you've previously deleted—see Hack #40, "Use File History to Recover Your Files". It's a great feature, although at first glance you may worry that it doesn't
back up SkyDrive folders because by default it only works with your Libraries, Desktop,
and Internet Explorer favorites.

Fear not: if you install the SkyDrive app, File History works with the files in your Sky-
Drive folder as well. First, make sure that you've turned on File History. Once you've
done that, there are several ways to recover a deleted file or an older version of an
existing file.

To make sure that you've turned on File History, first get to the Control Panel by making
the Windows 8 Charms appear—move your mouse to the right side of the screen or
swipe from the right. Then click the Search charm, type **Control** and click the Control
Panel app that appears on the left side of the screen. From the Control Panel, click
"Save backup copies of your files with File History." The screen that appears, shown
in Figure 5-6, tells you whether it's turned on or not. If it's not turned on, turn it on (see
Hack #40, "Use File History to Recover Your Files" for details). Keep in mind, though, if it's not
turned on, you won't be able to recover any old files.

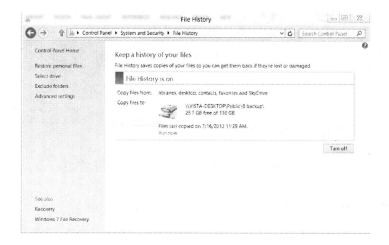

Figure 5-6.
You can recover deleted files from SkyDrive using the windows 8 File History feature

If it's turned on, open File Explorer, navigate to the folder with the files you want to recover, and click History on the Home tab. A screen appears like the one in Figure 5-7. To see earlier versions of the files in the folder and earlier deleted files in the folder, click the left arrow; to see later versions, click the right arrow. Right-click any file you want to restore or whose earlier version you want to see. You can first preview the file if you'd like. Choose Restore to restore the file to its original SkyDrive location, or "Restore to" to restore it to a different location.

Figure 5-7.
Restoring deleted files from SkyDrive

See Also

- Hack #44, "Use SkyDrive to Sync Your Files Everywhere"
- Hack #45, "Make SkyDrive Play Nice with Other Windows Folders"
- Hack #47, "More SkyDrive Hacks"

HACK 47   More SkyDrive Hacks

Here are a few more hacks for getting the most out of SkyDrive.

Make OneNote Notebooks Available on SkyDrive

OneNote is one of Microsoft's biggest secrets—the best piece of software you may never use. OneNote gives you a way to organize all your notes and projects into notebook-like documents, and it comes free in some versions of Microsoft Office. I use it constantly for big projects, including for the writing of this book.

There's one thing that OneNote isn't good at, though: making itself available on multiple PCs. Out of the box, if you've got OneNote notebooks on one PC, those notebooks won't show up for use in other PCs.

SkyDrive solves the problem. Open the notebook you want to share with your other PCs, then click File→Share, and in the "Web location" section, click the Sign-in link under Windows Live SkyDrive. You'll be prompted to sign in with your ID.

Then, select the folder where you want to have your OneNote notebook synced (or create a new folder), and then click Share Notebook (Figure 5-8). Your notebook will be synced to SkyDrive and available wherever you use SkyDrive. (Note that you may need to have the OneNote app installed on the device to access it; check the device's OneNote app for details.)

You can even use OneNote when you're on a computer that doesn't have OneNote on it, because it's also available on SkyDrive in the cloud.

Scan Documents into SkyDrive

Strange but true: some documents still exist on paper. But it's easy to turn those paper documents into electronic ones and put them into SkyDrive, where you can access them anywhere, even if you don't have a scanner. You can instead use your smartphone.

If you're a Windows Phone user, get the Handyscan for Windows Phone app [search for it in the Windows Store; see it on the Web (*http://bit.ly/SYN3k8*)]. iPhone users

 shows a OneNote window with the File menu open to Share. The navigation pane shows: Info, Open, New, Share (highlighted), Save As, Send, Print, Help, Options, Exit. The title bar reads "Intermountain Interview - Microsoft OneN". Menu tabs: File, Home, Insert, Share, Draw, Review, View.

Share Notebook

1. Select Notebook:
My Notebook

2. Share On:
Web — Access from any computer or browser. Share with others (optional).
Network — Shared with others on the network or SharePoint.

3. Web Location:
Microsoft SkyDrive (Not Preston Gralla?)   New Shared Folder

Personal Folders
Budget — Shared with: Just me
Documents — Shared with: Just me
Music — Shared with: Just me
Office Live Documents — Shared with: Just me
OneNote — Shared with: Just me
Pictures — Shared with: Just me
Windows 8 Hacks — Shared with: Just me

Shared Folders
Kaspersky — Shared with: Some people
Public — Shared with: Everyone (public)

Share Notebook

Figure 5-8.
Making your OneNote notebooks available on SkyDrive

can opt for Docscan for iPhone (search in the App Store). Android users should look for CamScanner or Scan to PDF in the Google Play store. They're all free, and all scan documents to PDF files. You'll need to make sure that you've got SkyDrive installed on your phone, so you can save the files to your SkyDrive.

Change SkyDrive Options

Little-known fact: there are several ways in which you can change how SkyDrive works on your local PC. Right-click the SkyDrive icon in the notification area, then click the Settings tab (Figure 5-9). If you want the files from the PC to be available to other devices, make sure the box is checked next to "Let me use SkyDrive to fetch any of my files on this PC." When you check that box, when you go to SkyDrive.com on another device, you'll be able to download files from this PC's SkyDrive folders to that device.

Figure 5-9.
Changing SkyDrive settings

If you don't want to sign into SkyDrive every time you log into Windows 8, turn off the "Start SkyDrive automatically when I sign into Windows" checkbox.

If for some reason you want your SkyDrive folders and files to stop syncing with Sky-Drive on the web and other devices, click "Unlink SkyDrive" and follow the directions. And if you want to send Microsoft information about SkyDrive problems you experience, check the box next to "Automatically send log files to SkyDrive when I experience a problem."

Click the "Choose folders" tab for a very nifty SkyDrive feature. From here, you can choose to only have some folders sync to SkyDrive and other devices. Click "Choose folders" and follow the instructions.

See Also

- Hack #44, "Use SkyDrive to Sync Your Files Everywhere"
- Hack #45, "Make SkyDrive Play Nice with Other Windows Folders"
- Hack #46, "Recover Deleted Files on SkyDrive"

> Want to give SkyDrive competitors a try? They're free, so why not? You just might find something you like.

SkyDrive isn't the only cloud-based syncing storage service out there—in fact, it's a bit of a latecomer compared to many of the others. None of the others have Windows 8 native apps (as I write this, anyway), but aside from that, they tend to be every bit as good as SkyDrive, and some have even better features. Here's a quick rundown on alternatives, including one that's my favorite.

Google Drive

Like SkyDrive, Google Drive (Figure 5-10) is a cloud-based storage service that stores your files online, but will also let you sync them locally to multiple devices. Also like SkyDrive, it installs as a separate drive on your computer and devices.

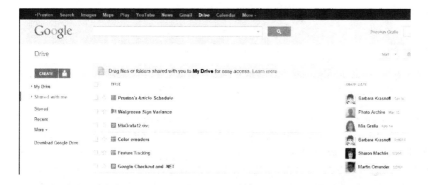

Figure 5-10.
The cloud-based interface of Google Drive

To run it on your PC, get the free Google Drive app (*https://drive.google.com*). You'll need a Google password, so if you don't already have one, you'll have to sign up. And if you already use Google Docs, using Google Drive for your cloud storage is a no-brainer.

Google Drive installs like a separate drive on your PC, and works much like SkyDrive. Head to the Web version of Google Drive and you'll see not only your files, but be able to share them with others. You'll also see people with whom you've shared files in the past, and the date you shared them.

Dropbox

This cloud-based storage, backup, and sync service has been around far longer than SkyDrive and Google Drive, and the company claims that it's been installed on 250 million different devices. It syncs files to the cloud and multiple devices, and allows sharing folders with others. Get it at *http://www.dropbox.com*.

Box (Formerly Box.Net)

This storage and sync service is targeted more to businesses than individuals, although individuals can certainly use it. Among its business-focused features are administrative controls which offer fine-grained features for setting permissions about sharing, as well as group-management tools. It's at *http://www.box.com*.

Tip: You can use several of these services simultaneously if you'd like. I use SkyDrive and Google Drive as well as SugarSync, and they work on the same computer without any problems.

SugarSync

This is my favorite cloud storage and sync service, and the one I use most regularly. I find it far more flexible than SkyDrive, Google Drive, and the rest.

Rather than install as a separate drive, which forces you to change the way you work with your folders and files, Sugar Sync instead works directly with your existing folders and files. Install the software, then tell it which folders you want synced to the cloud and other devices. Then install it on each device, and you decide which folders to sync to and from the cloud. It's the one I use every day. Get it at *http://www.sugarsync.com*.

HACK 49 Configure Windows 8 Syncing

> There's more to cloud-based syncing in Windows 8 than SkyDrive. Here's how to sync your Windows settings and more.

If you want your files to sync automatically to SkyDrive, you'll have to use the SkyDrive app, as outlined in previous hacks. But even if you don't do that, Windows 8 can automatically sync your most important settings, such as the colors you use, your account picture, your desktop theme, language preferences, some app settings, your browser history, and more.

When all that is synced, if you use another Windows 8 devices, such as a second computer or a tablet, those settings are sitting there waiting for you. And when you make a change to your settings on another device, they're synced back to your original device.

Windows 8 syncs on an account-by-account basis. So if you have multiple accounts on Windows 8 devices, each of those accounts syncs separately. Let's say you have a Windows 8 account named Pboy, and another Windows 8 account called Richboy. Each of those accounts syncs separately. So log into a Windows 8 PC with your Pboy account and you'll see your familiar Pboy settings; log in with the Richboy account and you'll see Richboy settings.

You're not stuck with simply syncing all settings on each account, though. You can easily customize which settings you want synced across all of your devices, and which you don't want synced.

Make the Windows 8 charms appear by moving your mouse to the right side of the screen or swiping from the right. Then select Settings→Change PC Settings→"Sync your settings" (Figure 5-11). From here it's straightforward—switch on those settings you want synced, and turn off those you don't want synced.

Note: You must be signed in to a Microsoft account to make changes to your sync settings. Changes you make affect only that account; sign into other accounts with Microsoft IDs to change their sync settings.

If you're using a mobile device such as a tablet or Windows 8 smartphone, and you're using a service that charges you for data or limits your data use, you may not want to use up your data for syncing—when you sync, you're sending and receiving data. If that's the case, scroll down to the bottom of the screen, to the "Sync over metered connections" section (Figure 5-11). Change one or both of the settings there. The top one turns off all syncing when you're on a metered connection (one in which you have a data-use limit). The bottom one, "Sync settings over metered connections even when I'm roaming," controls whether to sync while you're on a roaming connection; in other words, a connection that isn't your cellphone's native provider, which you can use and get charged a higher fee for data use.

Figure 5-11.
Customizing your sync settings

The choice you make here is important, because roaming charges can add up quickly. By default, the setting is turned off, which means you won't sync while roaming. Only turn it on if you absolutely need to sync your settings everywhere, and paying for that doesn't bother you.

Hacking the Hack

Are you having problems syncing your account among multiple devices? There are plenty of things that might be causing the problem, ranging from proxy setting issues to connectivity woes. First, though, check whether you've actually created a Microsoft account, because you may have accidently created a local account instead, which doesn't sync. Select Settings→Change PC Settings→Users. Look toward the top of the screen, where your current account is listed. Under your name, you can see whether it's a local account or a Microsoft account. Local accounts don't sync, so if you're using a local account rather than a Microsoft one, that's your problem. To create a Microsoft account, click "Switch to a Microsoft account" and follow the onscreen instructions.

When you use a Microsoft account, it can be tough to track down the cause of your non-syncing. Here's a simple solution: download the Microsoft Accounts Trouble-shooter (*http://bit.ly/VY5pre*). Then launch it and follow the directions when it tracks down your problem.

See Also

- Hack #50, "Create a Non-Syncing Windows 8 Account"

- Hack #51, "Power Hacks for Windows 8 Syncing"

HACK 50   Create a Non-Syncing Windows 8 Account

> Not a fan of the cloud and syncing? No problem. Create an account that
> lives all by its lonesome and syncs nowhere.

Don't like the idea of your sync settings following you everywhere—or just don't like
the idea of using a Microsoft account in Windows 8? You don't actually need one.
Instead, you can use what's called a *local account*, which doesn't tie into any Microsoft
services, and doesn't do any syncing.

Make the Windows 8 Charms appear by moving your mouse to the right side of the
screen or swiping from the right. Then select Settings→Change PC Settings→Users.
At the bottom of the screen, click "Add a user." On the screen that appears, go to the
bottom and click "Sign in without a Microsoft account." At the bottom of the next
screen, click "Local account." Fill in the required information, and you're ready to go.

See Also

- Hack #49, "Configure Windows 8 Syncing"
- Hack #51, "Power Hacks for Windows 8 Syncing"

HACK 51   Power Hacks for Windows 8 Syncing

> Windows 8 offers straightforward options for syncing your preferences
> among multiple devices. Here's how you can use the Local Group Policy
> Editor to fine-tune them even more.

As you've seen in the previous hack, it's pretty straightforward to set your sync settings for multiple computers and tablets. But given that you're reading this book,
you're not content with straightforward—you want a lot more when it comes to
syncing.

That's where the Local Group Policy Editor comes in. It gives you more power over the
ways that Windows 8 PCs and tablets sync.

Essentially, the Local Group Policy Editor lets you turn syncing off for certain Windows
8 features—and even turn those features off completely. So even if someone goes into
the Windows 8 sync settings as outlined in the previous hack, they can't use them.
You might do this if, for example, you're worried that someone will overwrite settings
on another PC or tablet, and you don't want that to happen.

First, log in as an administrator. Then you need to run the Local Group Policy Editor:
press Windows key+C to display the Charms bar, and then select Search. Make sure
that the Apps button is highlighted, and then type `gpedit.msc`.

Highlight the app when it appears, and press Enter. The Group Policy Editor launches. Go to *Computer Configuration→Administrative Templates→Windows Components* and scroll down until you see the Sync your settings entry (Figure 5-12). Highlight it, and you'll see the settings you can customize on the righthand side of the screen.

Figure 5-12.
Navigating to the "Sync your settings" entry in the Local Group Policy Editor

Notice that most of what you see mirrors the basic syncing options outlined in the previous hack. Click any of the settings that you want to turn off. In this hack, we'll use "Do not sync app settings" as an example (Figure 5-13). At the bottom of the screen, make sure you're on the Extended tab; that's where you can see a description of the option, what it does, and how you might want to customize it.

Double-click the setting. You'll have three options: Not Configured, Enabled, and Disabled (Figure 5-14). Not Configured means that you haven't touched it yet with the Local Group Policy Editor, so you can ignore that. That leaves you with two choices—Enabled or Disabled. Here's where you need to get used to a little bit of counterintuitive thinking. If you select Enabled, you'll turn off the ability to sync app settings across Windows 8 PCs and tablets for anyone who uses the PC or tablet. (The setting affects just that PC or tablet, of course.) This way, if someone goes into the normal sync settings, they won't be able to have app settings sync across devices.

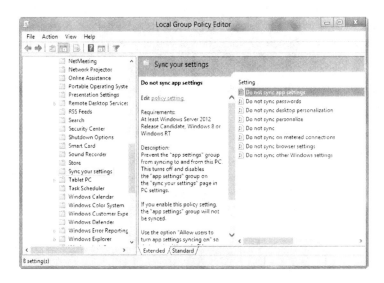

Figure 5-13.
Examining the "Do not sync app settings" option

Figure 5-14.
Three options for changing sync in the Local Group Policy Editor

Choose Enabled if you want to turn off syncing. You can also choose Disabled, but that doesn't really do anything if you haven't yet enabled the setting. By default, this setting is Disabled. So you need to choose Disabled only if you've previously enabled the setting.

Click Apply, and you'll turn off the syncing. Go through every setting here and decide which you want to allow, and which you want to turn off.

Note that there's a kind of nuclear option here—the "Do not sync" entry. This one disables *all* syncing in Windows 8.

Note: These settings don't affect SkyDrive—it's separate from all the other sync settings in Windows 8. So even if you don't allow any Windows 8 syncing at all, SkyDrive will still do its syncing thing.

- Hack #49, "Configure Windows 8 Syncing"
- Hack #50, "Create a Non-Syncing Windows 8 Account"
- Hack #121, "Hack Away at Windows with the Group Policy Editor"

HACK 52 Mastering the People App

> Windows 8's People app is Command Central for social networking in the operating system. Here's how to get the most out of it.

If you're a user of social media, there's no doubt that one of the best things about Windows 8 is the built-in People app. The app pulls in information from all of your social networking sites (Facebook, LinkedIn, and Twitter, among others), and displays it in a single location so you don't need to check into separate services one by one—instead, use the People app. And the app does all that automatically: you don't need to head out to the individual social networking sites. The information is delivered straight to you.

For the most part, the app is straightforward. Run it, and choose from three big links at the top:

People

Lists all of your contacts; click any to get more information about her, including sending her an email, viewing her profile on various services, and mapping her address, as you can see in Figure 5-15.

What's new

Shows you updates from all of your social networking services.

⊖ Lydia Gralla

Figure 5-15.
Getting information about someone in the People app

Me

Shows information about you, including your postings, notifications send to you, and more.

Looks simple, and it seems that's about all you can do with the People app. But there are a few nooks and crannies and hidden features potentially worth exploring.

Let's start with the simple one: what if there's a new social networking site you want to add? At first it seems there's no way to do it. Here's where it's hiding: click the upper-right portion of the screen, where it says "Connected to..." A list of your accounts appears, along with an "Add an account" link at the bottom of the pane. Click that link, and a list of available social networking services appears (Figure 5-16). Click the service to which you want to connect. Then click the Connect button. On the next screen, you'll link your Microsoft ID to the social networking account, which lets the two talk to each other.

Tip: The People app also works with the Mail app. When you send an email from Mail, the app lets you tap into all of the contacts in all of your social networking services.

You likely have plenty of contacts, and don't want to have to spend too much time scrolling or swiping through the app to find them. Here's a quicker way: choose the Search charm, and when you do a search, you'll be able to search for specific people.

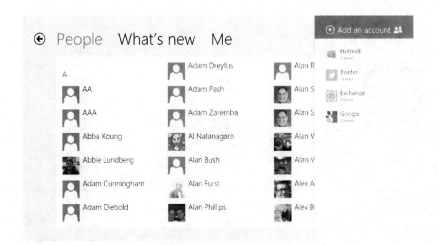

Figure 5-16.
Getting information about someone in the People app

Sometimes you'll feel as if you've hit a dead end when using People and can't get back to the main app. For example, if you do a search, find multiple people, and then decide you don't want to see those people, there seems to be no way to get back to the main app.

Here's the hidden navigation: right-click with your mouse or swipe up from the bottom of the screen, and you'll see a People icon at lower right. Click it to get back to the main People app.

You can also customize how some (but only some) of the accounts work on Windows 8—for example, how frequently to check for updates and new content, and for how long to keep the content.

Click the upper-right of the screen to display the accounts you've got. Then click the account you want to customize. As I write this, Facebook, Twitter, and LinkedIn don't allow Windows 8–specific customization. You can click to get to the Web, and select options from there, although not Windows 8-specific ones. For Microsoft and Google, you can make changes right in Windows 8 for Windows 8, but they're limited to things such as how often to check for new content (Figure 5-17). That may change over time, though.

Figure 5-17.
The Microsoft account and syncing settings

HACK 53 Share and Share Alike in Windows 8

> Sharing is built right into Windows 8's DNA, but it's not immediately apparent how to use it. Here's how.

Social networking on Windows 8 is different than it is on other versions of Windows, not only because a social networking app is built right into it, but because sharing with others is built into other parts of the operating system as well. For example, when you're considering buying music, you can share the album with others with whom you've connected on social networking sites.

It's not obvious at first how to do it, but once you know how, it's a snap. Sharing only works on Windows 8 native apps, not on Desktop apps. When you're looking at something you'd like to share with others, move your mouse to the right side of the screen or swipe from the right to display the Charms. Click the Share charm (it's the second from the top). You'll be able to share either via email or the People app—the social networking app. Sharing via email is straightforward; click the mail icon and follow directions.

To share via social networking sites, click People, and on the right side of the screen a panel slides into place showing the content you want to share. Up toward the top of the screen, you'll see which social networking sites you've installed on which you can share; click to select the one you want (Figure 5-18). You can also type a message. Click the Send icon on the upper right, and away it goes.

Figure 5-18.
Sharing music via Facebook

> *Note: Although there's a lot you can share in this way, there's a lot you can't share as well. Sharing has to be built directly into a Windows 8 native app, and not all apps include it. And even if an app does include it, there may be legal or other limits on what can and can't be shared.*
>
> *How do you find out what can be shared and what can't? The only way is to follow the instructions here for sharing, and if you get a message saying you can't share... that means the app can't share.*

HACK 54 Other Social Networking Apps

The People app is a great starting point for using social media on Windows 8. But there are plenty more apps, both Windows 8 native-based and for the Desktop, that you can use as well. Here are the best.

The People App built into Windows 8 is a very good one, but there are plenty of other social networking apps you might want to give a try. Here are a few of my favorites; some Windows 8 native-specific, some not.

Tweetro

This is a Windows 8 native app, so get it from the Windows 8 store by searching for its name. It's Twitter-specific, and shows a Twitter timeline, makes it easy to share photos via Twitter, shows you all mentions of you on Twitter, and more. It's great for Twitter-holics who want a Windows 8 native app.

Rowi

Here's another Windows 8 native Twitter-specific app. It's specifically built for tablets and touch, so if you've got a tablet, it's a good choice. Search for it in the Windows 8 Store.

MetroTwit

This Windows 8 native Twitter app also works best on tablets and touch. It sports a very simple, clean interface.

TweetDeck

This is my favorite Desktop Twitter app, with an enormous number of power user features. What I like best is that from a single interface, you can post updates not just to Twitter, but to LinkedIn and Facebook as well. It's the one I use every day, and it's free. Get it at *http://www.tweetdeck.com*.

6

Music, Media, and Video

Windows 8 was built for a media-centric world, where digital video, music, and photos are part of daily life. For the most part, the media apps built into Windows 8 are simple and easy to use. But that doesn't mean Windows 8 isn't hackable when it comes to media. In this chapter, you'll find plenty of ways to hack away at it.

HACK 55   Open Graphic Files In Photo Viewer Instead of the Windows 8 Native Photos App

Prefer the old favorite Desktop app Windows Photo Viewer over the Windows 8 native Photos app? Here's how to make sure your pictures and graphics open to the Desktop app, not the Windows 8 one.

Windows 8 native apps are not to everyone's liking, and for good reason. As a general rule they're pretty to look at, but not always so pretty to use, because they offer only the most basic capabilities.

That's certainly the case with the Windows 8 Photos app. Essentially, it lets you look at photos stored on your computer, and that's about it. A much better bet is to use the older, but much more useful, Desktop-based Photo Viewer, which has many more features than the Windows 8 native Photos app.

But there's a problem: if you double-click a photo or graphics file using File Explorer, Windows 8 opens it in the Photos app rather than Photo Viewer. Luckily, there's a simple way to solve the problem. You can tell File Explorer to open the Photo Viewer rather than the Photos app.

Launch Control Panel by typing *Control Panel* at the Start screen, highlighting the Control Panel icon on the left side of the screen, and then pressing Enter. Then go to Programs→Set your default Programs. Scroll down to the Windows Photo Viewer listing and click "Set this program as default" (Figure 6-1). From now on, whenever you double-click a photo or picture in File Explorer, it will open in Photo Viewer.

Note: GIF images are the exception. Even when you set Photo Viewer as the default graphics program, .gif files will open in Photos. To select a different program, see the next section, "Hacking the Hack".

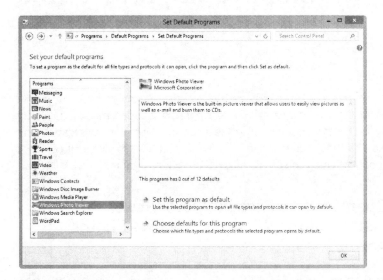

Figure 6-1.
Telling Windows 8 to use Photo Viewer as the default for viewing photos

Hacking the Hack

If you'd like fine-grained control over which file types Photo Viewer opens, and which the Photo app opens, instead click "Choose defaults for this program." You'll see a list of graphics file types (Figure 6-2). Select those you want to open in Photo Viewer. The ones you don't select will still open in the Windows 8 Photo app.

If you would prefer to keep the Windows 8 native Photo app as the default, but occasionally want to open a photo or graphic in Windows Photo Viewer, right-click the file and select Open With→Windows Photo Viewer. That will open the file in Photo Viewer one time, but won't change the default.

See Also

- Hack #56, "Add Facebook and Flickr to Your Windows 8 Photo Collection"

- Hack #57, "Hacking Through the Photos App"

- Hack #58, "Add Folder Locations to Photo and Video Libraries"

- Hack #61, "Power Up Windows 8 with a Free Movie Maker, Photo Gallery, and More"

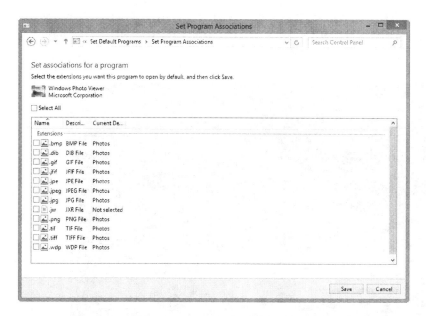

Figure 6-2.
Telling Photo Viewer which files it should open, and which should be left to the Windows 8 native Photo app

HACK 56 Add Facebook and Flickr to Your Windows 8 Photo Collection

> Got a photo collection in Facebook or Flickr? It's easy to view them in the Windows 8 Photos app... if you know how to do it.

Photos are for sharing. You've probably got photos on Facebook and on the photo-sharing site Flickr. Wouldn't it be nice if those photos would automatically show up, ready for use, in the Windows 8 native photo app?

It can be done, and without much heavy lifting, either. You simply need to connect the Microsoft account you use to sign into Windows 8 with your Facebook and Flickr accounts. You may have already done that when you first set up Windows 8, and if that's the case, you're done hacking. Your Facebook and Flickr photos are already in the Windows 8 Photos app. If not, however, follow these instructions. I'll give instructions for doing it in Facebook, but it's essentially identical to the steps you'll take for doing it in Flickr as well.

Tip: If you don't use a Microsoft ID to sign into Windows 8, then Windows can't grab your photos from Facebook or Flickr.

First, launch the Windows 8 Photos app. You'll see libraries of photos from various sources, including your own PC, PCs to which you're connected on your network, and SkyDrive, as you can see in Figure 6-3.

Figure 6-3.
The Windows 8 photo app

If you see Facebook and Flickr listed here, you don't need to go any further. If they're not there and you want to add them, press Windows key+I to pull up Settings, as shown in Figure 6-4. Click Options. A screen appears that lists all of the various locations where the Windows 8 Photos app displays photos from. A checkmark next to a location or account means Photos is currently displaying those photos (Figure 6-5). If you don't want photos from a particular location or account to appear in the Photos app, uncheck the box.

To add Facebook or Flickr (or to edit its options if you've already added it), click the Options link next to it. You'll need to provide your Facebook (or Flickr) user name and password, and confirm that you want to link your Facebook account to your Microsoft account. Once you do that, the link is made, and you're ready to go.

Hacking the Hack

When you connect your Facebook and Microsoft accounts, you're doing more than just displaying Facebook photos. You're also sharing lots of other content between the accounts. To see everything you're sharing, click that Options link again. You'll be sent to Internet Explorer, and a page appears that shows you what's shared between the accounts (Figure 6-6).

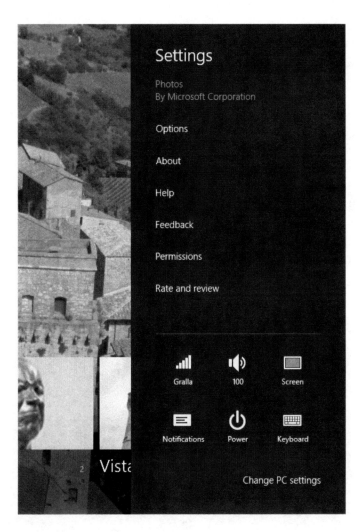

Figure 6-4.
The Windows 8 photo app settings screen

For example, you can see Facebook friends and updates in Windows 8—in the People app, primarily. In Microsoft's Messenger IM app, you can see Facebook friends who are available for chat. And the list goes on. Turn off the checkboxes next to any types of information you don't want to share, click Save, and you're done. If you want to remove the connection completely, click the "Remove this connection completely" link at the bottom of the page.

Figure 6-5.
A listing of the accounts from which the Photo app displays photos

Microsoft account

Facebook username:
Preston Gralla

Microsoft account:
Preston Gralla
pgralla@hotmail.com

When you sign in with your Microsoft account as pgralla@hotmail.com, your Facebook account comes with you. Customize what info you're sharing between Facebook and your Microsoft account.

☑ **See Facebook friends and their updates**
See what they're doing from your inbox, Messenger, or Windows Phone.

☑ **Chat with Facebook friends**
And show them when you're available from Messenger and Windows Phone.

☑ **View your Facebook photos and videos**

☑ **Publish photos and videos to Facebook**
With Photo Gallery and Movie Maker 2011, you can publish to Facebook and tag your Facebook friends.

☑ **Share to Facebook**
Share status updates, photos, and documents with your Facebook friends from Messenger, SkyDrive, and Windows Phone.

| Save | Cancel |

Remove this connection completely

https://profile.live.com/home/Services/connect?

Figure 6-6.
Here's what's shared between Facebook and your Microsoft account

See Also

- Hack #55, "Open Graphic Files In Photo Viewer Instead of the Windows 8 Native Photos App"

- Hack #57, "Hacking Through the Photos App"

- Hack #58, "Add Folder Locations to Photo and Video Libraries"

- Hack #61, "Power Up Windows 8 with a Free Movie Maker, Photo Gallery, and More"

Hacking Through the Photos App

> The Photos app has a lot more to it than meets the eye. Here's how to get more out of it.

Like most Windows 8 native apps, Photos isn't particularly powerful or sophisticated. Launch the app, and you can look at, print, and share photos, and that's about it.

Never fear. There are also ways to get much more out of the app than first appears—and make sure that the photos that show up there are the ones you really want.

First, you can tweak the display of photos onscreen. Go to a folder to see your photos, and depending on your screen size and size of photos, you'll usually see a handful of photos at most (Figure 6-7). However, if you want, you can see many more photos onscreen, in smaller sizes, by zooming out, as you can see in Figure 6-8.

Figure 6-7.
Here's the default size for pictures in the Photos app...

If you've got a tablet or touchscreen device, pinch your fingers together on the screen, and you'll zoom out. To zoom back in, pinch your fingers apart. To do this with a keyboard and mouse, press the Ctrl key while you move the mouse scroll wheel toward you to zoom out, and press the Ctrl key while moving the mouse scroll wheel away from you to zoom back in. The same gestures zoom in and out on when you're looking at individual pictures. In fact, when you're looking at a picture, if you zoom out enough like this, you'll zoom all the way out to the folder that contains the photos.

Note: If you're not connected to the Internet, you won't be able to see photos in locations outside your computer; for example, in Facebook, Flickr, or SkyDrive.

Figure 6-8.
...and here's the smaller size, so you can see more at a time onscreen

Fixing SkyDrive Woes

If you store photos on SkyDrive, they automatically show up in the Photos app... usually, that is. There's a chance some photos, or even entire folders, won't show up. Fortunately, there's a way to force the Windows 8 photo app to make them appear. First, you need to understand how SkyDrive works.

SkyDrive folders are designed to be of certain types—documents, pictures, and so on. SkyDrive does its best to figure out what type a folder is by looking at the types of files in it, and then designates that folder as a certain type.

The Photos app, for its part, only displays photos from folders that have been designated as Pictures. So if SkyDrive (or you) made a mistake in designating a folder full of photos as documents, that folder won't show up in Photos. To fix the problem, head to SkyDrive using Internet Explorer or another web browser (not the Windows 8 native SkyDrive app). Click any folder whose pictures you want to appear in Photos. On the right side of the screen, you'll see information about the folder, including its name, date it was added to SkyDrive, and so on. Next to "Folder type," you'll see how the folder is currently designated (Figure 6-9). To change it, click Change, select Pictures, and then click Save.

Also, keep in mind that if you've got pictures in a documents folder, they won't show up in the Windows 8 Photo app, so move them to a picture folder.

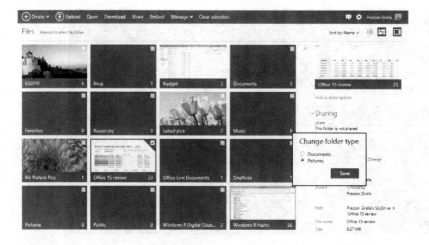

Figure 6-9.
From here, you can force SkyDrive folders to show up in the Windows 8 native Photo app

Tiles, Backgrounds, and Slide Shows

One of the niftier features of the Photos app is that you can use it to set any photo as your lock screen photo, be the background to the photo app itself, and more.

To do it, right-click a photo or press Windows key+Z while viewing it to bring up the app bar, as seen in Figure 6-10. Click "Set as," and you get these options:

Lock screen

Sets the photo as the background for your lock screen.

App tile

Normally, the Photos app tile cycles through your photos. If you prefer, you can have the tile be a static photo; select "App tile" to put the photo you're looking at on the tile.

App background

Want the photo you're viewing to form the background of the Photos app in its top-level view (as seen in Figure 6-11)? Just make this choice.

If you want Photos to play a slideshow of all the photos in the folder that you're currently viewing, click "Slide show" after you display the app bar.

Figure 6-10.
The app bar lets you create a slide show, use the photo as the lock screen background, and more

Figure 6-11.
The Photo app, using a photo as its background

See Also

- Hack #55, "Open Graphic Files In Photo Viewer Instead of the Windows 8 Native Photos App"

- Hack #56, "Add Facebook and Flickr to Your Windows 8 Photo Collection"

- Hack #58, "Add Folder Locations to Photo and Video Libraries"

- Hack #61, "Power Up Windows 8 with a Free Movie Maker, Photo Gallery, and More"

Add Folder Locations to Photo and Video Libraries

Windows 8 graphics apps look only in a few places for your photos and videos, not everywhere. Here's how to add other locations.

Windows 8 apps such as the Photo app and video apps look to your Libraries locations for photos to display that are on your computer—the Libraries→Pictures and Libraries→Videos folders.

> *Note: Photo and video apps also look to network and Internet locations for pictures and videos, such as SkyDrive, or shared picture and video folders in other PCs on your network.*

But you may not have all your photos and videos there. They may be spread out in multiple folders across your hard disk, or may even be on USB hard drives or other removable storage. It's relatively easy to get your Windows 8 apps to look there as well.

To do so, you add folders and drives to your Pictures and Video library. You don't need to move the folders and drives. Instead, you tell the libraries that those folders and drives should be included.

Launch File Explorer and right-click *Libraries\Pictures,* or *Library\Videos*, depending on whether the files in the folders are videos or pictures. Select Properties. The Pictures Properties (or Video Properties) dialog box appears, as you can see in Figure 6-12.

Click Add, navigate to the location that you want to be included in the Library, and select it. You can select folders and drives not just on your local PC, but on your Homegroup as well. When you select the location, the videos and the pictures from the new folder, drive, or location automatically show up in various Windows 8 picture and video apps.

Simple, yes? Well, yes and no. Windows 8 has some limitations that you need to keep in mind when adding folders and locations in this way:

- You can add USB-based hard drives but, as I write this, you can't add USB flash drives. There's a chance that Microsoft will have fixed this issue by the time you read this.

- You may not be able to add folders from networked Windows XP machines. In my tests, I haven't been able to do it. But if you have a Windows XP machine, give it a try, because that might be fixed as well.

Figure 6-12.
The Picture Properties dialog box

- Non-Windows network attached storage (NAS) may not work, either. There's a wide range of these devices, so perhaps some work and some don't.

See Also

- Hack #55, "Open Graphic Files In Photo Viewer Instead of the Windows 8 Native Photos App"
- Hack #56, "Add Facebook and Flickr to Your Windows 8 Photo Collection"
- Hack #57, "Hacking Through the Photos App"
- Hack #61, "Power Up Windows 8 with a Free Movie Maker, Photo Gallery, and More"

HACK 59 **Improve DVD and TV Watching in Windows 8**

When you're watching videos, are they too dark? Too light? Here's how to make them just right.

You use your PC screen primarily for computing, not watching movies, TV shows, and videos, and what's best for creating spreadsheets and Word documents isn't always what's best for entertainment. So when you're watching video, your screen may sometimes seem too dark, other times too bright, and still other times give you washed-out colors.

There's a simple fix. You can adjust the settings with just a few clicks, and you won't have to experiment or rely on hit-or-miss adjustments.

Head to the Desktop and right-click. Then select Graphics Options→Profiles→Media Profiles (Figure 6-13) and select from Brighten Movie, Darken Movie, Default Profile, and Vivid Colors. Then when you've stopped watching the video, change the profile back if you want.

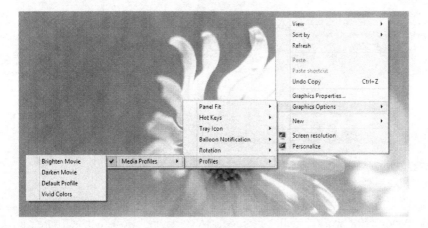

Figure 6-13.
Choosing a media profile to suit the video you're watching

Note: Depending on your video card and monitor, this option may not appear.

See Also

- Hack #64, "Get a Free Copy of Windows Media Center"

HACK 60 Using Windows 8 with Your Xbox 360

Got an Xbox 360 in addition to Windows 8? Good for you. Here's how to get them to work together.

Microsoft envisions Windows 8 and the Xbox 360 as being the centerpiece of your home entertainment; not as separate devices, but rather as part of an entire Windows ecosystem. It's currently more vision than reality, but at this point you can easily connect your Windows 8 device to your Xbox 360. When you do so, you'll be able to play games on your Xbox 360 directly from your Windows 8 device, play movies from your Xbox 360 device on your Windows 8 device, and more.

First, make sure that your Xbox 360 and your Windows 8 device are both connected to the Internet or the same network. Also, make sure that you're logged into both of them with the same Microsoft account.

On your Windows 8 device, click the Games tile on the Start screen. The Xbox Games app launches (Figure 6-14).

Figure 6-14.
The Xbox games app on Windows 8

Then, on your Xbox 360, from the Dashboard, select Settings→System→Console Settings→Xbox Companion. Select Available.

Next, go back to your Windows 8 device. In the Games app (also called Xbox Games), click the Connect button. In the app, you'll see a menu of items you can run on the Xbox 360, depending on what you've got installed. Click any game to play it in Windows 8.

In addition, the Xbox Games app on your Windows 8 device lets you create or customize your avatar (Figure 6-15), view your Xbox 360 achievements, and edit and share your profile. Scroll all the way to the left of the app and you'll find the screen that lets you do that.

Figure 6-15.
Creating an avatar using the Xbox Games Windows 8 app

Hacking the Hack

When you connect your Xbox 360 to Windows 8, that connection will remain integrated throughout Windows 8 apps. So, when you launch the Windows 8 Music app called Xbox Music, you'll be able to play music CDs on your Xbox, and when you launch the Windows 8 Video app (also called Xbox video), you'll be able to play videos from your Xbox.

HACK 61 ## Power Up Windows 8 with a Free Movie Maker, Photo Gallery, and More

> Windows 8 doesn't come with a movie creation tool or a particularly good photo gallery. That's simple to fix. Here's how to get all that and more, for free.

On its own, Windows 8 can't be called a multimedia powerhouse. It includes no software for creating movies and DVDs, and its photo viewing tools are rudimentary at best. That's a shame, because most Windows 8 hardware—especially newer hardware—is well-suited for multimedia.

Help is on the way. Microsoft offers several excellent, free programs you can download in a single package. For example, Windows Movie Maker is a surprisingly powerful movie-making and DVD-creation tool. Windows Photo Gallery offers a host of features for viewing, editing, and printing photos.

They're both available as part of Microsoft's free Windows Essentials (*http://download.live.com*). It's one download (an installer, actually), but contained in that one download are a variety of pieces of software. During installation, you get the option of which you want to install and which you don't. Here's the full list of what you get when you download:

Photo Gallery

A very good tool for viewing, editing, and printing photos.

Windows Movie Maker

Great tool for making movies and DVDs.

Microsoft SkyDrive

A very worthwhile piece of software for storing files in the cloud and syncing them among all of your devices, including PCs running various versions of Windows, Macs, tablets, and smartphones. This client software works well with the SkyDrive built into Windows 8, but offers more capabilities. (See Chapter 5, *Cloud and Social Networking Hacks* for many great hacks using this client version of SkyDrive.)

Mail

A mail program. You've already got a mail client built into Windows 8, so you may as well pass on this one.

Family Safety

You don't need this one as well, because it's already built into Windows 8. In fact, for that very reason, it won't even install.

Writer

Nice tool for creating blog posts, including features like embedding photos and videos. The tool publishes to your blog, as well.

Outlook Connector Pack

Connects Outlook.com (previously known as Hotmail) to the Outlook email client. If you don't have the Outlook email client, don't bother installing this.

Messenger

Microsoft's well-known IM client.

Note: You have to install both Windows Photo Gallery and Windows Movie Maker together, because they share a number of features.

At *http://download.live.com*, click "Download now" and save the file to disk. Then run the installer. When the installation starts, be sure to select "Choose the programs you want to install," rather than "Install all of Windows Essentials"; you'll see a screen like that shown in Figure 6-16. If you've already installed one of the programs, such as SkyDrive, you'll see a message saying it's already installed. And you won't see an option for installing Family Safety, because Windows 8 already has a feature for doing that, and the Windows Essentials version can't be installed.

Figure 6-16.
Selecting which Windows Essentials apps to install

Turn off the checkboxes next to any software you don't want to install. Then click Install. You're good to go. Figure 6-17 shows Windows Movie Maker, and Figure 6-18 shows Windows Photo Gallery.

Figure 6-17.
Windows Movie Maker in action

Figure 6-18.
Windows Photo Gallery

Hacking the Hack

Using Windows Movie Maker is generally straightforward, and you won't need much help for it. But there's a very useful feature you won't want to miss—video soundtracks. To be sure, getting music for your video can be tough, because it's hard to find music that fits the mood you want to create, and because you have to deal with copyright issues. For example, if you create a video, use a piece of commercial music from your collection, and then post the video to YouTube, you may run into problems, YouTube may even strip out the audio track because of rights violations.

Movie Maker has a simple solution. When you want to add a soundtrack to your video, head to the Home tab and click "Add music." You'll find options for AudioMicro, Free Music Archive, and Vimeo, as you can see in Figure 6-19. Select any music from those sources, and you won't have any rights issues; the music is free for you to use and post however you'd like.

Note: Depending on the music you choose, you may have to pay for the audio track.

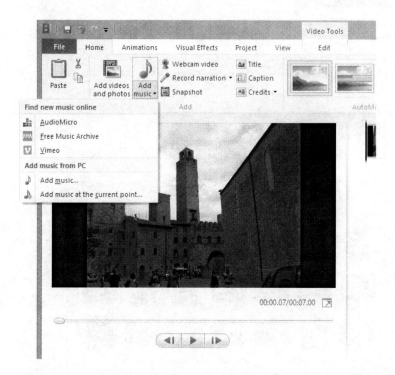

Figure 6-19.
Choosing rights-free music in Movie Maker

There's another nifty tool for using audio as well. If you've created videos, you know that getting the right level of background audio can be a challenge. You want it to be heard, but not overwhelm the narration. In Movie Maker, select the Project tab, and you'll see a variety of choices (Figure 6-20) about the background audio soundtrack: "Emphasize narration," Emphasize video," "Emphasize music," and "No emphasis."

Emphasize   Emphasize   Emphasize   No
 narration   video   music   emphasis

Figure 6-20.
Movie Maker lets you tweak your soundtrack's audio level

See Also

- Hack #62, "Organize Your Photos with Metadata"
- Hack #63, "Use RAW Photos in Windows Photo Gallery"

HACK 62 Organize Your Photos with Metadata

Photo Gallery offers a hidden way to easily organize your photos—add metadata to your files. Here's how.

If you've got plenty of photos on your hard disk, browsing through them to find ones you want can be time-consuming and frustrating. Organizing photos by folder helps only to a certain extent.

The free, downloadable Photo Gallery (Hack #61, "Power Up Windows 8 with a Free Movie Maker, Photo Gallery, and More") makes finding photos a snap because of a technology baked into Windows since Windows Vista—the Extensible Metadata Platform (XMP), which was created by Adobe, and is used in high-end, expensive photo-editing programs.

XMP is unique because it stores keywords—called *metadata*—as a part of each photograph. In Windows, because the keyword metadata is part of the files themselves, the metadata travels with the photos. And because the metadata is recognized by the operating system, you can use Windows Search to find the photos. For example, add the keyword *Florence* to all the photos of Florence, and you can easily search using that keyword in Windows.

Photos have several kinds of metadata in them, some of which are automatically placed there by the camera taking them. To see all the metadata in a file, right-click it, choose Properties, and then click the Details tab, as shown in Figure 6-21. You'll see all the metadata in the file, which has been divided into sections, such as Description, Origin, Image, Camera, and so on. Depending on how you acquired the photo, the metadata in many of these sections might be blank.

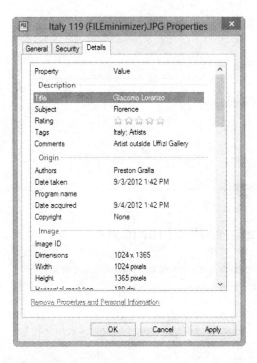

Figure 6-21.
Metadata in a photo file

If you've taken the picture with a digital camera, the file may have information in it such as the manufacturer of the camera and details about camera settings used when the photo was taken, such as F-stop, ISO speed, exposure time, and focal length.

In this hack, you'll see how to add metadata to your photos to more easily browse through, organize, and search for photos.

Editing and Adding Tags to Photos

Although photos taken by camera have metadata already in them, that metadata isn't particularly useful for sorting, searching, or browsing through photos. It's unlikely you're going to want to sort your photos by their ISO speed, for example. You're more likely going to want to sort them by the names of the people in them, or perhaps by date.

To do that, you add what Windows calls *tags* to your photo—keywords that describe the photo and become part of the photo's metadata. There are several ways to do this. The simplest is to double-click a file in Photo Gallery to view it (Figure 6-22), and then in the righthand pane, click Add Tags. Type the tags you want to associate with the photo, pressing Enter after each tag. You can add as many tags as you want, and each tag can be made up of multiple words although there's a limit of 255 characters per tag.

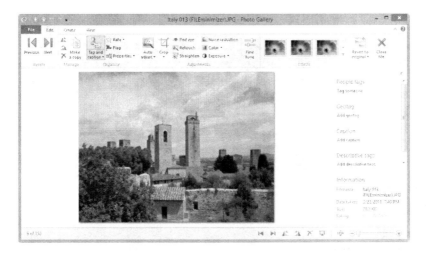

Figure 6-22.
Editing tags in Photo Gallery

If you've already added tags to other photos, when you click Add Tags, you'll see a list of the ten most recent tags you've used. Select any one to add it as a tag. In addition, as you type, an AutoComplete feature displays a list of existing tags that match the letters you've typed. Press the down arrow to select a tag, and then press Enter to add it to the photo.

You can also assign tags to multiple photos at once. Select multiple files, and add a tag as you would normally.

I've just described what I think is the simplest, most straightforward way to add tags, but there are other ways as well:

- In File Explorer or Photo Gallery, right-click a file, choose Properties, and then select the Details tab. Click in the Tags field, and type in your tags. Separate each tag from another with a semicolon.

- In File Explorer, make sure the Details pane is visible (View→Details Pane); see Figure 6-23. Click in the Tags field, and then type your tags. Separate each tag from another with a semicolon.

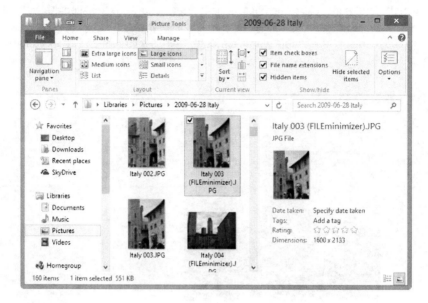

Figure 6-23.
Editing tags in File Explorer

- In Photo Gallery, select View→"Tag and caption pane." Select any photo or group of photos to which you want to add a tag, then in the pane, type the tags you want to use.

- In Photo Gallery, click the Home tag. You'll see icons for types of tags, including "People tag," "Descriptive tag," and Geotag. Click any icon, and then click "Tag an item."

Now that you've got your photos tagged, how will that help you display and find photos? Easy. In Photo Gallery, select View→"Tag and caption pane." On the tag and captions pane you'll see tags listed under "Descriptive tag," "People tags," and "Geotags." Click any of the tags, and you'll see all the photos associated with that tag (Figure 6-24). Also in Photo Gallery, click the File pane, then click the Tag icon and select from the tags to display photos associated with any tag (Figure 6-25).

Note: Geotags are commonly added automatically by cameras and smartphones, but you can also add them yourself manually, just like any other kind of tag.

Figure 6-24.
Viewing related photos by using tags

Figure 6-25.
Selecting tags to display files

In addition, when you do a search in Windows or in Photo Gallery, you can search by tags as well. Searching in Photo Gallery is an especially powerful, often overlooked tool. It will search only through your current selection, so it is a great way to find photos fast. For example, when you display all photos with a common tag, when you do a search, you'll only search through those photos. Similarly, if you display photos by date, or any other type of metadata, you'll only search through those photos. To search, select Home→"Text search" and type your search terms. Keep these things in mind when searching in Photo Gallery:

- If you type multiple search terms, Photo Gallery uses the AND search operator. When you type two search terms, *both* terms must be in a file's metadata for it to show up in your search results.

- The search looks through all of your files' metadata, including file names, tags, camera name, and so on.

- When you do a search in Photo Gallery, it searches for text strings, not keywords. So, for example, if you search for the term *vine*, you'll see results for files whose metadata includes Martha's Vineyard, bovine, and so on.

Using Other Metadata

As I explained earlier, tags aren't the only kind of metadata associated with each file. You can edit the metadata in a file by right-clicking it, choosing Properties, selecting the Details tab, and editing any metadata you see there. Photo Gallery also makes it easy to edit the most useful metadata, including the file name, the date, and time the picture was taken, as well as a rating on a one-to-five star scale you assign to the file. When you highlight a file, its details appear in the righthand pane. Click a star rating to assign it a rating, and click the date, time, or name to edit that information.

See Also

- Hack #61, "Power Up Windows 8 with a Free Movie Maker, Photo Gallery, and More"
- Hack #63, "Use RAW Photos in Windows Photo Gallery"

HACK 63 Use RAW Photos in Windows Photo Gallery

> Some digital cameras use the high-quality RAW file format to take photos. Photo Gallery doesn't seem to handle them—unless you use this hack, that is.

Digital cameras that take high-quality photos may take them in the RAW format, which are of higher quality than those taken in *.jpg*.

Photo Gallery, though, doesn't display RAW files. Transfer RAW files to your PC, and Photo Gallery won't be able to display them. You'll see the name of a file, such as *OPC_341.NEF,* but you won't see a thumbnail of it. And if you double-click the file, you won't be able to open it.

The problem is that RAW isn't really a commonly accepted standard. Each camera manufacturer implements RAW files differently. There is a way, however, to force Windows Photo Gallery to display the photos. The long and very difficult and annoying way around is to go to the camera manufacturers' websites and download codecs—

special software that can decode the photos so you can view them. There are several problems with doing this. One is that the manufacturers may not have posted the codecs, or it may be difficult to find or display them. Another problem is that if you have photos from different cameras, you may have to visit multiple sites and install each codec separately, which is not a particularly pleasant way to spend your time.

There's a much simpler fix: Download and install the free Microsoft Camera Codec Pack (*http://www.microsoft.com/en-us/download/details.aspx?id=26829*). This download includes codecs for dozens of cameras from multiple manufacturers, including Canon, Nikon, Sony, Olympus, Kodak, and others.

Once that's installed, all RAW photos from those cameras will show up in the Windows Photo Gallery. Oddly enough, though, they won't end in a *.raw* extension. Each camera manufacturer has its own specific file type for its highest-quality photos. Generally, they're called RAW files, but the extensions will differ. So, for example, Nikon RAW files have the *.nef* extension, while Canon uses a number of different ones, such as *.crw* or *.cr2*, depending on the camera.

If you edit any RAW files using Windows Photo Gallery, you won't actually change the RAW files themselves. Instead, Windows Photo Gallery leaves the original RAW images intact, and saves a *.jpg* copy of the edited file. The edited *.jpg* file will be of a lower quality than the RAW image.

See Also

- Hack #61, "Power Up Windows 8 with a Free Movie Maker, Photo Gallery, and More"
- Hack #62, "Organize Your Photos with Metadata"

HACK 64 Get a Free Copy of Windows Media Center

Want to get a free copy of Windows Media Center? Here's how to do it.

Notice something missing from Windows 8? That's right, it doesn't include Windows Media Center. There are reasons for that: One is that Microsoft doesn't think you want it. Another is that the company would prefer that you use other ways to watch TV and DVDs, such as the Xbox 360, which can be connected to your Windows 8 machine.

But if you really want to get a copy of Windows Media Center, you can get it. Depending on the version of Windows 8 you have and when you're reading this, it might be free, cost you $9.99, or instead a whopping $69.99.

If you've got a copy of Windows 8 Pro, you can get a copy for $9.99...or better yet, for free. Normally you'll have to pay $9.99 for it online, but until January 31, 2013 you can get it for free. To get it for free, first head here (*http://windows.microsoft.com/en-US/*

windows-8/feature-packs). Look for the free offer, enter your email address, and wait until you're sent an email with a product key for it. When you get the product key, press Windows key + Q, type `Add Features`, click Settings, then click "Add features to Windows 8," which appears on the left side of the screen. Enter the product key that you just got sent via email, and follow the instructions. After a few minutes your device will reboot, and Windows Media Center will be reinstalled (Figure 6-26).

Figure 6-26.
Windows Media Center, running in Windows 8

If you don't have Windows 8 Pro, head to *http://windows.microsoft.com/en-US/ windows-8/feature-packs* and follow the instructions for upgrading and buying Windows Media Center. If it's after January 31, 2013 and you do have Windows 8 Pro, follow the instructions for buying Windows Media Center for $9.99. If you don't have Windows 8 Pro, you'll have to pay $69.99 to upgrade to it and get Windows Media Center.

HACK 65 Play it Loud!

> You can pump up the volume and get high-quality surround sound on your PC—but you have to know where to look.

Do your PC speakers sound only ho-hum? The problem may not be that they're not good enough quality—you may simply not know the right settings to make them sound better.

Many PCs have Intel motherboards with High Definition Audio support, which means that they're capable of some pretty cool sound features. But normally, those features aren't turned on. To turn them on, choose Control Panel→Hardware and Sound→Sound. A screen like the one shown in Figure 6-27 appears. If your system supports High Definition Audio, it will say it right on the icon—for example, "Ready."

Figure 6-27.
Checking whether your system supports High Definition Audio

You first need to tell Windows 8 what kind of sound system you have—stereo, quadrophonic, 5.1, 7.1, and so on. Click the sound device you want to configure (you may have multiple ones on your system), and then click Configure. A screen like the one shown in Figure 6-28 appears. Select your sound system. To check whether a speaker is working, click it and a sound will come out of it. When you've tested each speaker, click Next to launch a wizard that will confirm your speaker setup.

Note: A 5.1 system is one in which there are five speakers and a subwoofer; a 7.1 system is one in which there are seven speakers and a subwoofer.

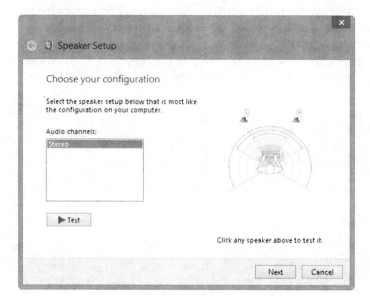

Figure 6-28.
Configuring your sound system

HACK 66 ## Convert Vinyl and Tapes to MP3s

> Got a retro music collection on vinyl and tapes, and wish you had them
> as digital files for your PC? Here's a groovy, far-out, psychedelic way to
> help them enter the electronic era.

Contrary to popular opinion, there was music before CDs and MP3s. Plenty of it. And plenty of it was good. And it was all on vinyl LPs and tapes.

What if you've got a collection of vinyl and tapes and want to bring them into the modern era, but don't want to pay for new CDs or digital downloads—or the music may simply not be available in a digital format? Join the club. There are plenty of us out there in the same boat. I've got a big vinyl collection myself, sitting in my basement, with plenty of old blues players like Bukka White, Skip James, and Robert Johnson, not to mention their oddball revivers such as the duo of Backwards Sam Firk and Delta X.

Fear not; it doesn't take much work to bring that collection into the modern world by turning these recordings into MP3s.

One expensive way to do it is to buy a special turntable or tape deck that connects to your PC via a USB port, then play the music on the turntable, and record it using music recording software such as the free program Audacity (*http://audacity.source-forge.net*). But that won't be cheap. A USB turntable like the Ion iTTUSB Turntable (*http://www.ion-audio.com/ittusb.php*) has a list price of $200, for example.

There's a much cheaper way to do it, it only costs about $10, and it's not any harder, either. All you'll need is an inexpensive stereo cable from Radio Shack or other electronics store.

First, you need to connect your old turntable or tape player to your PC. (Don't have one anymore? Head over to eBay or a yard sale.) The exact cable you need varies according to the kind of stereo equipment you have. If you have a cassette deck, or a turntable and pre-amplifier that's part of a larger stereo system, you'll most likely need something called a Y-cable. On one end, it has two RCA plugs that hook up to the back of your stereo gear, and on the other end, it has a 3.5-millimeter stereo miniplug that hooks right into your PC's sound card.

If you're going to record from a portable cassette player, you instead need a cable that has stereo miniplugs on both end of it. One miniplug connects to the cassette player, and the other end to your PC's sound card.

If you care about sound quality, consider getting the highest quality cables you can find. Poor quality plugs can create audio noise, and your MP3s will have that noise in them.

Plug everything in. Before you can start recording, though, you need to find out where you can control your PC's audio line-in level—set it too low, and you'll barely be able to hear your MP3s; set it too high, and you'll get distortion and noise.

In Windows 8, right-click the audio icon in the far right of the System Tray, and select Recording Devices. Make sure the device is configured properly by highlighting it and clicking Configure, then walking through the configuration screen. Click OK. Then double-click the audio icon to bring up the volume control.

You'll need software to record your music. A popular freebie is Audacity (*http:// audacity.sourceforge.net*), but there are others as well. Using Audacity will take some work, though, because you have to go through both a recording and conversion process. And one more problem with Audacity and other free recording programs is that, although they come with a lot of useful filters, cleaning up audio from vinyl and cassette may be something of a manual process. There's a good chance that your file is going to have scratches, pops, clicks, and hiss on it. Vinyl-recording software can automatically clean it up for you, as well as make recording a one-step process rather than a several-step process.

A good bet is the shareware program Spin It Again (*http://www.acoustica.com/spinitagain*). You can try it for free; it's $34.95 if you decide to keep it.

It's remarkably easy to use. To record from a vinyl LP, for example, connect the cables, click "Record a Vinyl LP" or "Record a Cassette Tape," and follow the wizard that appears. It even walks you through setting up the right sound levels. Once you've recorded your tracks, play each of them, and from the Cleaning & Effects Processing dropdown list, select the clean-up you want the program to perform, such as Vinyl Declick & Decrackle, Damaged Records, or Clean Anything, and the program does the rest.

Networking, the Web, Wireless, and the Internet

Using a computer without the Internet is about as unthinkable as using a computer without a display or screen. The Internet has become thoroughly entwined in the way we compute. In fact, it has become so much a part of how we use technology that there no longer seems to be a dividing line between our computer and the vast resources of the Net and the Web. And increasingly, accessing the Internet means using wireless networking.

In this chapter, you'll learn to hack all things related to the Internet—your home network, wireless technologies, Internet Explorer and other web browsers, and more. Whether you're looking to replace your Windows 8 native Internet Explorer browser with something else, make Windows 8 play nice with your home network, hack Windows 8 wireless networking, get down and dirty with your home wireless router, speed up Web browsing, remotely control another computer, or more, you'll find it all here.

HACK 67 Make the Desktop Version of Internet Explorer the Default Rather than the Windows 8 Native Version

> Not a fan of the Windows 8 native version of Internet Explorer? Here's a way to make the Desktop version the default browser—even when you're using the Start screen interface.

There's a good chance that you've been confused at times when using Internet Explorer in Windows 8, because there are two Internet Explorer apps—the Windows 8 native version and the Desktop version. The Windows 8 native version is more visually attractive, but when you use it, you don't get many familiar buttons and options, and you also can't use add-ons, or even use ActiveX.

These shortcomings can be a problem because the Windows 8 native version is the default, so when another app triggers the use of Internet Explorer, you're sent to the Windows 8 native version, not the Desktop version.

There's a quick hack that solves the problem. You can make the Desktop version of Internet Explorer the default.

First, run the Desktop version of Internet Explorer. Click the gear icon on the upper-right of the screen and select Internet Options→Programs. Click in the "Choose how you open links" section, select "Always in Internet Explorer on the Desktop," and then click OK (Figure 7-1). Also make sure to turn on the "Open Internet Explorer tiles on the Desktop" checkbox. That way, the Internet Explorer tile will appear on the Start screen, and any pinned sites will also open in the Desktop version of Internet Explorer.

Warning: This hack changes the setting only for the currently logged on user. If you want to change it for all accounts on the computer, use Group Policy. To do so, press Windows key+R, type `gpedit.msc` *in the Run box, and then press Enter. That runs the Group Policy Editor. You'll need to change two policy settings, both located in Computer Configuration→Administrative Templates→Windows Components→ Internet Explorer→Internet Settings. Double-click "Set how links are opened in Internet Explorer" and set it to Enabled. Then double-click "Open Internet Explorer tiles on the desktop" and exit the Group Policy Editor. (Note: Group Policy Editor is available only in Windows 8 Pro and Windows 8 Enterprise.).*

Hacking the Hack

Maybe you're a fan of the Windows 8 native version of Internet Explorer, but sometimes when you're using it, you want to use the Desktop version. Simple. Display the app bar of the Windows 8 native version of Internet Explorer by right-clicking anywhere on the page, or pressing Windows key+Z. Then click the small wrench icon and select "View on the desktop" from the pop-up menu.

See Also

- Hack #68, "Change Your Default Native Windows 8 Browser to Chrome"

HACK 68 ## Change Your Default Native Windows 8 Browser to Chrome

At first, there seems no way to change your default Windows 8 native browser from Internet Explorer 10. But with a bit of tweaking, you can do it.

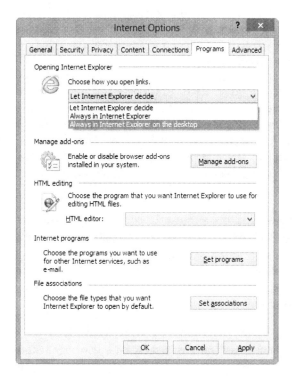

Figure 7-1.
Making the Desktop version of Internet Explorer the default

No matter what browser you use on the Windows 8 desktop, when it comes to the Start screen, there seems to be only one choice: Internet Explorer. Even if you have another browser installed on the desktop, you won't find a way to run it as a Windows 8 native app.

Part of the problem is that the Start screen lets you run only your default browser—there's simply no way to run another browser. Internet Explorer is the default browser, and there seems to be no way to change that.

That's not really the case, though. You can, in fact, use a different browser, as you'll see in this hack. I'll show you how to do it using Google's Chrome browser, but you can use similar techniques for other browsers as well.

First, of course, you have to install Chrome. Make sure you're installing the Windows 8 native version of Chrome. (As I write this, the Windows 8 native version of Chrome was only available in Google's Dev channel, although that might be changed as you read this.)

First, to go to the normal Chrome download page (*http://www.google.com/intl/en/ chrome/browser/*). If the Windows 8 version isn't there, head to the Dev channel (*http://dev.chromium.org/getting-involved/dev-channel*). Click the Dev channel for Windows link. Download and install the browser.

That by itself won't make Chrome your Windows 8 native browser—and oddly enough, the first thing you need to do to make it your default on the Start screen is head to the Desktop. Launch Chrome on the Desktop, and go into Chrome's settings to make it your default Desktop browser. To do so, click the icon with three horizontal stripes on Chrome's toolbar, then select Settings. Down in the Default Browser section, click "Make Google Chrome my default browser." Finally a message box pops up asking you to select the default browser.

That makes Chrome your default Desktop browser, but it still won't work as the default on the Start screen. To do that, get to the Control Panel. For the quickest way to get there, first press Windows key+Q to access the Search charm. Then search for **Control Panel**, and then click on the Control Panel icon when it appears. You'll be sent to the Desktop Control Panel. Go to Programs→Default Programs→Set Your Default Programs. Now click on Google Chrome and select "Set this program as default."

Finally, go back to the Windows 8 interface and click the Google Chrome icon. You'll now be able to run Chrome as a Windows 8 native app. Just click the icon on the Start screen.

Hacking the Hack

Now that Chrome is your default Start screen browser, make sure to take advantage of one of its niftiest features—its ability to sync your bookmarks, Chrome extensions, history list, password, and more among Chrome running on different computers. In fact, it even lets you sync open tabs among all computers running Chrome. Click the Settings icon, and in the Sign In area, click "Advanced sync settings" to make sure you're syncing.

See Also

- Hack #67, "Make the Desktop Version of Internet Explorer the Default Rather than the Windows 8 Native Version"

HACK 69 Make Windows 8 Play Nice with Your Home Network

You may run into problems accessing other PCs on your home network when you're using Windows 8. Here's how to do it easily.

When you sign into Windows 8, you typically use your Microsoft account (previously called your Windows Live ID). There are a number of benefits to doing that, notably that you can sync settings with other computers using Windows 8.

But there's a drawback as well—you may have problems accessing other PCs on your home network because you're using your Microsoft account rather than whatever account you previously used on your network. Here's how to solve these problems.

Using Homegroup with Windows 8

If you use a Homegroup sharing network, you'll probably need to configure it properly for Windows 8. First, get to the Homegroup settings by displaying the Settings charm (easiest way: Windows key+I) and selecting Change PC Settings→Homegroup (Figure 7-2). On the righthand side of the page, enter the Homegroup password.

Tip: If you don't yet have a Homegroup, Windows 8 will set it up for you. To have other Windows 8 or Windows 7 PCs join, give them the password, which might have already been set up for you. Scroll to the Membership area on the right side of the screen to find it.

Figure 7-2.
Windows 8 Homegroup settings

You've logged into Homegroup. Now configure which folders, documents and devices you want to share. You'll find options for doing that on the righthand side of the screen.

To use Homegroup, launch File Explorer (previously called Windows Explorer), and click the Homegroup icon in the navigation pane (Figure 7-3).

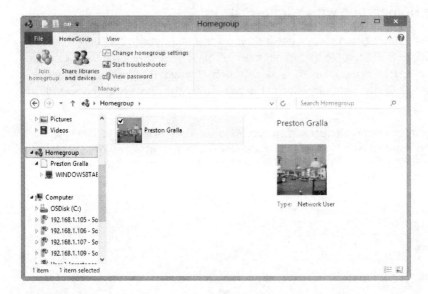

Figure 7-3.
Windows 8 Homegroup

Using Windows 8 with Network Shares

If you've got Windows Vista, Windows XP, or earlier Windows versions on your home network, they can't access Homegroup. So you must instead use the older Network shares Windows technology.

If all you want to do is access the public and shared folders of other PCs, you don't really need to do much. Just launch File Explorer, click the PC whose public and shared files and folders you want to access, and then navigate to the files and folders you want (see Figure 7-4). It's a snap.

If, however, you want to access the rest of the computer, including your Documents folder and other folders, you're in for trouble. The machine likely won't recognize you

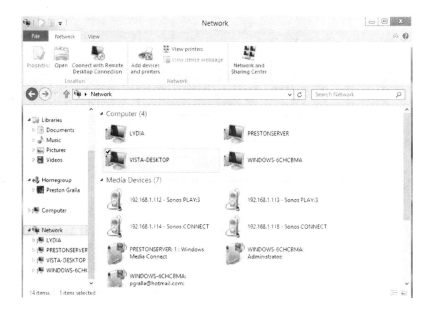

Figure 7-4.
Accessing a home network using Network sharing

because you're using your Microsoft account rather than the user account you pre-viously used to access the PC. You'll be presented with a login screen to authenticate to the machine if you're using a different set of credentials than the accounts the remote computer knows of.

There's a hack to solve the problem. You'll have to create what's called a Windows Credential. Then, using that stored credential, you'll be able to access all of another computer's folders and files.

When you're on the Start screen, type **Vault**, click Settings on the righthand side of the page, then select Settings as the category of your search. From the screen that appears, click Manage Windows Credentials. The Credential Manager appears (Figure 7-5).

Click "Add a Windows Credential." In the "Internet or network address" area (Figure 7-6), first type the name of the machine you want to access. (If you're unsure of the name of the computer you want to access, open a command prompt window on it and type **hostname**. This will return its NetBIOS name.) Just type the machine's name, without the \\ marks in front of it. So you'd type **BigMommaPC**, not **\\ BigMommaPC**. After that, type the user name and password you normally use for that machine. You'll have to create a separate credential for each machine.

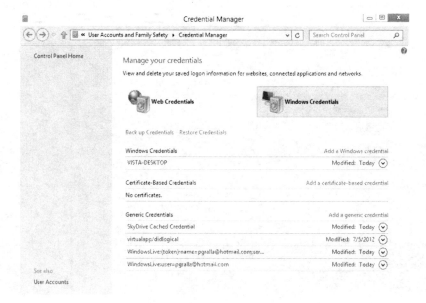

Figure 7-5.
Use the Credential Manager to create a credential that will let you access other machines on your home network

Figure 7-6.
Adding a Windows Credential to the Credential Manager

Once you've created all the credentials, reboot Windows. Then start File Explorer, and explore your networked PCs to your heart's content.

See Also

- Hack #72, "Hack Windows 8 Wi-Fi, Wireless, and Network Settings"
- Hack #77, "Troubleshoot Wireless Interference Woes, and Extend Your Range"
- Hack #90, "Protect Your Home Wi-Fi Network"

> No matter how fast your Internet connection is, it's never fast enough. Here's a quick way to speed up your Web browsing, no matter at which speed you're connected to the Internet.

Sometimes no matter how fast your Internet connection, Internet pages seem to load like molasses. You'll likely blame the problem on your service provider, but they may not be at fault. Sometimes the issue is related to the Domain Name System that controls the way your PC interacts with the Internet in order to get web pages delivered to it.

Here's a brief primer on how the Domain Name System works. You use the Web by typing in hostnames, such as *www.oreilly.com*, but web servers and Internet routers can't understand plain English words, so they need those letters translated into numeric IP addresses. Whenever you type a hostname, it needs to be resolved to its IP address, such as 208.201.293.101. DNS servers provide that name resolution automatically behind the scenes as you surf the Web.

Sometimes, though, those servers can get bogged down. If they're slow in acting, your page is slow in loading, because your PC has to wait while the hostname is resolved to the numeric IP address.

There's a simple solution: Use the free OpenDNS service. You can tell your computer to use OpenDNS's DNS servers rather than the ones your service provider automatically uses.

Note: Using OpenDNS has other benefits in addition to speeding up Web browsing. If the DNS servers your service provider uses go down, you can't surf the Web normally. However, if they go down and you're using OpenDNS, you'll be able to surf normally.

To set up OpenDNS, you'll need to get to your Internet IP settings. From the Control Panel, select Network and Internet→Network and Sharing Center, then click your Internet connection and select Properties. Highlight "Internet Protocol Version 4 (TCP/IPv4)" and click Properties. As shown in Figure 7-7, choose "Use the following DNS server addresses" and, in the first box beneath it, type **208.67.222.222**; in the second, type **208.67.220.220**. Click OK, and then OK again. You're now using OpenDNS's servers. (To configure IPv6, open the "Internet Protocol Version 6 (TCP/IPv6)" and click Properties. Select "Use the following DNS server addresses" and type **2620:0:ccc::2** and **2620:0:ccd::2**.)

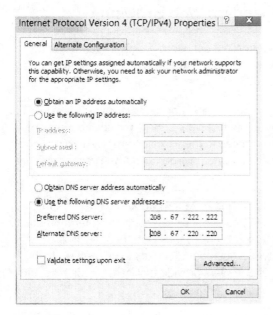

Figure 7-7.
Telling your computer to use OpenDNS's servers

Tell Your Entire Network to use OpenDNS

Telling an individual PC to use OpenDNS is well and good. But what if you've got multiple PCs, tablets, smartphones, and other devices on your home network? You don't want to have to perform this step on every one of them. And in some instances, devices might not give you access to making this kind of change.

There's a simple solution: You can change your home router's settings so that all requests for web pages go through OpenDNS servers.

How you do this varies from router to router, so I can't include instructions for all of them. However, the same general rules will apply from router to router, so check your router's instructions, and use the following instructions as your guide. I'll give instructions for how to make the changes using the popular Linksys WRT-160n router. (You can also head to *https://store.opendns.com/setup/router*, choose your router, and follow the instructions.)

In a Linksys router, you typically log into the setup screen by opening your browser and going to *http://192.168.1.1*. When the login screen appears, leave the username blank. In the password section, type **admin**, and then press Enter. (That's the default. If you've changed the user name and password, use those.) You should be at the Basic Setup page. If you're not, click Setup at the top of the screen, and then click Basic

Setup. As shown in Figure 7-8, in the "Static DNS 1" box, type **208.67.222.222**, and in the "Static DNS 2 box" type **208.67.220.220**. Click Save Settings. That'll do the trick. If the router uses a native IPv6 Internet connection and offers DHCPv6, be sure to also add both IPv6 addresses for the OpenDNS servers: **2620:0:ccc::2** and **2620:0:ccd::2**.

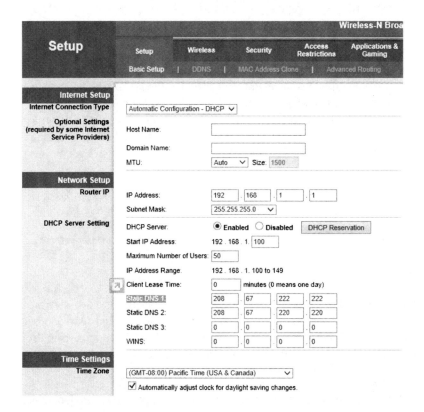

Figure 7-8.
Telling your router to use OpenDNS's servers

Hacking the Hack

OpenDNS does more for you than just speeding up Web browsing. You can also use it to filter websites for parental controls. For details, go to *http://www.opendns.com* and sign up for the free home service.

Control Another PC with Remote Desktop

You can control a computer—virtually moving its mouse, typing on its keyboard, and running it just as if you were sitting at it—over a network or the Internet, using either Windows 8's built-in features or a third-party program.

When you're using one PC on your network, wouldn't it be nice to be able to take complete control of another, just as if you were sitting at the keyboard? Say you use a primary computer for most of your work, but the sun is shining outside, the porch beckons, and you'd like to spend some time outside, but need to access your main computer for things like checking email with Outlook. You can do it using a Windows 8 feature called Remote Desktop Connection.

Note: Using Remote Desktop, you can also control a PC over the Internet rather than your home network, in theory. But it can be very difficult, frustrating, time-consuming, and sometimes even impossible, so for controlling a PC over the Internet, I suggest using a free program you can download, as I'll explain later in this hack.

Controlling a PC in Windows 8 using a Remote Desktop Connection is a two-step process. First, you have to tell the PC that you want to control that it should allow another computer to control it. Then, you actually take control of it. The PC you want to control won't have to use Windows 8; it can be an earlier Windows version, as long as that version of Windows lets you use this feature.

First, go to the PC you want to control and configure it so it can be controlled. Make sure that you're logged in as an administrator. If you're going to control a Windows 8 PC, in the Control Panel do a search for Remote and then click "Allow Remote access to your computer." Then, as shown in Figure 7-9, select "Allow remote connections to this computer." If you've set up your PC to go to sleep or hibernate when it's not being used, you'll get a message saying that you need to reconfigure those options, or else you won't be able to wake your computer and take control of it. To turn the setting off, head to Power Options in the Control Panel. If you don't care about waking the PC from sleep or hibernation, click OK when the message appears.

You'll find a somewhat confounding box toward the bottom of the screen: "Allow connections only from computers running Remote Desktop with Network Level Authentication (recommended)." Remote Desktop with Network Level Authentication is only available on Windows 7 and Windows 8, so if you plan on controlling the Windows 8 PC with a PC running one of those operating systems, turn on this box. (If you plan to control it with an earlier version of Windows, don't use this setting.)

Now it's time to choose who can connect to take control of your computer. Click Select Users. Windows automatically allows connections from the current user, along with all users in the local Administrators group, so there's no need to add either the current user, or any administrator. If you want to let others control the PC, click Select Users, and then add them.

Note:Only users who have accounts that require a password for logging into Windows can take control of a remote computer.

Figure 7-9.
Configuring a Windows 8 PC to accept Remote Desktop Connections (step 1)

Tip: If you're using an earlier version of Windows than Windows 8, you configure the PC to be controlled much the same way you configure it for Windows 8.

Click OK. Now you're ready to take control of that PC. You can use either the Desktop client or the Windows 8 native client. Each has its pros and cons. With the Windows 8 native client, you can control multiple PCs at a time. But you can only run the app full screen, while the Desktop client lets you change the size of the remote desktop window.

To run the Desktop client, from the Windows 8 Start screen, type *Remote*, highlight Apps on the right side, and the Remote Desktop Connection app appears on the left. Click it, and then click Show Options when it appears (Figure 7-10). In the Computer box, type the name of the computer you're going to control. Make sure that you type it correctly. Type the user name of an account that has access to the remote computer. Then click Connect.

Figure 7-10.
Configuring a Windows 8 PC to accept Remote Desktop Connections (step 2)

After a few moments, you may see a screen warning you that the identity of the remote computer can't be verified. You can safely ignore the warning, so click Yes. If you don't want to see the message each time you connect, also check the box next to "Don't ask me again for connections to this computer."

In a few moments, you'll connect to the remote computer. If you haven't connected before, you'll be asked to type your password. (If you choose to make Windows remember it, the set of credentials will be added to the Credential Manager) Once you're logged in and connected, the connection will appear in its own separate window. The window has controls across the top right for minimizing and resizing the windows. Using that window, you can do everything you normally would do on the computer, as if you were sitting in front of it (Figure 7-11). Keep in mind that this means that when you print, you'll print to the printer attached to the computer you're controlling, not the printer attached to the computer taking control. You'll be able to cut and paste information from the remote client window to other windows. To end the connection, click the X in the window. That ends the connection, but not the actual session. To properly log off and end the session, sign out from the remote Start screen or remote Start menu.

Figure 7-11.
Controlling a Windows Vista PC from inside Windows 8 using the Remote Desktop Connection

Using the Windows 8 Native Client

If you prefer Windows 8 native apps to Desktop apps, you can use the Windows 8 native Remote Desktop app. It may or may not be built into your version of Windows 8—there seems to be inconsistency from machine to machine. And some people have even reported their Windows 8 native Remote Desktop unaccountably vanishing.

That doesn't matter, though, because you can download it for free from the Windows Store. You'll find it in the Productivity area.

After it installs, run it, then at the bottom of the screen, type in the name of the machine that you want to control, using the same rules as described for the Desktop app. Then click the Connect button. As with the Desktop version, you may get a message telling you that it can't verify the identity of the remote PC. Ignore the message and click "Connect anyway." You'll then make the connection and can control the remote PC.

The Windows 8 native app improves on the desktop app in one way: it automatically scales the remote screen so that it fits perfectly inside the Remote Desktop app. You won't have to fiddle with any settings to get it right.

There's another benefit as well—you can make multiple remote connections from the app and control multiple PCs, switching from PC to PC. To do it, once you've made one connection and you're controlling a remote PC, move your mouse to the top of the screen and click the icon that appears. The current remote connection appears as a thumbnail at the top of the screen, next to a + sign. Click the + sign and you can make a second connection. When you're in either of your two connections, move your mouse to the top of the screen and click (Figure 7-12). Both connections appear as thumbnails. Click the one to which you want to connect.

Once you've made a connection, that connection shows up as a tile. Click to run it again to connect to the remote PC.

Figure 7-12.
The Remote Desktop app remembers past connections; click one to connect

Control a Remote PC with LogMeIn

It's theoretically possible to control a PC over the Internet using the Remote Desktop Connection, but I wouldn't recommend it. It's hard to do, if you can do it at all. There's a much better solution—and not only is it free, it has more capabilities as well.

The program is called LogMeIn (Figure 7-13), and there are free and paid versions. Get the free version unless you need remote HD video and sound. Install it only on any PCs that you want to control, and remember the user name and password, because you'll need it in order to control that computer.

There are many reasons to use LogMeIn for remote control, and here's a big one: You don't need to install software on the computer you'll use to control the remote computer. All you need is any browser.

Once you've installed LogMeIn on the computer you want to control, head to *www.logmein.com* on the computer you want to use to control the remote computer. Log in with the user name and password you used to register LogMeIn on the remote PC. Then click LogMeIn. You'll see an icon representing the PC that you want to control.

Click it. If you use Internet Explorer, you may be prompted to install an ActiveX plug-in. But the Windows 8 version of Internet Explorer doesn't run plug-ins, and you may have problems with the Desktop version as well, so you can safely ignore that, and instead proceed to connect normally, without the plug-in.

Next you'll be prompted for a user name and password. This isn't the LogMeIn user name and password; it's the user name and password for the machine to which you're connecting. In other words, use your Windows login information. Then click Enter. In a moment or two you'll make the connection, and you'll have remote control of your computer, using just your browser.

Figure 7-13.
Controlling a remote PC over the Internet using LogMeIn

You may need to fiddle around a bit with LogMeIn in order to match the resolution of the remote computer with the computer doing the controlling. The way you match it varies from browser to browser. In Firefox, for example, there's a LogMeIn add-on that makes it easier to connect and manage the connection, so use that. In Internet Explorer, you can change the zoom level using the control on the upper left until you match the resolution properly.

Hacking the Hack

If you're the kind of geek who loves connection details, you'll love LogMeIn. On the PC that was being controlled, double-click the LogMeIn icon in the Notification Area and a LogMeIn control panel appears. Click "Connection and Event Details," and on the Connections tab, you'll see information about past remote control sessions, including the IP address of the computer that remotely controlled the computer, the user name who did the controlling, the length of the connection, the time of connection and disconnection, and more. On the Events tab, you'll see many more details, including the kind of browser that did the connecting.

And here's one more nifty thing about LogMeIn: you can remotely control your PC using an iPhone, Android phone, iPad, Android tablet, or, of course, a Windows 8 or Windows RT tablet.

HACK 72 Hack Windows 8 Wi-Fi, Wireless, and Network Settings

Whether you want to see a report on your total bandwidth use, create a metered connection to make sure you don't exceed bandwidth limits, or more, there are tweaks here for you.

Windows 8 was built with wireless connections in mind. And that means that you'll get capabilities that no other versions of Windows offer—and that no other operating system offers, period. The most important of them have to do with checking your bandwidth use. If you use a wireless service provider, rather than a cable or DSL provider, that's important because service providers typically have bandwidth limitations—exceed them and you'll pay through the nose. And as I write this, even cable and DSL providers are talking about bandwidth limitations. So if you have a wireless network at home connected to cable or DSL, you'll want to check and possibly limit your bandwidth as well.

You'll have to dig into Windows 8 a bit to get at these settings; they don't appear where you think they would. So if you look in the normal wireless settings, you'll be disappointed.

There's two different ways to get where you want to go, depending on whether you're on the Desktop or on the Start screen. On the Desktop, click the wireless icon in the Notification Area, and the Networks pane slides into place. In the Start screen, press Windows key+I to get to the Settings panel, and then click the wireless icon towards the bottom of the screen.

Whichever way you get there, click the icon of the network you're currently using down toward the bottom of the screen, and you'll come to the Networks panel. You'll see a list of networks, including the one to which you're currently connected, networks you've connected to in the past, and any wireless networks within range. Hover your mouse over any network, and you'll get details about what kind of security, if any, it uses (Figure 7-14).

Figure 7-14.
Getting details about the security of a wireless network

Note: The Networks panel will show your wired connections as well as wireless ones. So you can display bandwidth, meter your bandwidth usage, and so on, just as you can for wireless networks.

Right-click your active connection and you get a series of choices (Figure 7-15).

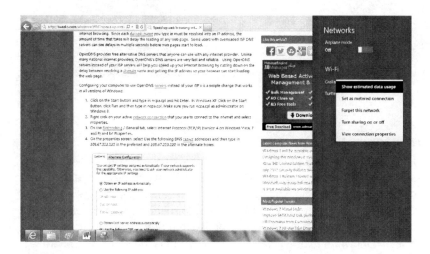

Figure 7-15.
The right-click options for a network

Here's what each does:

Show estimated data usage

Select this option, and you'll see your estimated data use for a given period of time, typically a month, or else the last time you reset it (see details in the next section). This information is useful if you're worried about bumping up against data limits. When you move away from this screen and come back again, you won't see your data use. But it's there waiting for you—just click the network and you'll see it (Figure 7-16).

Tip: Want to stop showing the estimated data use? Right-click the network icon and the options change—"Hide estimated data usage" replaces "Show estimated data usage."

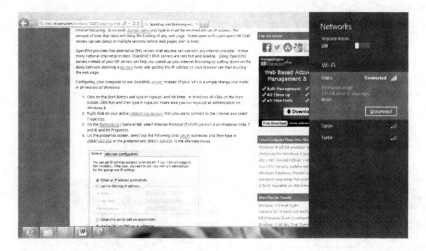

Figure 7-16.
Showing your estimated data use

Set as a metered connection

Use this option only if you're using a tablet or other mobile device, you're connected to a network such as a cellular wireless one that charges for data use, and you know that at some point you're going to connect to a non-metered network, such as Wi-Fi. When you set a network to be a metered connection, it won't download Windows updates until you're on a different connection, and will also try to save bandwidth in other ways. The exception is if a Windows update is a critical one; in that instance, it will download and install. To turn off this setting, click the network again and choose "Set as non-metered connection."

Forget this network

Windows remembers networks, and then automatically connects to them if they're in range. Select this option if you don't want Windows to automatically connect to the network.

Turn sharing on or off

When sharing is turned on, other devices on the network can use devices to which your PC is connected, such as printers. Click here to choose whether sharing should be on or off for the network. It should be off for public networks such as Wi-Fi hot spots at cafes, and on at home.

View connection properties

Click here to get to the Network Properties dialog box (Figure 7-17), and change more connection options if you'd like. You'll find two tabs. The Security tab lets you choose the kind of encryption used on the network, and includes your network password. The Connection tab has options for deciding whether to have Windows connect to the network automatically; whether to connect to the network even if it's not broadcasting its network name, called an SSID; and whether Windows should look for other networks to connect to, even when you're connected to this one.

See Also

- Hack #73, "Use Task Manager to Track Bandwidth Use of Individual Apps and Overall Network Use"

HACK 73   Use Task Manager to Track Bandwidth Use of Individual Apps and Overall Network Use

Not sure where all your bandwidth is going? You may have an app that's a bandwidth hog. Here's how to find it, plus other network tricks using the Task Manager.

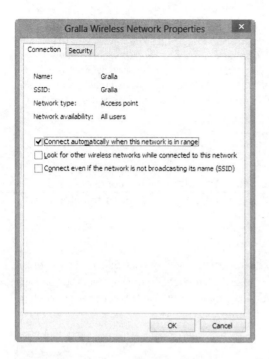

Figure 7-17.
The network properties dialog box

As you've seen in Hack #72, "Hack Windows 8 Wi-Fi, Wireless, and Network Settings", you can easily track your bandwidth use on a network-by-network basis. That's certainly useful. But there's one thing that it doesn't do for you: track which apps are bandwidth hogs. This information may be important if your Internet provider sets monthly bandwidth limits and you can't find out why you're bumping up against them. And if your web browsing seems unnecessarily slow, it may be because you've got an invisible bandwidth hog.

There's a very simple way to find out how much bandwidth every app on your PC is using. Not only will you be able to see how much they're using right then, but you can also view their historical usage over time. To do it, run the Windows 8 Task Manager. Not only will it show you bandwidth use for individual apps, but you can see your current overall bandwidth use, and plenty more about your network as well (Figure 7-18).

Note: Task Manager does a lot more than just track your bandwidth use, as you'll see in Hack #37, "Speed Up System Performance with the Task Manager".

WINDOWS 8 HACKS

Run the Task Manager by pressing Ctrl+Alt+Delete and choosing Task Manager. If you're not on the Processes tab, click it. (If you don't see multiple tabs on the Task Manager, click the More Details arrow at the bottom to reveal them.)

Name	Status	10% CPU	30% Memory	1% Disk	0% Network
Apps (2)					
> Internet Explorer		2.4%	112.3 MB	0.1 MB/s	0.4 Mbps
> Task Manager		1.3%	7.8 MB	0 MB/s	0 Mbps
Background processes (23)					
Adobe® Flash® Player Installer...		0%	1.6 MB	0 MB/s	0 Mbps
COM Surrogate		0%	1.0 MB	0 MB/s	0 Mbps
Device Association Framework ...		0%	5.5 MB	0 MB/s	0 Mbps
Internet Explorer		0%	5.2 MB	0 MB/s	0 Mbps
Internet Explorer (32 bit)		0%	1.8 MB	0 MB/s	0 Mbps
IPoint.exe		1.2%	3.5 MB	0 MB/s	0 Mbps
Live Communications Service		0%	7.8 MB	0 MB/s	0 Mbps
> Microsoft Office Software Prote...		0%	1.5 MB	0 MB/s	0 Mbps
Microsoft OneNote Quick Laun...		0%	0.4 MB	0 MB/s	0 Mbps
Microsoft SkyDrive (32 bit)		0%	6.4 MB	0 MB/s	0 Mbps

Figure 7-18.
Showing the bandwidth use of your currently running apps

Look at the far-right column, the one for Network. For each app, it lists its current bandwidth use in megabits per second (Mbps). As for the percentage number on top of Network, you might as well ignore it. There's nothing logical that it measures. In theory, it should measure the percentage of your total available bandwidth that you're currently using. In practice, though, Windows 8 doesn't know your total available bandwidth, and so it can't really measure this. Scroll down the list and see if there are any apps or processes that are taking up an undue amount of bandwidth. That may well be your bandwidth hog.

There is a shortcoming in this, though. It only shows you the current bandwidth use, and it's possible that what's happening right now is an anomaly. So it's a good idea to check bandwidth use like this regularly.

Even so, that still won't give you the most accurate picture of what apps are the biggest bandwidth users. There's an easy way to find out, though. Click the "App history" tab.

Look at the Network and Metered network columns. That shows you the total amount of data downloaded per app, either on a normal network or metered network (Figure 7-19). (For details about metered networks, see Hack #72, "Hack Windows 8 Wi-Fi, Wireless, and Network Settings".) As for the time period it measures, look toward the upper-left of the screen, just below the tabs. It tells the usage time period it's measuring. If you want to start from scratch, click "Delete usage history."

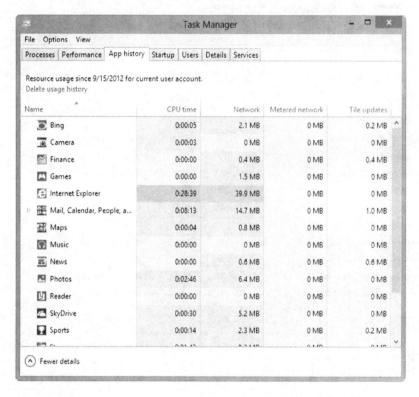

Figure 7-19.
Seeing how much data each app has downloaded

Task Manager does even more than that. It shows you a moving graph of your bandwidth use over the last sixty seconds. Click the Performance tab and then click Wi-Fi. You'll see the chart right there. It also includes a lot more information, including the name of your network, your network SSID (network name), the DNS server you're using, the type of network you're using (for example, 802.11g), the signal strength if it's a wireless network (Figure 7-20), the current sending and receiving bandwidth, and your IPv4 and IPv6 Internet addresses.

See Also

- Hack #72, "Hack Windows 8 Wi-Fi, Wireless, and Network Settings"

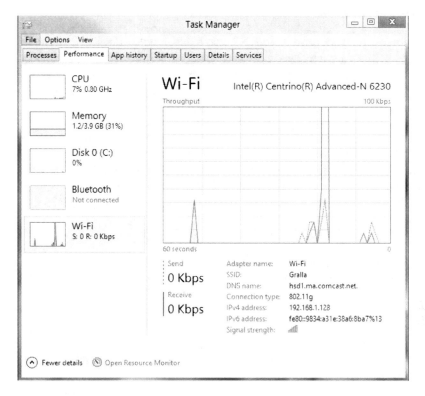

Figure 7-20.
Seeing your Wi-Fi signal strength

HACK 74 ## Map a Network Drive or Network Location

> Got a location on a network or the Internet that you'd like to get to quick-
> ly? Use this simple quick hack to get there fast.

Windows 8's Homegroup and other network tools are fine for browsing through your
network, but they're not particularly fast. If there's a folder on one of your networked
PCs—or on the Internet—that you access frequently, you'll spend plenty of time slog-
ging your way through a series of clicks to get there.

There's a better way. You can map a network drive or other kind of network location
(such as an Internet FTP server) to your PC so you can hop there in a single click.
Here's how to do both.

Map a Network Drive

When you map a network drive to your PC, you make it look like just another drive letter on your PC, but it's actually a folder on another computer on the network. Once you map it, the folder will look like any other drive—it will show up in File Explorer (called Windows Explorer in previous versions), and in your apps. Use it just like any other drive, so you can save files to it, open it, and so on.

To map a network drive, open File Explorer. Make sure that you open it to Computer—if you open it to any other location, you won't be able to map a network drive to it. On the File tab, click "Map network drive" and then select "Map Network Drive" from the drop-down list. As shown in Figure 7-21, in the Folder box, browse to the folder on another PC that you want to map to, and then choose it. From the Drive list, choose the letter that you want to use for the folder when you access it.

Note: You can only map network drives to folders on other PCs that you have access to. So first make sure that they're part of your Homegroup, or that they're accessible via the Network location in File Manager.

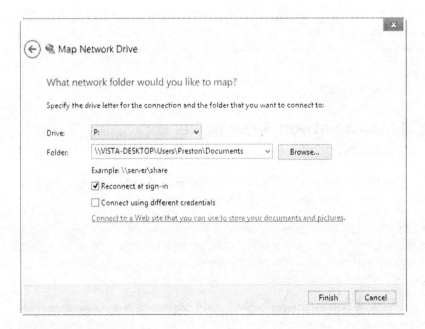

Figure 7-21.
Mapping a network drive

Turn on the "Reconnect at sign-in" checkbox. If you don't do that, you'll have to manually reconnect to the drive every time you want to access it. When you've made your choices, click Finish.

Now that the mapping is done, you can access that drive from everywhere. So, for example, in Microsoft Word, to open files from the folder from another PC that you've mapped to your local PC, simply open Word, and navigate to it like you would any other drive on your PC. You can do the same using any app on your PC, including File Explorer.

Map a Network Location

Mapping a network location to your local PC sounds a lot like mapping a network drive, and there's a basic similarity—in both instances, you make a remote location appear as if it's a drive right on your PC. But there's a difference as well. When you map a network drive, you're typically connecting to a folder on another PC on your network. When you map a network location, you're typically connecting to a service or site on the Internet—for example, an ftp server or a SharePoint document library.

Note: As a practical matter, I've found that I can use the Network Location and Network Drive features interchangeably.

Launch File Explorer and make sure you're at Computer. Then choose "Add a network location," click Next, and then click Next again. Type the network location that you want to map; for example, `ftp://ftp.myftpsite.com`, or `\\server\sharefolder`. Then click Next. Depending on the kind of resource you're going to add, you may need to type a user name and/or a password—what you normally use to connect to the network resource (Figure 7-22).

Note: If you're connecting to an anonymous ftp server that doesn't require a name or password, make sure to turn on the box next to "Log on anonymously."

Type a name for the resource and then click Next. Then from the final screen, click Finish. You can now use the network location from your PC (Figure 7-23).

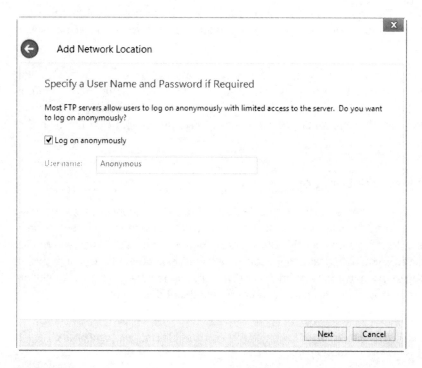

Figure 7-22.
Mapping a network location

Figure 7-23.
File Explorer, showing a mapped network drive and a mapped network location

HACK 75 Troubleshoot Network Connections with ping, tracert, and pathping

> When you need help tracking down network connection problems, the command line is the place to go.

If you're having problems with your network and network connections, your best first bet is to try to get Windows to fix it with a built-in troubleshooter. Launch the Control Panel (type **Control** on the Start screen, then click Control Panel when it appears on the left side of the screen), and select Network and Internet→Network and Sharing Center→Troubleshoot Problems. A troubleshooting wizard launches that may fix the problem.

Or it may not.

If the wizard doesn't get to the root of the problems, time to roll up your virtual sleeves. You're going to have to get down and dirty with command-line tools. The `ping` and `tracert` commands are familiar tools that you might have used on occasion, but you may not know the depth of their power or the command line switches available to use with them. And you probably haven't heard of `pathping`, a quasi-combination of the two commands.

Troubleshoot TCP/IP Problems with ping

The quickest, most commonly used, and, frequently, most helpful TCP/IP trouble-shooting tool is the command-line tool `ping`. Use `ping` to find out whether the resource or server you're trying to connect to on your network or the Internet is active, and to see whether there are any problems with the hops along the way to that resource or server. The `ping` command sends Internet Control Message Protocol (ICMP) Echo Request messages to the destination you're checking on, receives responses in return, and reports to you information about the connection path between you and the destination and how quickly the packets made their trip. For example, if you're having trouble getting email from a server, your first step in troubleshooting should be to ping the server to see whether the server is live, and to see how responsive it is. To use `ping`, open the command prompt and type **ping target**, where `target` is either a hostname or an IP address—for example, *pop3.catalog.com*, *computerworld.com*, or *65.221.110.98*. In response, you'll get information in this format:

```
Pinging computerworld.com [65.221.110.98] with 32 bytes of data:

Reply from 65.221.110.98: bytes=32 time=83ms TTL=242
Reply from 65.221.110.98: bytes=32 time=73ms TTL=242
Reply from 65.221.110.98: bytes=32 time=91ms TTL=242
Reply from 65.221.110.98: bytes=32 time=91ms TTL=242
```

```
Ping statistics for 206.16.6.208:
    Packets: Sent = 3, Received = 3, Lost = 0 (0% loss),
Approximate round trip times in milli-seconds:
    Minimum = 73ms, Maximum = 91ms, Average = 82ms
```

If the host isn't active, instead of getting this report, you'll get the message "Request timed out."

If you enter a hostname, `ping` reports back with its IP address and then gives details about its four attempts to contact the host, a measurement of how long (in milliseconds) the packet took to make the round trip between your PC and the host, the TTL information about each packet, and a summary of its findings.

The TTL field can tell you how many hops the packets took to get from your PC to their destination. TTL initially specified the amount of time a packet could live, in seconds, before it expired, as a way to make sure packets didn't simply bounce around the Internet forever and create traffic jams. However, it can be reinterpreted to mean the maximum number of hops a packet will be allowed to take before it reaches its destination. The default number is 255. Each time a packet takes another hop, its TTL is reduced by one. The TTL number that `ping` reports is the packet's final TTL when it reaches its destination. To find out the number of hops a packet takes, subtract its initial TTL (by default, 255) from the TTL reported by `ping`. In our example, the packets took 13 hops to get to their destination.

You can use `ping` with switches, like so:

```
ping -a -l 45 208.201.239.237
```

This command changes the packet size sent from its default size of 32 bytes to 45 bytes, and resolves the IP address to a hostname; it lists the IP address's hostname in the output.

The `ping` command has a wide variety of useful switches that you can use for all kinds of troubleshooting. You use the basic `ping` command to check whether an Internet or network resource is live and to see if there are any delays in reaching it. But, as Table 7-1 shows, you can use `ping` and its switches for many other purposes as well—for example, to find out the IP address of a hostname, and vice versa.

Table 7-1. Useful ping switches

SWITCH	WHAT IT DOES
-a	Resolves an IP address to a hostname.
-f	Turns on the Don't Fragment flag for a packet. This lets you send packets that don't get broken up, and it can be useful when you want to test whether packets of a certain size are getting through.

SWITCH	WHAT IT DOES
-i value	Sets the value of the TTL field, using a number from 0 to 255. When you use this option, note that the ping report will report back as if it were set to 255. For example, if you set a TTL of 20, and the packet takes 15 hops, the TTL value ping reports will be 240.
-l value	Specifies the size of the ping message in bytes.
-n count	Specifies the number of ICMP Echo Request messages sent, instead of the default number of 4.
-r count	Displays the IP addresses of the hops taken along the route to the destination. Specify a number between 1 and 9. If the number of actual hops exceeds the number you specify, you will get a "Request timed out" message.
-s count	Displays a timestamp for the Echo Request and the Echo Reply Request for hops along the route. Specify a number between 1 and 4. If the number of actual hops exceeds the number you specify, you will get a "Request timed out" message.
-t	Keeps sending the Echo Request message continually until stopped by pressing Ctrl-Break, Pause, or Ctrl-C.
-w value	The maximum amount of time (in milliseconds) to wait for an Echo Reply message for each Echo Request message before issuing a timeout message. The default is 4000 (4 seconds).
-4	Forces ping to use IPv4.
-6	Forces ping to use IPv6.

Trace Your Network and Internet Data Path with tracert

Frequently, you encounter a connection problem over your network or the Internet not because your final destination is down, but because there's a problem with a router somewhere between you and your final destination. For troubleshooting those kinds of problems, use tracert. It displays the path that data takes en route to the server or service you're trying to reach, either on your network or across the Internet. As with ping, it does this by sending ICMP Echo Request messages to the destination you're checking on. To use it, type **tracert destination** at a command prompt, where desti nation can be either an IP address or a hostname. Following is a typical response from a tracert command:

```
Tracing route to redir-zdnet.zdnet.com [206.16.6.208]
over a maximum of 30 hops:


  1    9 ms  11 ms  10 ms  10.208.128.1
  2    8 ms  8   ms   7 ms  bar02-p0-1.cmbrhe1.ma.attbb.net [24.128.8.53]
  3    9 ms  *      32 ms  bar03-p7-0.wobnhe1.ma.attbb.net [24.147.0.193]
  4    8 ms  14 ms   9 ms  12.125.39.213
  5   12 ms  10 ms   9 ms  gbr2-p70.cb1ma.ip.att.net [12.123.40.102]
  6   25 ms  26 ms  24 ms  gbr4-p80.cb1ma.ip.att.net [12.122.5.65]
  7   36 ms  39 ms  64 ms  gbr4-p40.cgcil.ip.att.net [12.122.2.49]
```

```
 8  33 ms  33 ms  48 ms  gbr3-p60.cgcil.ip.att.net [12.122.1.125]
 9  72 ms  80 ms  78 ms  gbr3-p30.sffca.ip.att.net [12.122.2.150]
10  72 ms  77 ms  73 ms  idf26-gsr12-1-pos-6-0.rwc1.attens.net [12.122.255.222]
11  76 ms  78 ms  79 ms  mdf3-bi4k-2-eth-1-1.rwc1.attens.net [216.148.209.66]
12  73 ms  72 ms  74 ms  63.241.72.150
13  72 ms  74 ms  71 ms  redir-zdnet.zdnet.com [206.16.6.208]
```

If the destination can't be reached, you will get the message "Destination unreachable."

As you can see, `tracert` shows the IP address and hostname address of each hop, along with timing data for each hop. If you're having problems on your network, this information can help you locate the source of the problem; if a hop has a particularly long delay, you know that's the cause.

You can use several switches with `tracert`, like this:

```
tracert -d -h 45 zdnet.com
```

This command traces to zdnet.com, displaying only the IP addresses of each router and specifying a maximum number of 45 hops en route to the destination. Table 7-2 shows the most useful `tracert switches`.

Table 7-2. Useful tracert switches

SWITCH	WHAT IT DOES
-d	Does not display the hostname of each router
-h value	Sets a maximum number of hops for the trace to the destination
-w value	Sets the maximum amount of time in milliseconds to wait for a reply

Troubleshoot Network Problems with pathping

The `pathping` command works like a combination of `ping` and `tracert`. Type `pathping` from the command line, like this: `pathping target`, where `target` is either a hostname or an IP address—*pop3.catalog.com* or *209.217.46.121*, for example. You then get a two-part report: first a list of every hop along the route to the destination, and then statistics about each hop, including the number of packets lost at each hop. It uses switches—for example:

```
pathping -n -w 1000 oreilly.com
```

This command tells `pathping` to not resolve the IP addresses of routers, and to wait one second (1,000 milliseconds) for an Echo Reply message. Table 7-3 lists the most important `pathping` switches.

Table 7-3. Useful pathping switches

SWITCH	WHAT IT DOES
-n	Does not display the hostname of each router.
-h value	Sets a maximum number of hops for the trace to the destination. The default is 30 hops.
-w value	Sets the maximum amount of time (in milliseconds) to wait for a reply.
-p	Sets the amount of time (in milliseconds) to wait before a new ping is issued. The default is 250.
-q value	Sets the number of ICMP Echo Request messages to transmit. The default is 100.
-q	Sets the number of queries per hop.
-i	Uses the specified source address.
-4	Forces the use of IPv4.
-6	Forces the use of IPv6.

See Also

- Hack #76, "Troubleshoot Network Connections with netstat and ipconfig"

HACK 76 Troubleshoot Network Connections with netstat and ipconfig

Here are a few more command-line tools for tracking down problems with your network connection.

In addition to well-known command-line network utilities such as ping, tracert, and pathping (Hack #75, "Troubleshoot Network Connections with ping, tracert, and pathping"), two additional all-purpose utilities can help you troubleshoot network connections: net stat and ipconfig.

Use netstat to Get Information About Open Network Connections

If you want to get a snapshot of all incoming and outgoing network connections, use the netstat command. At a command prompt, type **netstat**. It lists all connections, including the protocol being used, the local and Internet addresses, and the current state of the connection, like this:

```
Active Connections
  Proto  Local Address       Foreign Address        State
  TCP    PrestonGralla:1031  localhost:2929         ESTABLISHED
  TCP    PrestonGralla:2887  192.168.1.103:netbios-ssn  TIME_WAIT
```

```
TCP    PrestonGralla:2899 www.oreillynet.com:http  ESTABLISHED
TCP    PrestonGralla:2900 www.oreillynet.com:http  ESTABLISHED
TCP    PrestonGralla:2932 mail.attbi.com:pop3      ESTABLISHED
TCP    PrestonGralla:2936 vmms2.verisignmail.com:pop3  ESTABLISHED
```

It will help you know whether connections are live, the network or Internet device to which they're connected, and which local resource is making the connection. It's best suited to when you're troubleshooting network problems and want to find out whether certain ports are open, why certain computers on the network are having connection problems, and similar issues. You can use command-line switches with netstat. For example, you can display open ports and open connections with netstat -a. Table 7-4 lists netstat switches.

Table 7-4. Useful netstat switches

SWITCH	WHAT IT DOES
-a	Displays all open connections and ports.
-b	Displays the application (such as *firefox.exe*) responsible for the connection.
-e	Displays Ethernet statistics about packets transmitted and received. Can be combined with the -s switch.
-n	Displays the addresses and ports in numeric, IP address form.
-o	Displays the process identifier (PID) that owns each connection.
-p proto	Displays the connections used by the protocol, which can be IP, IPv6, ICMP, ICMPv6, TCP, TCPv6, UDP, or UDPv6.
-r	Displays the network's routing table.
-s	Displays statistics for each protocol. It lists all statistics for all protocols, but you can list only those for a specified protocol if you combine it with the -p switch.
interval value	Runs netstat repeatedly, pausing value seconds between each new display. To stop the display, press Ctrl+C.
-x	Displays Network Direct connections, listeners, and shared endpoints.
-y	Displays the TCP connection for all connections. This cannot be combined with other switches.

Use ipconfig to Troubleshoot TCP/IP

One of the most powerful tools for analyzing and troubleshooting TCP/IP problems is the ipconfig command-line utility. It provides information about each of your adapters, including the assigned IP address, subnet mask, default gateway, MAC address, DNS servers, whether DHCP is enabled, and a variety of other data. To see basic information about your adapters, type **ipconfig** at a command prompt, and you'll see output like this:

```
Windows IP Configuration
Ethernet adapter Local Area Connection:
        Connection-specific DNS Suffix  . : ne1.client2.attbi.com
        Link-local IPv6 Address . . . . . : fe80::1569:46d4:f862:4837%8
        IPv4 Address. . . . . . . . . . . : 192.168.1.100
        Subnet Mask . . . . . . . . . . . : 255.255.255.0
        Default Gateway . . . . . . . . . : 192.168.1.1
```

As you can see, ipconfig provides basic information about your IP address, subnet mask, default gateway, and a connection-specific DNS suffix, if any. However, you can get much more detailed information using the /all switch, like this: ipconfig /all. For most troubleshooting purposes, use the /all switch. You get a much more comprehensive listing, as shown here:

```
Windows IP Configuration
        Host Name . . . . . . . . . . . . : PrestonGralla
        Primary Dns Suffix  . . . . . . . :
        Node Type . . . . . . . . . . . . : Mixed
        IP Routing Enabled. . . . . . . . : No
        WINS Proxy Enabled. . . . . . . . : No
Ethernet adapter Local Area Connection:
        Connection-specific DNS Suffix  . : ne1.client2.attbi.com
        Description . . . . . . . . . . . : CNet PRO200WL PCI Fast Ethernet
Adapter
        Physical Address. . . . . . . . . : 00-08-A1-00-9F-32
        Dhcp Enabled. . . . . . . . . . . : Yes
        Autoconfiguration Enabled . . . . : Yes
        IP Address. . . . . . . . . . . . : 192.168.1.100
        Subnet Mask . . . . . . . . . . . : 255.255.255.0
        Default Gateway . . . . . . . . . : 192.168.1.1
        DHCP Server . . . . . . . . . . . : 192.168.1.1
        DNS Servers . . . . . . . . . . . : 204.127.202.19
                                            216.148.227.79
        Lease Obtained. . . . . . . . . . : Wednesday, June 27, 2007
9:11:29 AM
        Lease Expires . . . . . . . . . . : Wednesday, July 04, 2007
9:11:29 AM
```

You can also use ipconfig to release and renew DHCP addresses, and to perform other troubleshooting functions as well. For example, to renew an adapter's IP address, use this command:

```
ipconfig /renew "adapter name"
```

where `adapter name` is the name of the adapter whose IP address you want to renew. Make sure to put quotes around the adapter name and use spaces if there is more than one word in the adapter name. Table 7-5 lists other switches you can use with `ipconfig`.

Table 7-5. Command-line switches for ipconfig

SWITCH	WHAT IT DOES
/all	Displays complete TCP/IP configuration information!
/displaydns	Displays information from the DNS resolver cache
/flushdns	Clears the DNS resolver cache
/registerdns	Refreshes all DHCP leases and reregisters DNS names
/release "adapter"	Releases the IPv4 address for the specified adapter
/renew "adapter"	Renews the IPv4 address for the specified adapter
/release6 "adapter"	Releases the IPv6 address for the specified adapter
/renew6 "adapter"	Renews the IPv6 address for the specified adapter
/setclassid "adapter" newclassid	Resets the DHCP Class ID for the specified adapter
/showclassid "adapter"	Displays the DHCP Class ID for the specified adapter
/showclassid6	Displays all the IPv6 DHCP IDs allowed for the adapter.
/setclassid6	Modifies the IPv6 DHCP class id.

See Also

Hack #75, "Troubleshoot Network Connections with ping, tracert, and pathping"

HACK 77 Troubleshoot Wireless Interference Woes, and Extend Your Range

> The efficiency and throughput of Wi-Fi networks can vary dramatically. Make sure you get maximum throughput from your wireless network.

Here's the promise of wireless home networking: turn everything on, and you're done. Everyone in your house gets full access to the network and high-speed Internet.

Ah, if life were only that simple.

In the real world, using a wireless network at home can be maddening. Put the router downstairs, and your upstairs PCs may barely make the connection; put the router upstairs, and the downstairs PC goes without.

Worse yet, everything may work according to plan, but every once in a while, your PCs may lose their connection for no apparent reason.

Don't put it all down to cosmic rays, sunspots, or the will of the gods. There are a number of reasons why your home wireless network may have problems. And there are many simple ways you can extend your network's range and make sure that all the PCs in your house can connect. Here's what you should do:

Centrally locate your wireless access point

This way, it's most likely that all your wirelessly equipped PCs will get reasonable throughput. If you put your wireless access point in one corner of the house, nearby PCs might get high throughput, but throughput for others might drop significantly.

Change your Wi-Fi channel

You may have neighbors with Wi-Fi networks, and if so, those networks may interfere with yours. In the United States, Wi-Fi networks should broadcast on any one of three channels (eleven are available, but only three do not overlap: 1, 6, and 11), and if you're using the same channel as a neighbor, your reception can suffer. To find out what channel your neighbor's Wi-Fi network uses, you'll need to use software. A great free one is InSSIDer (*http://www.metageek.net*). Run the software (Figure 7-24), and see if any nearby networks use the same channel as yours. (Your router may also come with a tool that detects nearby Wi-Fi networks and channels in use, and recommends a network channel for you. Check its documentation for details.)

Interference can be caused not only by networks using the same channel, but nearby channels as well. It's best to have a spacing of about five channels. So if you use channel 3, and a nearby network uses channel 2, and you're running into problems, set your network to use channel 7. However, in the United States, you can get the largest number of non-overlapping channels by choosing 1, 6, and 11. If you live in a densely populated area, you'll have to coordinate channel assignments with your neighbors.

Note: Many routers ship with a default channel of 6, so if you're using that channel, you're most likely to run into interference from nearby Wi-Fi networks.

How you change the channel depends on your specific router. For most Linksys routers, though, open a browser to *http://192.168.1.1* and log in. By default, there's no username, and the password is admin. Click the Wireless tab (Figure 7-25), and from the Standard Channel drop-down box, select the channel you want to use. Then click Save Settings.

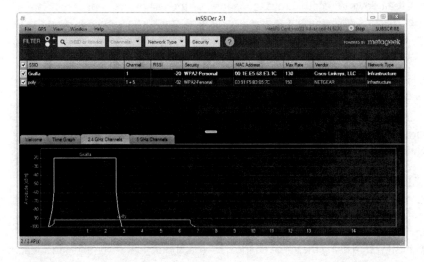

Figure 7-24.
Checking whether any nearby networks use the same Wi-Fi channel as a home network

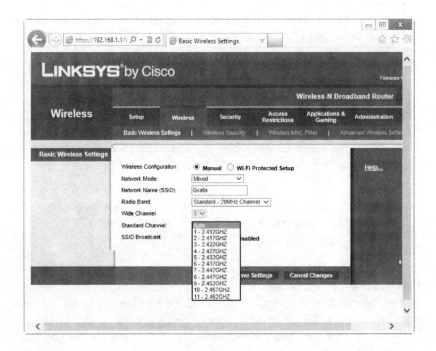

Figure 7-25.
Changing the wireless channel on a Linksys router

Check for interference

Cordless telephones, microwave ovens, and other devices may use the same frequency as your Wi-Fi network. They may be the cause of intermittent connection problems. Move your access point away from any cordless phones or microwave ovens. If you're using a 2.4-GHz phone system, consider switching to a 5-GHz phone, which won't interfere with anything but the less common 802.11a (so if you are using 802.11a, you should avoid 5-GHz devices).

Change the orientation of your access point's antennas

Moving them from vertical to horizontal, or vice versa, or anywhere in between may have a surprising effect on signal strength to distant PCs. So experiment with antenna orientation until you find one that's best.

Point the antennas of your wireless PCs toward the access point

Although 802.11 technology does not require a direct line of sight, pointing antennas in this way tends to increase signal strength. USB wireless cards generally have small antennas that can be positioned, but frequently wireless PC cards don't, so you might have trouble figuring out the antenna orientation in a wireless PC card. If you have a wireless PC card that doesn't have what appears to be an antenna, the antenna is generally located at the periphery of the card itself, so point that at the access point. If Wi-Fi is built into your notebook, the antenna may be built into the frame of your display.

A newer standard, 802.11g, operates in the same part of the spectrum and has a maximum throughput of 54 Mbps, significantly faster than 802.11b. Much of what you'll buy these days is 802.11g.

The equipment for the 802.11b and 802.11g standards work with each other, although with one "gotcha" you need to watch out for. If you mix and match 802.11g and 802.11b equipment, your entire network may operate at the lower 802.11b speed, depending on your manufacturer. If you have an 802.11g router and 802.11b adapters, the network will run at the slower speed, of course. But in some instances, if you have an 802.11g router, three 802.11g adapters, and one 802.11b adapter, the entire network may *still* run at the lower speed, even between the 802.11g adapters and the 802.11g router. The upshot: to be safe, make sure every piece of your equipment is at least 802.11g, not 802.11b.

You'll also find 802.11g routers and adapters that promise speeds far greater than 802.11g, commonly at 108 Mbps. This technology goes by different names from different vendors, such as Linksys's SpeedBooster. It works only when you buy all the hardware from the same manufacturer because they use proprietary protocols to reach those speeds. If you mix and match components from different manufacturers, you'll get normal 802.11g speeds, not the faster ones.

There's a newer, higher-speed standard as well, 802.11n. This promises exceedingly high speeds over greater coverage areas. It uses the 2.4-GHz spectrum, like 802.11b and 802.11g, and has a maximum data rate of a whopping 540 Mbps. It promises an indoor range of 50 meters, compared to 25 meters for 802.11g.

Don't place your access point next to an outside wall

If you do that, you'll be broadcasting signals to the outside, not the inside, of the house. That's nice if you want to give your neighbors access to your network, but not great if you want to reach all the PCs in your house.

Avoid placing the antennas of access points or PCs near filing cabinets and other large metal objects

They can cause significant interference and dramatically reduce throughput.

Consider using external and booster antennas

Some wireless routers accept booster antennas. Check the router manufacturer's website to see if yours does.

> Note: Other manufacturers sell similar products, so check your router manufacturer's website for details.

Update your firmware

Manufacturers regularly update the firmware of their routers to squash bugs and improve performance. So update your router's firmware. How you update firmware varies from router to router, so check for instructions.

Try and try again

The ultimate way to find the best placement for your access point and wireless PCs is to continuously experiment and see what kind of throughput you get. Each house and office is so different that no single configuration can suit them all.

8

Security

Windows 8 is the most secure version of Windows yet released, but that doesn't make you free of dangers. Even when you use Windows 8, your PC is frequently at risk—just connect to the Internet and there are malware peddlers and other evil-doers out to do you harm, steal your private information, or even turn your PC into a spam-spewing zombie.

In this chapter, you'll learn how to dig deep into Windows to make sure that you're well protected, and then customize it so that you're protected in exactly the way you want. So this chapter includes hacks to do things such as hack the Windows firewall, use BitLocker encryption to protect USB flash drives as well as your hard disk, create a safe Windows 8 "picture password," create restore disks if your system ever crashes, better protect yourself on your home network, and much more.

HACK 78 Keep Portable Storage Secure with BitLocker to Go

> If you've got Windows 8 Pro or Enterprise, you've got an excellent built-in security tool for protecting your portable storage: BitLocker to Go. Here's how to use it.

USB flash drives (often called *thumb drives*) are ubiquitous. You've likely used them many times because they carry tremendous amounts of storage in a small package. But they're also easy to misplace or even lose to theft. And that means whatever files you've stored on the drive can be viewed by anyone who finds it.

Not if you use BitLocker to Go, though. BitLocker to Go is a security feature built into Windows 8 Pro or Enterprise that lets you encrypt portable storage devices like USB flash drives so that no one can read them except someone who has a key to unlock it.

To use it, insert a USB flash drive into your Windows 8 device. Then, launch the Control Panel by typing *Control Panel* at the Start screen, highlighting the Control Panel applet, and pressing Enter. In the Control Panel search box, search for BitLocker. You'll come to a screen like that shown in Figure 8-1.

BitLocker Drive Encryption

Help protect your files and folders from unauthorized access by protecting your drives with BitLocker.

Operating system drive

OSDisk (C:) BitLocker off

Turn on BitLocker

Fixed data drives

Removable data drives - BitLocker To Go

USB DISK (D:) BitLocker off

Turn on BitLocker

Figure 8-1.
Set up BitLocker and BitLocker to Go from here

Click the "Turn on BitLocker" link near the removable drive you want to protect. After a few moments, a screen appears asking how you would like to unlock the drive when you plug it in. If you use smart card-based security, turn on the option at the bottom, which is specifically for smart cards. Like most people, though, you likely don't have a smart card, so turn on the checkbox for the top option: "Use a password to unlock the drive." Type a password, type it again to confirm, and then click Next. (See Figure 8-2.)

Tip: If you don't see a "Turn on BitLocker" link, click the down arrow to the right of the name of your removable drive.

Next, you're asked how you want to back up your recovery key (your password). This is an extremely important step, because if you lose it, you won't be able to read the data on the drive you're protecting. You can print it out and put it somewhere for safekeeping, save it to a file, or save it to your Microsoft account. Make your choice then click Next. (See Figure 8-3.)

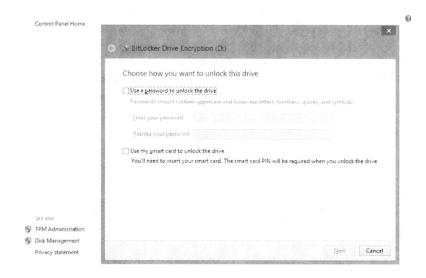

Figure 8-2.
Creating a password to unlock your removable storage

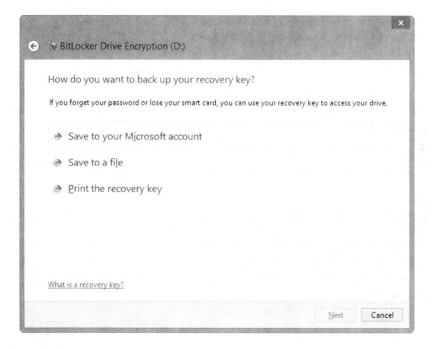

Figure 8-3.
Choosing where to back up your recovery key

After a short while, you're told that your recovery key has been backed up. Click Next. Now you choose whether to encrypt the entire drive, or only the space that's already being used. There's a good chance that you'll be confused by this option. But it's actually a simple decision. If the flash drive is new and hasn't been used before, choose "Encrypt used disk space only" (Figure 8-4). This is the fastest choice. It will encrypt any new data you add, so you know for sure it will protect all your data. If you already have data on the drive, or once had data on it, choose "Encrypt entire drive." Make this choice even if you've had data and deleted it, because otherwise, someone may be able to recover your deleted data. Click Next, and then from the screen that appears, click "Start encrypting."

Figure 8-4.
Choosing whether to encrypt the entire drive, or only part of it

After a while, depending on the size of your drive, how much data is on it, and your processor speed, you'll get a message that the encryption is complete (Figure 8-5). You can now take it out of your Windows device and take with you. Only someone with the right password will be able to read it.

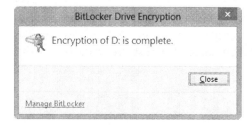

Figure 8-5.
Congratulations—you've encrypted a drive

When you plug it in, you'll get a notice that a BitLocker-protected drive has been inserted into a drive. Tap the notice, type your password on the screen that appears, and you're ready to go.

Tip: If you don't get a notice, you can still unlock the drive. Go to the same screen you used to start the BitLocker encryption, and you'll see an "Unlock drive" next to the drive. Click that and type in your password from the screen that appears (Figure 8-6).

Figure 8-6.
Unlocking a BitLocker-protected drive

Note that if you click the "More options" link, you'll be able to tell BitLocker that from now on, whenever this drive is inserted into the computer you're using, it should be opened automatically, without a password needing to be typed in. However, on other devices, you'll still need to type a password.

When you use File Explorer, a BitLocker-protected removable disk has a different icon than an unprotected one. If you haven't yet unlocked it, you'll see a locked padlock icon, as shown in Figure 8-7. To unlock it, click it and type in the password from the screen that appears. Once it's unlocked, it shows up in File Explorer with an unlocked icon.

Figure 8-7.
Unlocking a BitLocker-protected drive

Hacking the Hack

You can also protect your hard disk with BitLocker. When you get to the initial screen for protecting portable storage, click BitLocker next to the disk you want to protect with it, and follow the instructions.

See Also

• Hack #79, "Hide Folders and Files with the Encrypting File System"

HACK 79 Hide Folders and Files with the Encrypting File System

> Protect all the information on your PC from prying eyes using Windows' built-in encryption scheme.

If you're looking to protect files on a file-by-file basis or a folder-by-folder basis, rather than all at once, you don't need to use BitLocker. Instead, you can use Windows 8's Encrypting File System (EFS), which lets you easily encrypt individual files or groups of files.

EFS lets you encrypt only the files and folders of your choice; you can encrypt a single file or folder or all your files and folders. Encrypted files and folders show up in File Explorer in green, so you can tell at a glance which have been encrypted. You can work with encrypted files and folders transparently; in other words, after you encrypt them, you open and close them as you normally would any other file. They're decrypted on the fly as you open them, and then encrypted as you close them. You're the only person who can read or use the files. Encryption is tied to your account name, so even other accounts on the same computer can't read or use them, unless you specifically grant access to certain accounts.

Note: Each time you encrypt a file, EFS generates a random number for that file called the file encryption key *(FEK). EFS uses that FEK to encrypt the file's contents with a variant of the* Data Encryption Standard *(DES) algorithm, called DESX. (DESX features more powerful encryption than DES.) The FEK itself is encrypted as well using RSA public key-based encryption.*

EFS has a few minor limitations you should be aware of:

- EFS works only on NTFS volumes.

- EFS won't work on compressed files. You'll have to decompress them if you want to encrypt them. Similarly, if you want to compress an encrypted file, you'll have to decrypt it.

- EFS can't encrypt files in the *C:\Windows* folder or any files marked with the System attribute.

When you work with encrypted files and folders, they appear to behave like any other files on your hard disk. In fact, though, their behavior is somewhat different, and you may notice files you thought were encrypted suddenly become decrypted for no apparent reason. So, before you turn on encryption, you should understand the common actions you can take with encrypted files and folders, and what the results will be. Table 8-1 lists what you need to know.

Table 8-1. How encrypted files and folders behave

ACTION	RESULT
Move or copy unencrypted files into an encrypted folder.	The files are automatically encrypted.
Move or copy encrypted files from an encrypted folder to an unencrypted folder.	The files remain encrypted.

ACTION	RESULT
Move or copy encrypted files from an encrypted folder to a non-NTFS volume.	The files are decrypted, though first you are given a warning and a chance to cancel the move or copy operation.
Back up files using Windows' backup utility.	The backed-up files and folders remain encrypted.
Rename an encrypted file.	The file remains encrypted after it is renamed.
Delete an encrypted file.	The restorable file in the Recycle Bin remains encrypted.

Encrypting Files and Folders

To encrypt a file or folder, right-click the file or folder in File Explorer and choose Properties→General→Advanced. The Advanced Attributes dialog box appears, as shown in Figure 8-8.

Figure 8-8.
Encrypting a file

Turn on the "Encrypt contents to secure data" checkbox. Note that you can't turn on both this box and the "Compress contents to save disk space" box. You can either compress the item or encrypt it, but not both.

Click OK, and then OK again. If you're encrypting a folder with subfolders underneath it, the Confirm Attributes Changes dialog box appears (Figure 8-9). You have a choice of encrypting the folder only, or encrypting the folder plus all subfolders and all the files in the folder and subfolders. If you encrypt the folder only, none of the files currently in the folder will be encrypted, but any new files you create, move, or copy into the folder will be encrypted.

If you're encrypting a file in an unencrypted folder, the Encryption Warning box will appear. You have the choice of encrypting the file only, or the file and the parent folder.

Figure 8-9.
Encrypting files or folders using the Advanced Attributes dialog box

As a general rule, you should encrypt the folder as well as the file, because if you encrypt only the file, you might accidentally decrypt it without realizing it. Some applications save copies of your files and delete the originals; in those instances, the files become decrypted simply by editing them.

If you encrypt the folder as well, all files added to the folder are encrypted, so the saved file is automatically encrypted. Click OK after you make your choice.

If this is the first time you're encrypting a file or folder, you'll get a pop-up notice (see Figure 8-10) asking whether you want to back up your file encryption certificate and key, which is a good idea. Click "Back up Now" and follow the wizard's instructions; your best bet is to simply choose the defaults.

Decrypting Files and Folders

You decrypt files and folders in the same way you encrypt them. Right-click the file or folder, choose Properties→General→Advanced, clear the checkmark from the "Encrypt contents to secure data" box. Click OK and then OK again.

Letting Others Use Your Encrypted Files

When you encrypt files, you can still share them with others and let them use them as if they were not encrypted—a process that Windows defines as *transparent*. You'll be able to share them this way only with other users on the same computer or with others on your network. You designate who can use the files and who can't. To allow specified people to use your encrypted files, right-click an encrypted file, and choose Properties→General→Advanced. The Advanced Attributes dialog box appears. Click Details. The Encryption Details dialog box appears, as shown in Figure 8-11. It lists all the users who are allowed to use the file transparently. Click Add.

Figure 8-10.
A pop-up notice asking whether you would like to back up your encryption key

Figure 8-11.
Choosing to share an encrypted file with others

The Select User dialog box appears. Choose the users you want to be able to use your encrypted files, and click OK. Only users whose computers have Encrypting File System certificates will show up on this list. The easiest way for someone to create a certificate is to encrypt any file; that automatically creates their certificate.

Encrypting and Decrypting from the Command Line

If you prefer the command line to a graphical interface, you can encrypt and decrypt using the *cipher.exe* command-line tool. To find the current state of encryption of the directory you're in, type `cipher` without parameters at a command prompt. `cipher` tells you the state of the directory. For individual files, it lists a U next to files that are not encrypted and an E next to those that are encrypted.

When used with parameters, `cipher` can encrypt and decrypt files and folders, show encryption information, create new encryption keys, and generate a recovery agent key and certificate.

To encrypt or decrypt a folder or file, use the complete path, filename (if you're acting on a file), and any appropriate switches, as outlined in Table 8-2. The /E switch encrypts folders or files, and the /D switch decrypts them. To perform the task on multiple folders or files, separate them with single spaces. For example, to encrypt the \Secret and \Topsecret folders, issue this command:

```
cipher /E \Secret \Topsecret
```

Table 8-2 lists the most useful command-line switches for `cipher`. For more help, type `cipher /?` at the command line.

Table 8-2. Command-line switches for cipher

SWITCH	WHAT IT DOES
/D	Decrypts the specified file or folder.
/E	Encrypts the specified file or folder.
/H	Displays all files in a folder, including those that have hidden or system attributes. (These are not displayed by default).
/K	Creates a new file encryption key for the user running `cipher`. If this option is chosen, all the other options will be ignored.
/R	Generates an EFS recovery agent key and certificate, then writes them to a *.pfx* file (containing the certificate and a private key) and a *.cer* file (containing only the certificate).
/S	Performs the operation on the folder and all its subfolders.
/U	Updates the user's file encryption key or recovery agent's key on every encrypted file.
/U /N	Lists every encrypted file and does not update the user's file encryption key or recovery agent's key.

SWITCH	WHAT IT DOES
/W	Wipes data from unused disk space on the drive. (When a file is deleted, its data remains untouched until another file claims the unused space. /W deletes all vestiges of this data. It does not harm existing data.)
/X *filename*	Backs up your certificate and keys to *filename*.
/ADDUSER *user*	Adds the specified user to the file.
/REMOVEUSER *user*	Removes the specified user.
/REKEY	Updates files to use your current EFS key.

See Also

- Hack #78, "Keep Portable Storage Secure with BitLocker to Go"

HACK 80 Tell Windows 8 Apps Not to Snoop on Your Location

Windows 8 was built to use location-based information as a way to deliver more relevant services and information to you. If you're worried about being snooped on, here's how to turn that off.

When you first set up Windows 8, you were asked whether to allow the operating system and its apps to find your location and then use that information to deliver better services and information to you. So if you're using Windows 8 on a portable device like a tablet or notebook, it can know where you are. When you use Maps, for example, Windows 8 can let you know about stores nearby, give you directions, and so on.

But not everybody likes the idea of their operating system and its apps knowing quite so much about them. If you feel that way, it's easy to turn this feature off.

Press the Windows key+I to bring up the Settings screen and select Change PC Settings→Privacy. You'll see the screen pictured in Figure 8-12.

There are only three settings here. Turn the top one off if you want to ban apps from using your location. (If an app requires your location, it will ask if you want to turn location information back on.) The next one doesn't allow apps to use your name and your account picture. And the final one sends the URLs from apps you use to the Windows Store. Microsoft claims that this information will help improve the Windows Store, although they haven't detailed how.

Privacy

Let apps use my location

On

Let apps use my name and account picture

On

Help improve Windows Store by sending URLs for the web content that apps use

On

Privacy statement

Figure 8-12.
Changing your privacy settings

Hacking the Hack

Wondering what information Windows 8 gathers about you and how Microsoft uses it? Head to Microsoft's Windows 8 privacy statement (*http://windows.microsoft.com/ en-us/windows-8/release-preview-privacy-statement*).

HACK 81 Turn off the Windows 8 SmartScreen Filter

> The Windows 8 SmartScreen filter protects you from visiting dangerous websites and downloading dangerous software. Some people worry that the feature sends private information to Microsoft, so here's how to turn it off, or customize how it works, if you want.

The Internet is filled with plenty of sites that could invade your privacy or do you harm, including nasty downloads that could harm to your computer, or invade your privacy. To help combat these demons, Microsoft uses a feature called the SmartScreen filter, which warns you away from dangerous websites, and blocks downloads of dangerous files.

The SmartScreen filter was available in earlier versions of Windows, but in Windows 8, it's been expanded. Earlier versions of the SmartScreen filter didn't block malicious downloads; the one in Windows 8 does.

Some people worry that the new feature itself could invade your privacy, by allowing Microsoft to find out what apps you're running. No need for going into the details here, but Nadim Kobeissi laid out his warnings at *www.tinyurl.com/win8hacks2*. Microsoft discounts his arguments, as do many other people, such as the folks at Ars Technica at *http://ars.to/RaSb2t*.

I'm not here to referee the argument. But I am here to give you the power to turn off the SmartScreen Filter in Windows 8 if you're so inclined. Just keep in mind that if you do turn it off, you'll be removing a level of protection from Windows 8.

That said, here's how to go about turning it off. First, launch the Control Panel by typing *Control Panel* at the Start screen, highlighting the Control Panel applet and pressing Enter. Select System and Security→Action Center and click the down arrow next to Security to display a long list of security-related options.

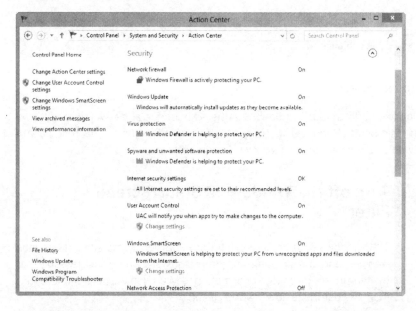

Figure 8-13.
Among the security options for Action Center is one to turn off the SmartScreen Filter

Click Change Settings underneath the Windows SmartScreen option. A screen appears with three options (see Figure 8-14).

Get administrator approval before running an unrecognized app from the Internet

This is the default setting. It means that the SmartScreen filter is in full force. Only an administrator can override SmartScreen after receiving a warning that an app may be dangerous.

WINDOWS 8 HACKS

Warn before running an unrecognized app, but don't require administrator approval

This means that someone will still be warned when an app is unrecognized, but that the person can override the warning and run the app even if he's not an administrator. Keep in mind that with this option, under the theory put forward by Nadim Kobeissi, Microsoft would still get information about your apps.

Don't do anything (turn off Windows SmartScreen)

As the name says, this turns off SmartScreen completely. You're on your own when it comes to Internet dangers.

Figure 8-14.
Among the security options for Action Center is one to turn off the SmartScreen Filter

HACK 82 Protect Yourself with a Windows 8 Picture Password

> The weakest link in the security chain is often your password. Here's how to log in to Windows 8 using a picture instead.

The common image of a dangerous hacker is someone with an almost supernatural ability to crack code. The reality is much more mundane. Many attacks are instead launched by much simpler methods, such as guessing or stealing someone's password. Many people use easy-to-guess passwords. Furthermore, because people need so many passwords, they tend to reuse the same one or a variant of it over and over.

Windows 8 provides a very clever way around the password problem. It lets you use something called a *picture password*, which really isn't a password at all. Instead, it's a drawing that you make based on an existing picture that has to be replicated for someone to log into your Windows 8 system.

To use this feature, press Windows key+I to bring up the Settings screen, and then select Change PC Settings→Users→"Create a Picture Password." You'll first have to confirm your current password. Then you'll be presented with a screen like the one in Figure 8-15.

Figure 8-15.
The first step in creating a picture password

Once you do that, you're sent to a screen that lets you choose a picture to use the basis for your picture password. Choose the picture, and then draw right on the touchscreen (or use your mouse on a non-touchscreen) using a combination of three circles, taps, and straight lines. When you've finished setting it up, the next time you log into Windows, you'll see the picture that was the basis of your picture password. Draw on it in the way you set up and you'll log into Windows. Of course, when you're having trouble entering the picture password, or are located at a place where password shoulder surfing might be an issue, you can switch to using your password at the logon screen.

HACK 83 Create a Windows 8 Recovery Tool

> Plenty of things can go wrong in Windows to make it impossible to boot. Here's how to create a tool that will help you recover from disaster.

It's your worst nightmare: for some reason, Windows 8 won't boot, and not only have you lost access to the operating system, but to your files as well. One solution is to use a recovery tool built right into Windows 8. This feature lets you build a recovery drive with a USB flash drive, or CD-RW, or recordable DVD, and then boot using that drive. Once you do that, you'll be able to recover your data and possibly fix Windows 8 as well.

On the Start screen, type *Recovery*, click Settings, and choose "Create a Recovery Drive." On the first screen that appears, you'll see an option for copying information from your system's recovery partition, if it has one (Figure 8-16). Doing so is a good idea, because it may give you extra features during recovery. Click Next. (If your device doesn't have a recovery partition, unfortunately, this option will be grayed out.)

Figure 8-16.
The first step in creating a recovery drive

Note: In order to use a recovery drive, your Windows 8 device needs to be able to boot from a CD or DVD, or from a USB drive. Check your system's documentation to make sure it can, and if it can, how to enable that feature.

On the next screen, you'll be prompted to insert or use a USB flash drive (Figure 8-17) or use a CD or DVD for recovery. (Previous versions of Windows couldn't use a USB flash drive for recovery.) Choose which you want to use and click Next, and then click Create. (The recovery drive will start building, as shown in Figure 8-18.)

Warning: Everything already on the USB flash drive or disk will be deleted, so if you have data you want to save, copy it off the drive or disk first.

Figure 8-17.
Choosing a USB flash drive for your recovery medium

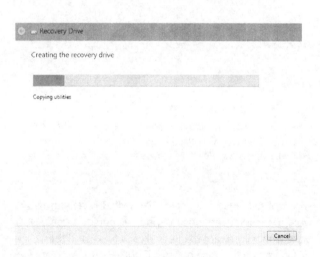

Figure 8-18.
Windows 8 at work, creating a recovery drive

After a few minutes, you'll get a message that the recovery drive is ready. Make sure to keep it in a safe place, and hope that you don't have to resort to using it.

WINDOWS 8 HACKS

If your system won't boot, plug in the drive and restart your device. You'll boot from the USB flash drive or disk instead of your device, where you'll be able to choose from a variety of options, depending on what your problem was, and what you want to do. You can, for example, try using System Restore; try an automated repair; perform a Refresh, which will reinstall Windows but keep your files and settings; or Reset, which wipes your files and reinstalls Windows.

HACK 84   Hack Windows 8's User Account Control

> Windows 8's User Account Control is there to protect you...and sometimes to annoy you. Here's how to bend it to your will.

Windows 8's User Account Control (UAC) is designed to protect you from yourself and against malware. When you try to make any one of a variety of important system changes to Windows 8, a UAC prompt appears, and you have to click the Continue button or enter a password before you proceed.

There's some method to this madness. UAC is designed to stop your system and its files from being tampered with. If malware gets loose on your PC, UAC will help stop it from doing damage because the malware won't be able to click a Continue button or type in a password. You'll get some warning before you try to make a change that will launch a UAC prompt. As you can see in Figure 8-19, a setting protected by UAC has a shield next to it.

Figure 8-19.
Settings protected by UAC have shield icons next to them

Note: The kind of UAC prompt that appears—either one that asks you to continue or one that asks you to type in your password—depends on whether you're logged in as a standard user or an administrator. If you're logged in as an administrator, you'll only have to click Continue. If you're logged in as a standard user, you'll have to type in an administrator's password. If there are multiple administrators set up on the computer, the prompt will include a list of all the administrators. You'll have to type the password underneath the right administrator account.

UAC and Elevating Privileges

Before you hack UAC, you need to understand its guiding principle—that of the *least-privileged user*. Under it, an account is set up that has only the minimum amount of privileges needed in order to run the computer for most tasks. A standard user, in Windows 8, is this least-privileged user.

But when a change needs to be made that can affect the overall operation or security of the operating system, the standard user's privileges aren't enough. Someone with greater privileges—usually called an *administrator* account—must make the change. That's why a standard user needs to type an admin password to make a change, and why an administrator must confirm whenever she wants to make a system-related change.

Hack UAC with the Control Panel

You're not stuck with Windows 8's default behavior when it comes to UAC; you can change how UAC works in any of several ways. If you're looking for the simplest way, although without fine-grained control, your best bet is to do it through the Control Panel. Launch the Control Panel by typing *Control Panel* at the Start screen, highlighting the Control Panel applet and pressing Enter. Then select "System and Security" and click "Change User Account Control Settings" toward the top of the screen. The screen shown in Figure 8-20 appears.

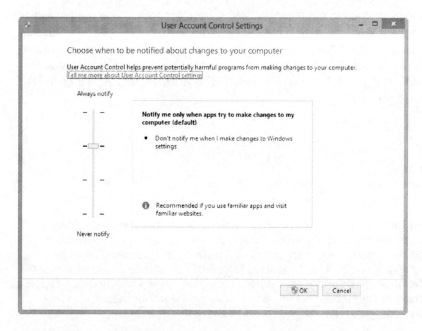

Figure 8-20.
Changing UAC settings through the Control Panel

You've got a choice of four settings here. The default settings vary depending on whether you're logged in as a normal user or an administrator. An administrator has settings that cause the UAC prompt to appear less often. Regular users, by default, have the "Always notify" setting, while administrators have the "Notify me only when apps try to make changes to Windows settings" default. To change your settings, move the slider to the one you want. They range from essentially turning off UAC ("Never notify me"), to the most restrictive ("Always notify me"). Here are more details on each setting, from most restrictive to least:

Always notify me

> With this setting, whenever apps or you try to make changes to your PC or settings that require administrator permissions, you'll be notified. During the notification, the Desktop dims, and you'll have to accept or deny the request before you can use your PC.

Notify me only when apps try to make changes to my computer (default)

> With this less-restrictive setting (the default for administrators), you won't be notified when you try to make changes that require administrator permissions. When apps try to make those changes, you'll be notified.

Notify me only when apps try to make changes to my computer (do not dim my desktop)

> Just like the previous setting, except your Desktop won't go dim.

Never notify me

> Turns off UAC completely. It's the least secure setting, but this way you'll never have to deal with UAC prompts.

After you make your choice, click OK. Naturally, there's a UAC prompt on the OK button. Your settings will go into effect immediately.

Hack UAC with Local Security Policy Editor and the Registry Editor

If you want even more fine-grained control over UAC, you can use the Local Security Policy Editor. But you'll only be able to use Local Security Policy Editor if you've got Windows 8 Pro or Windows 8 Enterprise.

Run Local Security Policy by pressing Windows key+R to launch the Run box, typing `secpol.msc` then pressing Enter. Now go to *Security Settings/Local Policies/Security Options*. This area lets you edit various security policies on your PC, including those related to UAC. To edit a policy, double-click it and fill in a dialog box—for example, choosing Enable or Disable.

You'll need to edit these policies to hack UAC:

User Account Control: Admin Approval Mode for the Built-In Administrator Account

Registry key: `FilterAdministratorToken`. This determines whether the main Administrator account is subject to UAC. Enabling it means that the account will be treated by UAC like any other administrator; the prompt will appear as normal. If it is not enabled, no prompt will appear for the Administrator account but will appear for standard user accounts.

> *Note: There's a great deal of confusion about administrator accounts in Windows 8. There are in fact two different types of administrator accounts—the single, all-powerful, built-in Administrator account, and accounts that are part of the Administrators group. The Administrator account can do anything on the computer, while members of the Administrators group run much as standard users, except they can elevate their privileges by clicking a Continue button in a dialog box when prompted.*

User Account Control: Behavior of the elevation prompt for administrators in Admin Approval Mode

Registry key: `ConsentPromptBehaviorAdmin`. This determines what prompt appears for administrators (members of the Administrators Group, not the built-in Administrator account). The default is Prompt for Consent, which means that a UAC prompt will appear, and the administrator needs to click Continue or Cancel. You can also choose Prompt for Credentials, in which case the administrator password will have to be typed in. If you choose No Prompt, a UAC prompt won't appear, and you can make the change.

User Account Control: Behavior of the elevation prompt for standard users

Registry key: `ConsentPromptBehaviorUser`. This determines what prompt appears for standard users. The choices are Prompt for Consent, Prompt for Credentials, or No Prompt. The default is Prompt for Credentials.

User Account Control: Detect application installations and prompt for elevation

Registry key: `EnableInstallerDetection`. By default, this policy is enabled, and so before software can be installed, UAC will ask for a prompt or a password. Disabling it allows software to be installed without the prompt.

User Account Control: Elevate only executables that are signed and validated

Registry key: `ValidateAdminCodeSignatures`. When enabled, UAC allows programs to be installed without a prompt if those programs have been properly signed and validated by their creators. By default, this policy is disabled, and all programs, whether signed and validated or not, require the prompt.

User Account Control: Run all administrators in Admin Approval Mode

Registry key: `EnableLUA`. This setting requires all administrators (except for the built-in Administrator account) to give consent or supply credentials (depending on the setting of `ConsentPromptBehaviorAdmin`). By default, it is enabled.

User Account Control: Switch to the secure desktop when prompting for elevation

Registry key: `PromptOnSecureDesktop`. This determines whether Windows 8 will switch to the secure desktop when the prompt appears. You'll notice that when the UAC prompt appears, the screen first goes black, and that when the prompt appears, the rest of the screen is dark. That's the secure desktop. By default, the secure desktop is enabled. This setting is particularly useful when you'll be using Remote Desktop to this computer a lot, since the secure desktop by default is inaccessible through Remote Desktop.

User Account Control: Virtualize file and Registry write failures to per-user locations

Registry key: `EnableVirtualization`. This controls whether changes to the Registry made by standard users should be written to a special, virtual area, rather than directly to the Registry. This protects the Registry. By default, it is enabled.

Hacking the Hack

When you try to run certain commands from the command prompt, you're told that you don't have administrative rights to run them, even if you're currently logged in as an administrator.

What gives?

The problem is that these commands are protected by UAC. So if you want to run them, you'll have to run the command prompt itself as an administrator—what's called running an *elevated command prompt*.

Note: You'll need to run gpupdate.exe to make the settings from secpol.msc apply, or perform a reboot when editing the Registry directly.

There's a simple way to run it in Windows 8. Press the Windows key+X or right-click in the lower-left portion of the screen. From the menu that pops up, select "Command Prompt (Admin)," as shown in Figure 8-21.

Figure 8-21.
Here's a quick way to run an elevated command prompt

Note: When a user is asked to type in an administrator password, it's called credential prompting; when an administrator is asked to permit an operation, it's called consent prompting.

See Also

- Hack #85, "Unlock Windows 8's Super-Secret Administrator Account"

HACK 85 Unlock Windows 8's Super-Secret Administrator Account

Hidden in the bowels of Windows 8 is a super-secret Administrator account. Here's how to unlock it, in case you ever need to use it.

Deep inside Windows 8, there's a secret Administrator account, and it's different from the normal administrator account you most likely have set up on your PC. (Note the differentiation between the secret Administrator account, and the administrator account you've set up. In this hack, we'll always use the capital "A" for the secret account, and a lowercase "a" for an administrator account you've set up.)

What's the difference between the secret Administrator account and a normal administrator account? The difference is more than the name: the Administrator account is not subject to User Account Control. So the Administrator can make any changes to the system without having to deal with UAC prompts.

Note: The Administrator account will still see the UAC shield on options that normally launch a UAC prompt. But the UAC prompt won't launch when those options are clicked.

For this reason, you may want to unlock the Administrator account, and use it only when you want to make a series of system changes and don't want to be bothered by UAC. True, you could instead simply disable UAC on your system, but that's a pain, and you may forget to turn it back on.

Turning on the Administrator account is straightforward. First, launch an elevated command prompt (a command prompt with administrator access) by pressing Windows key+X and choosing "Command Prompt (Admin)" from the screen that appears. Then enter this command:

```
Net user administrator /active:yes
```

Note: In Active Directory domain environments with the default password policies, you will need to set a password first, before you can enable the built-in administrator account.

From now on, the Administrator account will be one of the accounts you can log into. Use it like any other account. Be aware that it won't have a password, so it's a good idea to set a password for it. When you're logged in on that account, press Windows key+I to get to the Settings panel and select Change PC Settings→Users→Create a password and follow the directions for creating a password for it (Figure 8-22).

If you want to disable the account and hide it, enter this command at an elevated command prompt:

```
Net user administrator /active:no
```

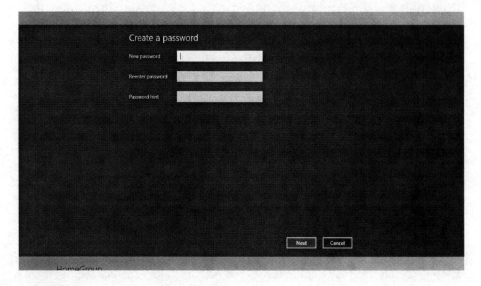

Figure 8-22.
Creating a password for the Administrator account

See Also

- Hack #84. "Hack Windows 8's User Account Control"

HACK 86 Punch an Escape Hole Through the Windows 8 Firewall

> Sometimes, firewalls offer too much protection; they may block unsolicited incoming traffic that you want to receive, for instance, if you're hosting a website. Here's how to open a hole in your firewall to let only specific incoming traffic through.

The Windows 8 firewall blocks unsolicited inbound traffic and connections, which can be a problem if you're running a website, an email or FTP server, or another service that requires you to accept unsolicited inbound packets. But you can punch a hole through it to let only that traffic in, while still keeping potentially dangerous intruders out.

First, decide what kind of unsolicited inbound traffic and connections you want to let through, and then find out which ports they use. For example, if you have a web server, you'll have to allow traffic through that's bound for port 80. Table 8-3 lists port addresses for common Internet services. For a complete list of ports, go to *http://bit.ly/ns3rrs*.

Table 8-3. Common Internet TCP ports

PORT NUMBER	SERVICE
7	Echo
21	FTP
22	SSH
23	Telnet
25	SMTP
42	Nameserv, WINS
43	Whois, nickname
53	DNS
79	Finger
80 or 8080	HTTP
81	Kerberos
101	HOSTNAME
110	POP3
119	NNTP
143	IMAP
161	SNMP
162	SNMP trap
1352	Lotus Notes
2500	Instiki Wiki
3389	Windows Remote Desktop
5631	PCAnywhere data
5632	PCAnywhere
5900 and higher	VNC remote control
6881 to 6990	BitTorrent

Once you know the port number, you're ready to get to work.

Allow a Program Through the Firewall

To allow a program through the firewall, first launch the Control Panel by typing `Control Panel` at the Start screen, highlighting the Control Panel applet, and then pressing Enter. Select System and Security→"Allow an app through Windows Firewall." On the screen that appears, click Change Settings. (See Figure 8-23.)

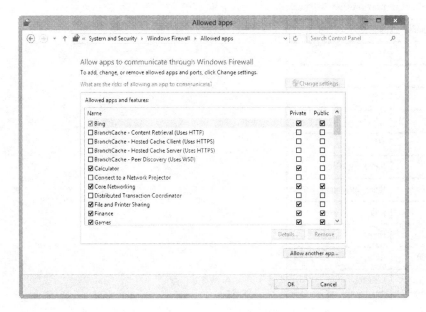

Figure 8-23.
Allowing a new app to get through the Windows 8 firewall

To enable a service and allow its incoming traffic through the firewall, put a checkmark next to the service you want to allow through, and click OK. For this screen, you won't have to know the port numbers for the services whose incoming traffic you want to let through; you just need to know which service you want to allow. Windows will know to block or unblock the proper port.

Note: If the program you want to let through the firewall isn't listed, click "Allow another app," browse to the program you want to let through, and click OK. It will now show up on the list.

Opening Up Ports

Taking the previous steps might not solve your problem, because the app you're interested in letting through may not be listed, and you may not have it on your hard disk. So you'll have to resort to a workaround. Tell the Windows 8 Firewall to open up the port that the service uses; by doing that, you'll allow through the service that uses that port.

First you have to know the port number of the service you want to let through. Table 8-3 lists common ports used by services; for a complete list, go to *www.iana.org/assignments/port-numbers*. Note that some services may use multiple ports, so write down all the ports.

Once you have that information, in Control Panel select System and Security→Windows Firewall→Advanced Settings. The Windows Firewall with Advanced Security app opens, as shown in Figure 8-24.

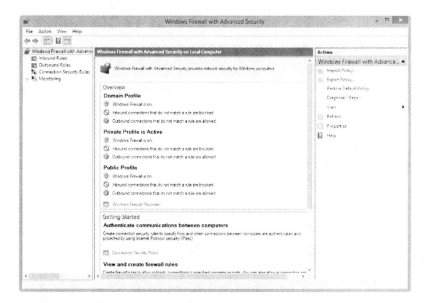

Figure 8-24.
The Windows Firewall with Advanced Security app

Click Inbound Rules and select New Rule from the right side of the screen. On the screen that appears (Figure 8-25), select Port and then click Next. Then type the port number you want to open, and select either TCP or UDP, depending on what the listing (*www.iana.org/assignments/port-numbers*) shows, and click Next. On the screen that appears, select "Allow the connection" and click Next. On the next screen, turn on all the checkboxes and click Next. And in the final screen, name your rule and click Finish, as shown in Figure 8-26. You've just opened up the port to allow the inbound connection.

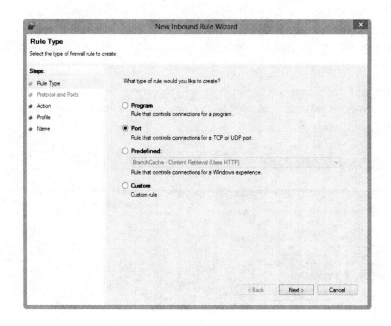

Figure 8-25.
Selecting the type of rule to create

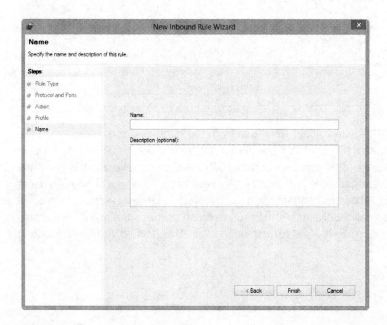

Figure 8-26.
Creating a rule for opening a port

See Also

- Hack #87, "Track Firewall Activity with a Windows 8 Firewall Log"

HACK 87 Track Firewall Activity with a Windows 8 Firewall Log

Get the rundown on would-be intruders who have tried to get onto your PC and then wreak revenge.

The Windows Firewall can do more than just protect you from intruders; it can also keep track of all intrusion attempts, so you can find out whether your PC has been targeted, and what kinds of attacks the Windows Firewall has turned back. Then you can send that information to your ISP so it can track down the intruders.

First, create a Windows Firewall log. To do that, you need to run Windows 8's "Windows Firewall with Advanced Security" feature. Press Windows key+R to open the Run box, type *wf.msc*, and press Enter. The "Windows Firewall with Advanced Security" screen appears.

On the right side of the screen, click Properties, and from the dialog box that appears, click the Private Profile tab. In the Logging section, click Customize. From the screen that appears in Figure 8-27, choose your maximum log size, location, and whether to log only dropped packets, or both logged packets and successful connections.

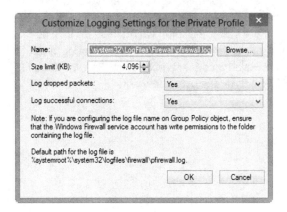

Figure 8-27.
Creating a Windows Firewall log

You'll need some help understanding that screen so you can make the best choices. First, here's what you need to know about dropped packets and successful and unsuccessful connections. A *dropped packet* is a packet that the Windows Firewall has blocked. A successful connection doesn't always mean an intruder has successfully connected to your PC; it refers both to incoming connections as well as any connection you have made over the Internet, such as to websites. If you decide to log successful connections, your log will become large quickly, and you'll need to search through the logs to find just the entries you are looking for. After you've made your choices, choose a location for the log (your best bet is to simply use the default location that's already there), set its maximum size, and click OK.

The log will be created in a W3C Extended Log format (*.log*) that you can examine with Notepad or another text editor or by using a log analysis program such as the free AWStats (*http://awstats.sourceforge.net*).

Next, click the Public Profile tab, and follow the same steps you did for the Private Profile tab. You've now turned on the log.

Now that you have a log, what can you do with it? Read it, of course, and send any information about attackers to your ISP.

> *Note: If, like many people, you use a wireless network or router, then incoming connections may be stopped at your router. Check your router's documentation to see if it keeps its own log (many routers let you get to the log through the router configuration utility or web-based interface).*

On the main "Windows Firewall with Advanced Security" screen, scroll down until you see the Monitoring link. Click it and go to the Logging Settings section (Figure 8-28).

Click the link for your log. The log will open in Notepad, as you can see in Figure 8-29. You can either examine it in Notepad or else in a program such as AWStats. It may look like gibberish, but there's plenty of information there, as long as you know what to look for. For example, if you found the following listing in the log, it would show you that PC (192.168.254.9) received a connection on port 139 (Windows file sharing) from another PC (192.168.254.5) on the same network:

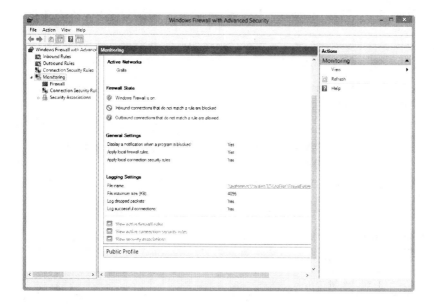

Figure 8-28.
The Monitoring section, showing the logging section

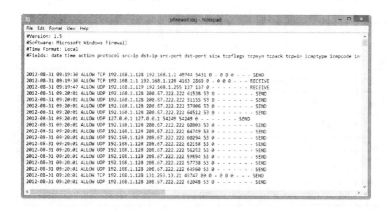

Figure 8-29.
Here's your firewall log

```
2012-07-18 02:22:45 OPEN-INBOUND TCP 192.168.254.5   192.168.254.9 55625 139
- - - - - - - - - -
2012-07-18 02:22:45 OPEN-INBOUND TCP 192.168.254.5  192.168.254.9 55626 139
- - - - - - - - - -
```

```
2012-07-18 02:23:01 OPEN-INBOUND TCP 192.168.254.5  192.168.254.9 55627 139
- - - - - - - - -
2012-07-18 02:23:01 OPEN-INBOUND TCP 192.168.254.5  192.168.254.9 55628 139
- - - - - - - - -
```

Each log entry has a total of up to 16 pieces of information associated with each event, but the most important columns for each entry are the first eight.

Note: In a text editor, the names of the columns may not align over the data, but they will align in a log analyzer.

Table 8-4 describes the most important columns.

Table 8-4. The columns in the Windows Firewall log

NAME	DESCRIPTION
Date	Date of occurrence, in `year-month-date` format
Time	Time of occurrence, in `hour:minute:second` format
Action	The operation that was logged by the firewall, such as DROP for dropping a connection, OPEN for opening a connection, and CLOSE for closing a connection
Protocol	The protocol used, such as TCP, UDP, or ICMP
Source IP (src-ip)	The IP address of the computer that started the connection
Destination IP (dst-ip)	The IP address of the computer to which the connection was attempted
Source Port (src-port)	The port number on the sending computer from which the connection was attempted
Destination Port (dst-port)	The port to which the sending computer was trying to make a connection
size	The packet size
tcpflags	Information about TCP control flags in TCP headers
tcpsyn	The TCP sequence of a packet
tcpack	The TCP acknowledgment number in the packet
tcpwin	The TCP window size of the packet
icmtype	Information about the ICMP messages
icmcode	Information about the ICMP messages
info	Information about an entry in the log

The source IP address is the source of the connection. You may notice the same source IP address continually cropping up; if so, you may have been targeted by an intruder. It's also possible that the intruder is sending out automated probes to thousands of

PCs across the Internet, and your PC is not under direct attack. In either case, you can send the log information to your ISP and ask them to follow up by tracking down the source of the attempts. Either forward the entire log, or cut and paste the relevant sections to a new file.

See Also

- Hack #86, "Punch an Escape Hole Through the Windows 8 Firewall"

HACK 88 Protect Your Privacy by Removing Windows 8 Metadata

> Nearly invisible metadata can reveal plenty of information you may wish remained private. Here's how to zap it.

A file's metadata contains plenty of information that's particularly helpful when you want to find files. For example, music files typically contain the name of the composer, type of music, and so on. A digital photograph contains when a picture was taken, who took it, the camera model, and other information such as ISO speed. Documents and spreadsheets contain a wide variety of information about their creators, including who created the document, how much time was spent editing it, who reviewed the document and so on. In many cases, programs automatically create their own metadata when a file is created. Users can also create metadata as well, as you'll see in this hack.

This metadata can be quite useful because some applications use it to search for information. And you might want to see some of that metadata yourself, such as the date a photograph was taken.

But there are times when you don't want your files' metadata to be viewed by others or by people outside your organization. The analyst firm Gartner points out that businesses might embed metadata into files about a customer—for example "good customer" and "bad customer"—and a company certainly wouldn't want others to see that metadata. It's easy to remove this metadata:

1. Open File Explorer and right-click the file.
2. Choose Properties.
3. Select the Details tab. A screen that displays the document's metadata appears, like the one shown in Figure 8-30.
4. Click "Remove Properties and Personal Information." The Remove Properties dialog box appears (Figure 8-31).

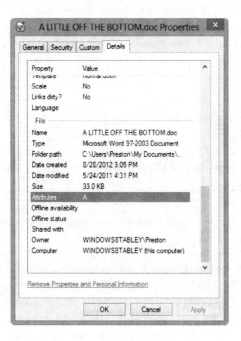

Figure 8-30.
Document metadata

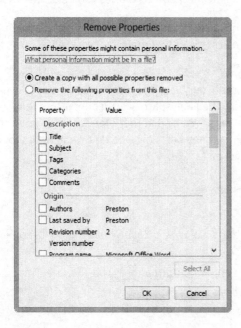

Figure 8-31.
Removing metadata

5. Check the boxes next to all of the metadata you want removed, and click OK. You can create a copy of the document with the metadata removed, and keep the original, or else you can remove the properties from the file.

Hacking the Hack

You can remove metadata from multiple files at once. Select all the files from which you want to remove metadata, then right-click them, and follow the directions in this hack for removing the data. The files, though, will have to have common metadata that can be removed in all of them.

You can also easily create metadata for files or edit existing metadata. Right-click a file, choose Properties, and select the Details tab. Then click any field and type metadata. (Some metadata can't be altered, such as the last time a file was printed.)

HACK 89   Impersonate Another Computer on the Network

> If you're looking to test your wireless security, a good way is to change your adapter's MAC address, which is a kind of serial number. Here's how to do it.

Every piece of networking equipment has a unique identifying number, called a Media Access Control (MAC) address. This MAC address is used for a variety of different purposes, but primarily as a globally unique identifier. For example, DHCP servers use the MAC address as a way of keeping track of devices before they've been assigned an IP address.

You can use MAC address filtering (Hack #90, "Protect Your Home Wi-Fi Network") to help keep malicious users from attaching to your wireless network; draw up a list of MAC addresses of all of the wireless adapters you want to grant access to, and then ban every other MAC address.

Tip: MAC address spoofing is commonly used by malicious hackers for a variety of different purposes. So be aware that any security system built using MAC addresses as its foundation will never be a truly secure one.

But how can you really know that's working? The simple way is to use a computer whose address is not in the list of permitted addresses. Once you've done that, you can change that computer's MAC address to one that is permitted and see if you can join the network. That's what you'll learn how to do in this hack.

Understanding MAC Addresses

Before you spoof a MAC address, it's a good idea to get a basic understanding of the addresses. MAC addresses are made up of six groups of two alphanumeric characters, separated by colons, like this: `00:0F:3D:EE:8E:F7`.

Those numbers and letters may appear to be random, but in fact they're not. There's some method to the madness. Manufacturers are assigned specific blocks of MAC addresses. For example, Netgear equipment typically has this prefix: `00-0F-3D`. Linksys equipment typically uses `00-18-F8`.

If you know a MAC address, it's easy to find out the manufacturer of the equipment because there's a public database you can search. Go to the IEEE Standards Association Organizationally Unique Identifier (OUI) database (*http://standards.ieee.org/regauth/oui*). Then type in the first three sets of numbers and letters, and press Enter. You'll see the name of the equipment manufacturer. Be aware, though, that the manufacturer you see listed may not match your hardware's name. That's because companies often subcontract out hardware or else buy it from other firms. So, for example, the MAC address of the built-in adapter for my Dell laptop is listed as the Taiwan-based Hon Hai Precision Ind. Co., Ltd., even though the adapter is a Broadcom wireless adapter.

Spoofing Your MAC Address

Before spoofing your MAC address, write down your real MAC address, so you can reinstate it. To find out your MAC address, go to a command prompt, and type *ipcon fig /all*. The MAC address will be listed as the Physical Address for the adapter.

Now you're ready to spoof the address. Download the free Technitium MAC Address Changer (*http://www.technitium.com/tmac/*). When you install it, you may receive a warning from the Windows security feature called SmartScreen that it has stopped an unrecognized app from running on your PC. Don't worry; the app is safe. If you get that warning, click "More Info," then click Run Anyway and proceed with the installation.

Make sure to install it on your Desktop, because otherwise Windows 8 might not recognize it on the Start screen.

Run the program, and then choose an adapter from a list of them at the top of the page. You may have an Ethernet adapter as well as a Wi-Fi adapter, and possibly others as well, such as a Bluetooth adapter. So make sure that you choose the correct adapter—it should be labeled Wi-Fi (Figure 8-32).

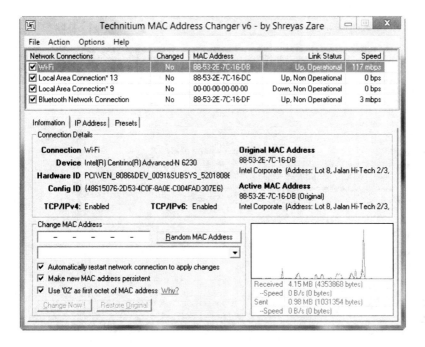

Figure 8-32.
Technitium MAC Address Changer can spoof your MAC address

Click the Random MAC Address button, and a MAC address will be generated and appear in the Change MAC Address field. It won't take effect yet, though. To make it take effect, click "Change Now!" You'll get a message that your MAC address was changed, as shown in Figure 8-33. Look at the Connection Details area, and you'll see a listing of your original MAC address, and the new one. To revert back to your original MAC address, click Restore Original. You'll get another message telling you that the address has been changed back. You'll see in the Connection Details area that it's been changed.

Warning: Don't use the same MAC address on more than one device on your network. If you do, you could cause conflicts, and devices may not work properly.

Now that you have a spoofed MAC address, test your wireless network's security. If you've filtered by MAC address, when you try to connect using a permitted address, you should be able to get in. If you can't get in, double-check to be sure you're using a MAC address from the permitted list. If your router has a log of denied connections, check it out to see if the attempt was listed.

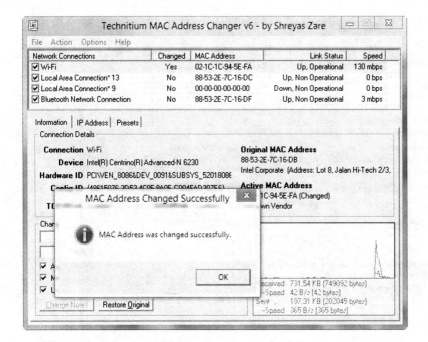

Figure 8-33.
Congratulations—you've just spoofed your MAC address

See Also

- Hack #90, "Protect Your Home Wi-Fi Network"

HACK 90 Protect Your Home Wi-Fi Network

> The bad guys don't just target corporate networks. If you have a Wi-Fi network at home, intruders are after you, as well. Here's how to keep your network and all your PCs safe from malicious intruders as well as prevent novice users from connecting to your network by mistake.

An unprotected home Wi-Fi network is an open invitation to intruders. It's like leaving your front door wide open and putting a sign out front saying, "Come in, and take anything you want."

That's because Wi-Fi broadcasting doesn't stop at your front door, or even the walls of your house or apartment. It leaks out through them. Anyone with a Wi-Fi-connecting device passing by can detect the signal and easily connect to your network. And once they've connected, they can do much more than just steal your bandwidth; if you've enabled folder-sharing on any PCs, they can get at your personal information and files, delete files, and wreak a lot more havoc than that.

And it's not necessarily even those bent on stealing your private information that you need to be concerned about. In recent years, it was revealed that Google, while collecting information for its Street View Google Maps feature, gathered information from people's home Wi-Fi networks, including private emails and more. Google said it never made use of the information, and has since stopped the practice and said it deleted the data. But it should be a warning to you that an unprotected home network is an invitation to abuse, intended or not.

However, there's a lot you can do to keep out intruders and protect your network and PCs. First and foremost, make sure you use encryption on your network. Just follow the instructions on the CD, onscreen, in the manual, or online; it's simple to do.

That's just the beginning, though. There's a lot more you need to do. No single hack will keep your network protected, so you should use all of what follows. (Note: In this hack, I'll show you how to do it using the popular Linksys WRT160N router; so your specific router may have different screens and slightly different steps than you see here, but the same general directions will apply.)

Tip: Even if you're not worried about malicious attackers connecting to your network, consider the damage that a novice user can cause. Suppose you purchase a Linksys router and don't configure anything—just take the plug-and-play route. A month later, your neighbor buys the same model of Linksys router but decides to lock it down with a new admin password, change the SSID from the default, and put a WPA2 password on the router. All of the sudden, you lose a few bars of signal. Can you guess why?

Turns out your neighbor accidentally reconfigured your router instead of his. And from that day on, you were connecting to his router, and he was connecting to yours. Even if you want to run a wide-open network that anyone can connect to, you should take a few steps (changing the SSID and putting a password on the configuration interface) to keep people from confusing your network with theirs.

Change Your Administrator Password

Before you do anything else, do this: change the administrator password on your router. Every model of router comes preconfigured with a standard password, which means that it is exceedingly easy for someone to hop onto your network, gain full control over administrative rights, and wreak havoc.

How you do it varies from router to router. In a Linksys router, you typically log into the setup screen by opening your browser and going to *http://192.168.1.1*. When the login screen appears, leave the username blank. In the password section, type `admin`, and then press Enter. Click the Administration link, then click Management. At the top of the page, you'll see the Router Password area. Type a password into the Router Password box, then retype it in the "Re-enter to confirm" box. From now on, when you log in, use that password instead of `admin` when you log into your router. Make sure to change the password at least once a year. Also, don't use the same password for your admin account and your WPA passkey. If a malicious user cracks the WPA passkey, he will have access to the settings of the network, too.

Stop Broadcasting Your Network's SSID

Your service set identifier (SSID) is your network's name, and if people know what your SSID is, it's easier for them to find your network and connect to it. Your router broadcasts its SSID, and that broadcast tells passersby there's a network there. It also gives out the name, which makes it easier to connect to.

So, if you turn off SSID broadcasting, you'll go a long way toward keeping casual users from seeing your network. But doing that by itself won't necessarily solve the problem. Even if you stop broadcasting your network's name, people might still be able to connect to your network. That's because manufacturers generally ship their wireless routers with the same generic SSID; for example, Linksys routers all have the SSID "Linksys" by default. So, even if you stop broadcasting your SSID, intruders can easily guess your router's name and log on.

The answer? First, change your SSID's name, and then hide it. That way, passersby won't see it, and they won't be able to guess it either. How you do this varies from manufacturer to manufacturer, and even from model to model from the same manufacturer. But for many models of Linksys routers, here's what to do.

To change your SSID name and stop broadcasting it, log into the setup screen by opening your browser and going to *http://192.168.1.1*. When the login screen appears, leave the username blank. In the password section type `admin`, and then press Enter. If you've changed the password, as outlined earlier in this hack, use your new password instead.

Note: Even with SSID broadcast turned off, a determined attacker using widely available tools can determine your SSID. As with all the security tips in this hack, combining layers of security will give you stronger protection.

Click the Wireless tab, as shown in Figure 8-34, and look for the Wireless Network Name (SSID) box. Enter the new name of your network. On the same screen, look for the Wireless SSID Broadcast setting, and choose Disabled. Then, click Save Settings. If you are doing this from a wireless PC, you will immediately lose your connection to the access point and the Internet.

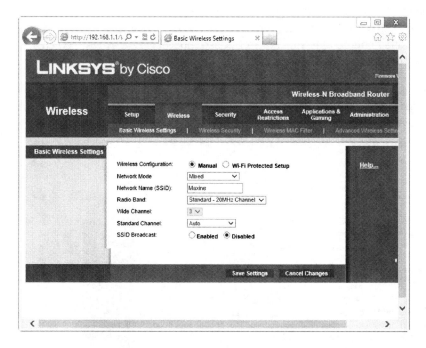

Figure 8-34.
Changing your SSID name from the default

After you change your network name, reconnect each Wi-Fi computer to the network, using the new network name.

Limit the Number of IP Addresses on Your Network

Your wireless router uses DHCP to hand out network addresses to each PC on your network. So another way to stop intruders from hopping onto your network is to limit the number of available IP addresses to the number of computers you actually have. That way, no one else will be able to get an IP address from your network's DHCP server, because your PCs will use up all the available IP addresses.

Warning: This will not deter a determined attacker, because she can simply use a static IP address. However, it will keep casual users from connecting accidentally.

Your router's built-in DHCP server hands out IP addresses whenever a computer needs to use the network, and the router lets you set the maximum number of IP addresses it hands out. To limit the number on a Linksys router, go to the Setup screen and scroll to the bottom. In the "Maximum Number of Users" box, type the number of computers that will use your network, and click Save Settings (see Figure 8-35). If you add another computer to your network, make sure you go back to the screen and increase the number of DHCP users by one.

If you use this technique, you'll also have to change the number of IP addresses your router hands out if you turn off one of your PCs or other devices or take it away from the network. For example, if you take a laptop with you on the road, remember to change the number of IP addresses your router hands out, and decrease the number by one.

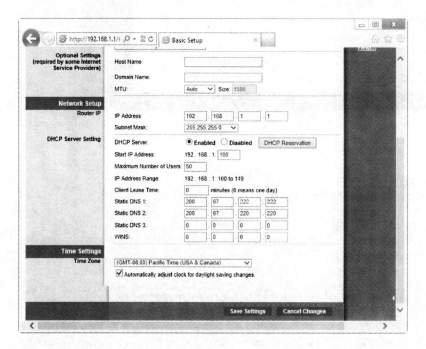

Figure 8-35.
Limiting the number of devices that can access your network

Tip: Keep in mind that you likely have more devices than just PCs on your network. You might also have tablets, smartphones, gaming devices, entertainment devices like the Sonos wireless music system and Roku streaming video players, and more. Limiting the number of devices that access your home network may not be as easy as it sounds.

Check and Filter MAC Addresses

The simplest way to check whether you have an intruder is to see a list of every device on your network. If you see an unfamiliar PC, it means you have an intruder.

To see all the computers currently on your network and their MAC addresses, log into the router's administrative interface. For example, on the Linksys WRT610N router, click Status, and then click Local Network. Click the DHCP Client Table button, and you'll see a list of all the devices on your network, their IP addresses, and their MAC addresses. If you see an unfamiliar computer listed there, you have an intruder. To kick the intruder off the network, turn on the checkbox next to its listing and click Delete.

That solves the problem only temporarily, though. The intruder can simply reconnect to your network and get a new IP address. You can, however, permanently ban all outside devices from ever connecting to your network.

To do so, you'll need to know the MAC address of all the wireless adapters on your PCs. You're going to tell the network to allow only those adapters to connect to the network; you'll ban all other PCs.

To find the MAC address of each adapter, open a command prompt on each computer, type `ipconfig /all`, and press Enter (if you have Mac OS X or Linux systems, use `ifconfig interface`, where `interface` is the name of your Wi-Fi network interface). The screen will display a good deal of information. Look for the numbers next to `Physical Address`, such as `00-08-A1-00-9F-32`. That's the MAC address. Write all those MAC addresses on a piece of paper. You'll also have to find the MAC addresses of all of your tablets, smartphones, and any other devices you connect to your wireless network. Check the manufacturer's website for details if it isn't in the manual or CD. You can also go to the DHCP Client Table as outlined earlier in this hack, and look for the names and MAC addresses of devices you want to let on—frequently the names of the devices will be listed along with their MAC addresses.

Now log back into your router, and configure MAC address filtering. For example, on the Linksys WRT160N, click Access Restrictions to get to the Internet Access Policy screen. Under status, select Enabled. Then click Edit List and type in MAC addresses into the text boxes. Click Save Settings. Now, only computers you specify will be allowed onto your network.

If you want to allow a new computer with a different MAC address onto your network, you need to add that MAC address.

Check Your Router Logs and Traffic

Your router may keep logs that track all the activity on your network. So, if you regularly check those logs, you can find out whether you've been targeted or whether an intruder has made his way onto your network.

How you check the logs varies from router to router. But on many Linksys routers, you can examine both your incoming and outgoing logs. Log into the router, click

Administration, and then click Log. If you see that Disabled is selected, it means you haven't yet enabled logging. So click Enabled. Once you do that, you'll see a screen with a dropdown list and a number of selections, such as Incoming Log, Outgoing Log, Security Log, and DHCP Client log.

Click Incoming Log to display a screen that shows the most recent inbound traffic, including the source IP from which the traffic is coming and the destination port number on a PC on your network. It's tough to decipher this screen, and there's not much immediately useful information here. Much more useful is the Outgoing Log, which shows all outbound traffic. It shows the LAN IP address of each piece of originating traffic, as well as the destination and the port number used. If you see unfamiliar destinations and LAN IP addresses, you have an intruder.

These two screens provide only a current snapshot of your network use, and they don't provide immediately useful information. But there's downloadable software that examines your router logs in much more detail and can give you much useful information, including whether you're under attack, where the attack is coming from, the type of attack you're under, and similar information.

The best of the bunch is shareware, rather than freeware. Link Logger (*http://www.linklogger.com'*) works with routers from Linksys, Netgear, and ZyXEL. When you run it, it automatically gathers information from your router logs, monitors your network, reports on what exploits and weaknesses are being targeted, and provides a wide range of reports and graphs. If you do find you're being attacked, it will list the attacker's IP address and computer name and identify the ports on his PC where the attack is coming from, as well as the IP address, computer names, and ports on your network being attacked

So, for example, you can create a report that lists for you all the attacks and alerts over a given period of time and includes a breakdown of the number of each type of attack. Also, if an attacker clears the logs on the router to cover his tracks, you'll have a record of the attacker clearing the log.

See Also

- Hack #89, "Impersonate Another Computer on the Network"

Email

Email—can't live with it, can't live without it. Can you name another technology that has so dramatically changed the way we communicate? It makes it immeasurably easier to keep in touch with friends and family, and to do business. And it makes life extremely annoying...just think of spam.

Windows 8 comes with a single email app, the Windows 8 native Mail app. It's not a particularly powerful app, and lacks plenty of features that power users crave, such as threaded messaging. So in this chapter, I'll offer hacks not just for the limited Windows 8 Mail app, but for other mail apps and services you'll likely use, such as Outlook, Outlook.com (the Microsoft mail service previously known as Hotmail), and Gmail.

No matter which mail client or service you use, odds are that you're not getting the most out of your email. Spam may bedevil you, Outlook may block you from getting attachments, and if you're a Gmail user, you may spend too much time doing unnecessary tasks.

This chapter shows you how to hack the Windows 8 Mail client, Gmail, Outlook, Outlook.com, and others, and tells you how to fight spam. And there's plenty more as well.

HACK 91 Trick the Windows 8 Mail App into Using POP Mail

Here's how to get around one of the Windows 8 Mail app's major short-comings—its inability to handle POP mail.

Let's face it: Windows 8's built-in Mail app isn't the swiftest kid on the block. There's plenty it doesn't do. And one of the most important things it doesn't do is let you read mail that uses the POP (Post Office Protocol). Many mail providers and Internet Service Providers use the POP protocol, which means that if you want to use the Windows 8 Mail app for reading email, you're out of luck.

Windows Mail instead lets you read mail from web-based mail services such as Gmail or its own Outlook.com mail service (previously called Hotmail). It also lets you read mail from a service that uses Microsoft Exchange. If you use Office 365, it lets you read that mail as well. And if your ISP or mail provider uses IMAP (Internet Message Access Protocol), you can read that too. But POP accounts? No go.

Unless, of course, you use a workaround, as you'll see later in this hack. But first, here's a quick review of the differences between POP accounts and IMAP accounts.

With a **POP account**, the POP server delivers email to your inbox, and the mail then lives on your local computer. Usually, once the mail is delivered, it's deleted from the server. (You can also usually configure POP clients to leave mail on the server after the mail is delivered, but that's not common.) So in typical use, you can't download another copy of that email, because it's been deleted from the server. Despite that, POP accounts remain the most popular type of email accounts.

On an **IMAP account**, on the other hand, the server doesn't send you the mail and force you to store it on your computer. Instead, it keeps all your mail on the server, so you can access the exact same mail from multiple devices—from a PC, a tablet, a smartphone, and so on. The IMAP server always remembers what you've done with your mail—which messages you've read and sent, your folder organization, and so on. So if you read mail, send mail, and reorganize your folders on your computer, when you then check your mail on a tablet or smartphone, or even another computer, you'll see all those changes, and vice versa.

With that as an introduction, let's get hacking.

Essentially, what you're going to do is to tell Microsoft's web-based mail service Outlook.com to get your POP-based mail—and then tell Windows 8 Mail to retrieve your Outlook.com mail. That way, your POP mail gets sent to Outlook.com, Windows Mail gets that mail, and all is right with the world.

Configure Outlook.com to Get your POP3 Mail

Head over to your Outlook.com mail account. If you don't yet have one, go to www.outlook.com and sign up. Note that if you already have a Microsoft web-based mail account, such as Hotmail or Windows Live Mail, you have an Outlook.com account, because Microsoft moved them over.

Once you log into Outlook.com, click the Settings icon in the upper-right of the screen, and select "More mail settings" (Figure 9-1).

Reading pane

  Off

● Right

  Bottom

More mail settings

Help

Feedback

Switch back to Hotmail

Figure 9-1.
To start configuring Outlook.com to grab your POP mail, select "More mail settings"

Under "Managing your account," click "Sending/receiving email from other accounts." From the screen that appears, click "Add an email account." A new page appears asking for your email address and password (Figure 9-2). Don't enter the address and password of the account yet, because you need to do some extra configuration. So click "Advanced options."

Tip: Outlook.com offers a feature that not all web-based mail services have (or, if they have it, offer flaky support)—POP3 over SSL. It's a nice security bonus.

On that screen, enter the information you normally need to access your POP account, including the server address, port number, and so on. If you don't have this info, ask your mail provider. You can also check the settings in whichever mail client you normally use, because it's in there, too. (For example, if you're using Outlook 2010, select File→Info→"Account settings"→"Account setting" and click the E-mail tab. Double-click the account, and you'll find the necessary information.)

O🔲 Outlook

Add an email account Inbox > Options > Sending/receiving

You can use Outlook to send and receive email from other accounts

Account info

Enter an email address below.

Email Address

[   ]

POP3 server information

Enter POP3 server information your email provider has given you.

Server address

[   ]

Port: [995 ▾]   ☑ Use SSL

☑ Leave a copy of my messages on the server

User name

[   ]

Password

[   ]

Privacy

[Next]   [Cancel]

Figure 9-2.
Configuring Outlook.com to retrieve mail from your POP-based email account

---

*Note: There's an important option you shouldn't overlook when configuring Out-
look to read your POP mail—whether to have your mail left on the POP server or
deleted from the server after delivery. If you're planning to use Windows Mail as
your only mail client for accessing your POP-based mail, it's probably a good idea
to turn on the "Leave a copy of my messages on the server" checkbox. However, if
you're going to have multiple devices access the mail, make sure to turn off this
setting so your email won't go away after one device grabs it.*

After you've filled in your account information, click Next. On the next screen, you're asked whether to create a new folder for the mail, or instead keep it in your Outlook.com Inbox; your best bet is to keep it in your Outlook.com Inbox. When you're done, click Save. Next, you'll get a verification email in your POP account. Click the link in that message, and you're sent to a page on Outlook.com telling you that you're set up.

Configure Windows 8 Mail to Get Mail from Outlook.com

Now you're ready for the next step—telling Windows 8 Mail to get mail from Outlook.com.

Note: If you've already configured Windows 8 Mail from Outlook.com you don't need to go through this step—you'll start getting your POP mail immediately.

Run the Windows 8 Mail app, press Windows key+C to display the Charms Bar, and select Settings→Accounts→"Add an account"→Outlook. Enter your Outlook.com email address and password in the form shown in Figure 9-3, click Connect, and you'll start getting the POP mail via Outlook.

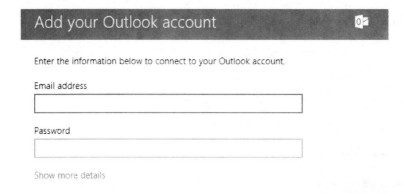

Figure 9-3.
Telling Windows Mail to read Outlook.com mail

See Also

- Hack #99, "Turn Outlook.com Into a Universal Inbox"
- Hack #102, "Use Gmail as a POP3 Server"

Use Different Live Tiles For Different Email Accounts

Get a fast view of your activity on separate email accounts, straight from the Windows 8 Start screen.

The Mail live tile on the Windows 8 Start screen can be frustrating if you've got more than one email account. As installed, the tile displays your latest emails from all your accounts. But what if you want to see mail from each account separately? It's simple to do.

After you've set up multiple email accounts, launch Mail and go to the main screen. Down at the bottom left, you'll see a list of all of your email accounts. Click the name of the email account that you would like to have its own tile. You'll go to that email account's inbox. Now right-click anywhere on the screen and from the menu bar that appears at the bottom of the screen, select "Pin to Start." A pop-up box appears with the name of the email account and the folder name, for example, "Gmail – Inbox" (see Figure 9-4). Rename it if you want, and then click OK.

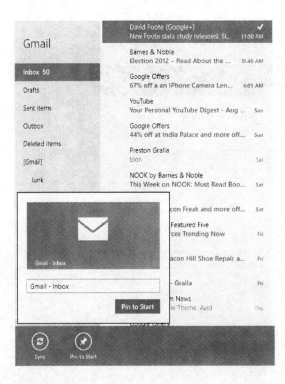

Figure 9-4.
Pinning a single email account's inbox to the Start screen

Now head to the Start screen. Scroll all the way over to the right, and you'll see a live tile for the email account you've added, as shown in Figure 9-5. It works just like the normal Mail tile, alerting you to new emails. Click it to read your mail.

You can move this tile to a new location if you want, in the same way you can move or arrange any of the Start screen tiles.

Figure 9-5.
The new live tile on the Start screen

Hacking the Hack

You're not limited to a single live tile for a single account. You can have multiple tiles for multiple folders on multiple accounts. So, for example, if you want to have one tile for your Gmail Work folder, another tile for your Gmail Home folder, another for Outlook.com's Inbox, another for Outlook.com's Family folder, and so on, you can do that. To do it, go to the folder that you want to have its own live tile, and then follow the directions in this hack for pinning a tile to the Start screen.

Keep in mind, though, that the Windows 8 Mail app doesn't let you create new folders. So if you want to create a new folder for any of your accounts, or delete existing folders, you have to go to the mail service itself.

You can also have information from the tiles show up on your Lock screen. To see how to do it, see the next hack.

See Also

- Hack #14, "Hack Your Way Through the Start Screen"
- Hack #93, "Hack Your Way Through your Windows 8 Mail Accounts"

Hack Your Way Through your Windows 8 Mail Accounts

There's a lot more ways you can control your Windows 8 mail accounts than you think. Here's how to do it.

Windows Mail looks like a simple app with not a whole lot of features or options. To a certain extent, that's true. But there's a lot more to Mail than meets the eye, especially when it comes to customizing features for different email accounts. You'll learn how to do that in this hack.

To start, launch the Windows 8 Mail app, launch the Charms bar by pressing Windows key+C, and then click Accounts. The screen that appears, as shown in Figure 9-6, lists all of your mail accounts and lets you create new ones.

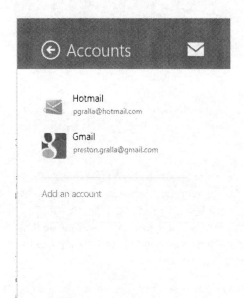

Figure 9-6.
Getting access to the settings for your email accounts

The listing of your mail accounts is more than merely informational, though. Click any account, and you can set plenty of options:

Account name

This one is straightforward; just type the name of the account. By default, the account is named after the service itself—Gmail, for example. But you can name it anything you like. So if you have multiple Gmail or Outlook.com accounts, you can have a different name for each.

Download new email

This drop-down menu lets you choose how often to check your account and download the latest mail. Click the box to choose your options. If you absolutely, positively, must get your mail as soon as it comes into your inbox, select "As items arrive." Otherwise, select every 15 minutes, every 30 minutes, or hourly. If you prefer to only have mail checked when you tell it to, select Manual.

> *Tip: It's easy to tell the Mail app to check your mail if you've chosen the Manual option. When you're in the Mail app, right-click any empty space, and then choose "Sync" from the app bar that appears at the bottom of the screen. In fact, no matter which option you choose, you can tell Mail to check for mail immediately in this way.*

Download email from

This confusingly named option lets you tell the Windows 8 Mail app how many days of mail you would like to see. You can choose from the last three days, seven days, two weeks, last month, and "any time," which really means all the mail you've ever received.

Content to sync

The options you see here change depending on the kind of account you're customizing. With Gmail, for example, you can tell it to sync not just your mail to your Windows 8 device, but also your Gmail contacts and Calendar as well. With some other services, you only have the option of syncing your mail.

Automatically download external images

Do you want to see not just the text in your mail, but images as well? Then turn this option on. There are pros and cons to getting images automatically. Turning this option on means your email will use more bandwidth and take longer to download. But given that email is increasingly graphically oriented, turning it off means that you may miss important content. However, even if you turn it off, there's still a way to see images. When you receive mail with images, but you've chosen not to download them, you'll see placeholder images indicating where the image should appear, as shown in Figure 9-7. To see all the images, click "Download all images in this message," just above the subject line. That will download them all, but just for that mail message (see Figure 9-8). You have to repeat this step in each mail message where you want to see the graphics.

> *Tip: Images in commercial email can be used to track who reads the message and who doesn't. So if you're worried about being tracked, that's another reason you may not want to automatically download external images.*

Figure 9-7.
Email with images turned off

Use an email signature

Do you want text automatically appended to each of your outgoing emails? If so, make sure this option is turned on. In the box underneath it, type in the text that you would like to appear when you send mail from that account. By default, email signature is turned on for all accounts, with the signature "Sent from Windows Mail." You'll likely want to change it.

Email address and password

These options do exactly what they say. If you change your account password, head here to change it.

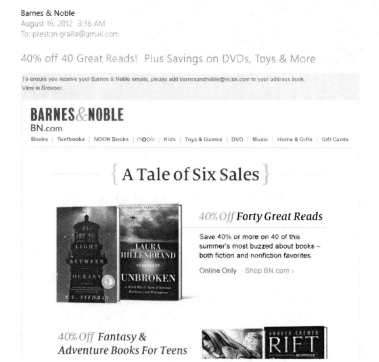

Figure 9-8.
Email with images downloaded

Show email notifications for this account

Email notifications are different from the information displayed on the mail app's live tiles. Notifications are even more in-your-face than the information on tiles. An email notification pops up as a separate window on the Start screen (Figure 9-9). That's in addition to the information shown on its live tile. By default, email notifications are turned off in Windows 8, but you can turn them on here.

Figure 9-9.
An email notification on the Start screen

Remove account

As the option says, click here to remove the account.

HACK 94 Understanding Windows Mail and Metered Networks

> Windows Mail works different on a metered network compared to an unmetered one. Here's what you need to know.

Windows 8 was built for many different kinds of devices, including mobile ones, such as tablets, that use many different ways of accessing the Internet. In an increasing number of cases, that Internet access is *metered:* essentially, you pay for a certain amount of bandwidth per month, and if you exceed it, you pay extra. Even some companies that provide home networks—such as cable providers—are eyeing this kind of pricing model.

As you've seen in Hack #72, "Hack Windows 8 Wi-Fi, Wireless, and Network Settings", you can tell Windows 8 that some networks are metered. When you do that, Windows 8 does its best to minimize the amount of bandwidth you use on those networks. On unmetered networks, by way of contrast, there are no limitations—use bandwidth to your heart's content.

Which brings us to Windows Mail. You many notice some odd behavior in Windows Mail and think there's a problem. But it may be no problem at all—you may simply be on a metered network and have forgotten it.

When you're on a metered network in Windows Mail, you'll only get the first 20KB of your message body, and no attachments. To get the rest of the message, just tap it, and it'll be downloaded, attachments and all. But if this annoys you, there's a simple fix: tell Windows Mail your network isn't a metered one.

To do it, you first need to get to the right settings screen. If you're on the Desktop, click the wireless icon in the Notification Area, and the Networks pane slides into place. If you're on the Start screen or in an app, press Windows key+I to get to the Settings panel, and then click the wireless icon towards the bottom of the screen. (On a touch-only device, slide the Charms Menu onto the screen from the right, touch Settings, then click the wireless icon towards the bottom of the screen.)

Then, right-click the network icon of the network you're currently using. If the network is a metered one, one of the options will be "Set as non-metered connection" (Figure 9-10). Make that choice, and you turn metering off. You can then read all email, no matter what size. To make the network a metered connection again, simply repeat these steps and select "Set as metered connection."

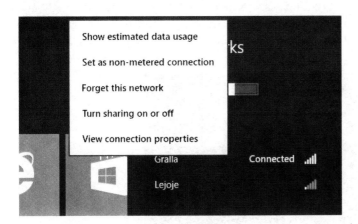

Figure 9-10.
Designating a network as a metered network

See Also

- Hack #72, "Hack Windows 8 Wi-Fi, Wireless, and Network Settings"

HACK 95   # Send Large File Attachments in Windows 8 Mail and Outlook.com Using SkyDrive

> ISPs sometimes block the sending or receiving of large file attachments via email. Here's a simple way to send and receive files of any size using SkyDrive.

ISPs don't like it when you send or receive large attachments via email, because these can quickly use tremendous amounts of bandwidth. Many of them block sending file attachments over a certain size. That's a problem if you need to send or receive large files.

In Windows 8 Mail and Outlook.com, there's a simple way around it—use SkyDrive. You can put the large file you want someone to get on SkyDrive, and then use built-in features of Windows 8 Mail and Outlook.com to send a link to the large file rather than the file itself. When someone receives the email, they click the link and download the file. No muss, no fuss, and no ISP blocking what you can send via email. Here's how to do it.

Sending Large Files via Window 8 Mail

Create your email as you would normally. Then right-click an empty spot on the screen and click the Attachments button. A screen appears letting you browse through your PC for files you want to send. Navigate to the files you want to send, click any you want to attach, and click Attach. You can attach multiple files this way. (See Figure 9-11.)

Figure 9-11.
Browsing files to send via the Mail app

When you're done, you'll see icons and thumbnails of the attachments you want to send. Just beneath the files, you'll see text that reads "Send using SkyDrive instead." Click that link. It doesn't matter whether the files you want to send are already on SkyDrive; Windows 8 automatically puts them into a SkyDrive folder for you. (If you change your mind and want to send the files themselves, click "Send using basic attachments instead.")

Now send your mail. When someone gets the mail, instead of attachments, there will be links in the mail which they can click on to view the file or files on SkyDrive or download them (Figure 9-12).

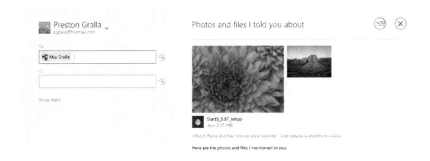

Figure 9-12.
Sending links to files on SkyDrive

Sending Large Files via Outlook.com

You handle attachments differently in Outlook.com than you do in Windows 8 Mail. Before creating your email, click the Settings icon in Outlook.com (it's the icon of a small gear on the upper right of the screen) and select "More mail settings." On the screen that appears, look for the "Writing email" section and click Attachments. The settings are shown in Figure 9-13.

You have the choice of telling Outlook to always send files as attachments, always send them using SkyDrive, or letting Outlook.com make the decision by using SkyDrive for large attachments and for Office documents (documents created in Word, File, Excel, PowerPoint, and so on).

Choose to either always send via SkyDrive, or let Outlook.com decide when to send via SkyDrive. Then go back to Outlook, create your mail and attach files as you usually do, and Outlook.com does the rest.

Hacking the Hack

This hack is also useful if you want to send attachments (like .exe files) that many mail programs, such as Outlook, block because they're potentially dangerous. Because you're sending a link to a file rather than the file itself, the mail gets through Outlook fine. The recipient clicks the link and downloads the file with no problems.

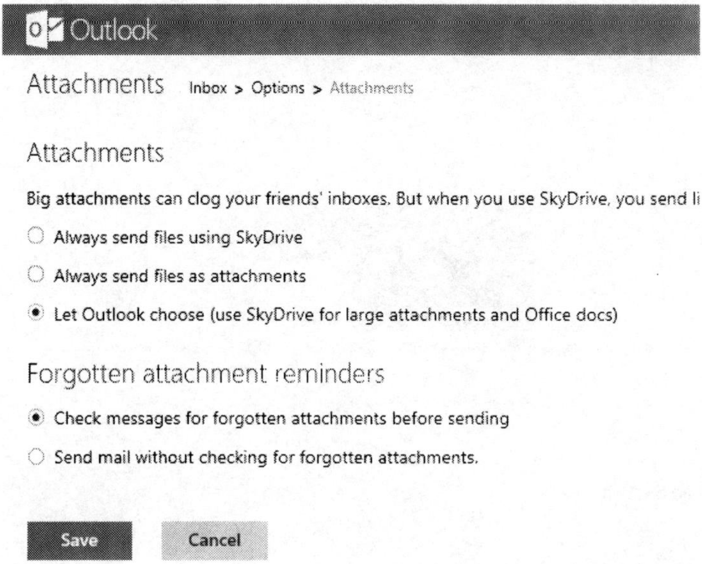

O꿈 Outlook

Attachments   Inbox **>** Options **>** Attachments

Attachments

Big attachments can clog your friends' inboxes. But when you use SkyDrive, you send li

○ Always send files using SkyDrive

○ Always send files as attachments

◉ Let Outlook choose (use SkyDrive for large attachments and Office docs)

Forgotten attachment reminders

◉ Check messages for forgotten attachments before sending

○ Send mail without checking for forgotten attachments.

| Save | Cancel |

Figure 9-13.
In Outlook.com, you send links to files in SkyDrive, rather than sending the attachments

A variety of other services let you "send" large files by sending a link to a file stored on the Web, each of which works a bit differently. Web-based storage and syncing services such as SugarSync (*http://www.sugarsync.com*) have features for doing this, as do standalone services such as SendThisFile (*http://www.sendthisfile.com*) and TransferBigFiles (*http://www.transferbigfiles.com*).

See Also

- Hack #106, "Open Blocked File Attachments in Outlook"

HACK 96 **Import Gmail Mail and Mail from other Web-Based Mail into Outlook.com**

> Making the switch to Outlook.com from Gmail or another service such as Yahoo Mail? Here's how to import your emails and information.

Leaving one Web-based mail service for another can be a distressing experience, notably because you'll generally leave all your information behind, possibly including years of emails as well as many contacts. It's so daunting to consider, you may have even decided not to do it.

But if you're making the move to Outlook.com, the process can be relatively simple, because of a wizard provided by a company called TrueSwitch. Head to *https://secure5.trueswitch.com/hotmail/* to fill out a form to do the import. You can see what you'll need to fill out in Figure 9-14.

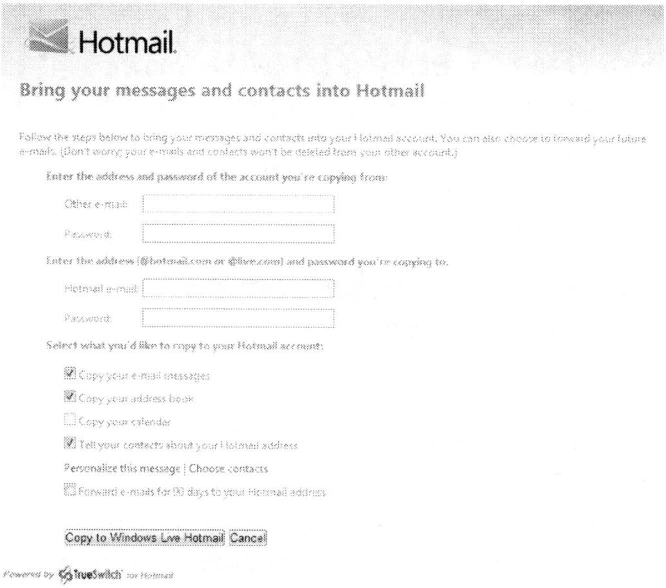

Figure 9-14.
Importing contacts and information into Outlook.com

Note: The import form may say that you'll be importing mail into Hotmail. But don't worry, it'll head into Outlook.com if Microsoft has already converted you. Microsoft has been gradually converting all Hotmail.com users to Outlook.com, so if you're not on Outlook.com yet, you will be soon. And if you're a Hotmail user, when you import your mail, it will all come with you to the new Outlook.com interface when Microsoft converts you to it.

Fill in the address and password of the Web-based mail service whose information you want converted into Outlook.com. Enter your Outlook.com mail address, and the wizard does the rest. However, there are a few things worth paying attention to:

Clean out your web-based mail first

If you don't want to end up with thousands of new imported messages, kill emails you don't need. Spend a little time and you'll find out that not that many email messages are truly vital.

Be careful about choosing "Tell your contacts about your Hotmail address"

Choosing this option will send an email to every person in your contact list with your new email address. You may have many people in your contacts who you don't know that well, so consider instead sending individual emails to those people who really matter, telling them about your new email address. You may also want to clean out your contact list before converting.

It's a good idea to forward new emails from the old webmail service

The option at the bottom of the screen, "Forward emails for 90 days to your Hotmail address" is unchecked by default. But you'll likely want to receive those emails in Outlook.com so you don't need to check two separate email accounts, so turn it on.

HACK 97 Configure Outlook.com for Windows Phone, Android Devices, and iPhones and iPads

Yes, you can access your Outlook.com email on your smartphone and tablet. Here's how to do it.

You need to get at your email not just when you're using your Windows 8 PC or tablet, but when you're using your smartphone or other tablet as well. How you access it varies according to your smartphone or tablet; here's how to do it for Windows Phone, iOS devices, and Android devices.

Windows Phone

As you might guess, it's pretty simple to get at your Outlook.com email on a Windows Phone. If the Microsoft account (formerly called Windows Live ID) you use to sign into your Window Phone is the same as the Microsoft account you use for Outlook.com, you're all set—there's nothing else you need to do. The Mail app, contacts, and so on work directly with Outlook.com. Case closed.

> *Note: In this chapter, I consistently refer to Outlook.com mail accounts. Remember that even if your mail address is a Hotmail.com or Windows Live Mail one, you may already have an Outlook.com mail account. Microsoft is converting all of its previous web-based mail accounts to Outlook.com.*

However, there's a chance that you use a different Microsoft account for your Windows Phone than you do for Outlook.com. If that's the case, you'll have to do a little more work. Go to Settings→Email & Accounts→Outlook. Select Outlook and type in your Outlook email address and password. After Windows Phone creates that account, it send you back to the "Email & Accounts" screen. Tap it. From here, choose what content to sync—choose from your email, contacts, calendar, and tasks. Also choose other settings, such as how often to check for new mail. After you've done that, you'll be set, and you'll be able to use your Outlook.com mailbox on your Windows Phone device.

Android Device

To use Hotmail on an Android device, go to Google Play and download Microsoft's Hotmail app (Figure 9-15). (Make sure it's from Microsoft and not from another company.) Outlook.com and Hotmail are the same service, so the Hotmail app works fine. (There may also be a specific Outlook.com app available by the time you read this; there were none as this book went to press.)

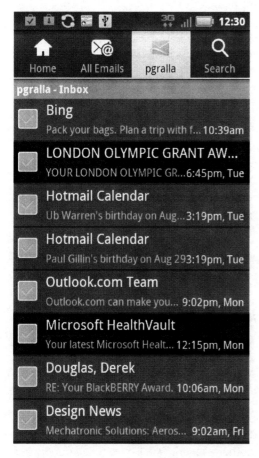

Figure 9-15.
The Android Outlook.com (and Hotmail.com) app

After downloading the app, sign in with your Outlook.com email address and password. When you do that, you'll come to a series of screens asking how you want to configure Outlook.com to work. You'll find the usual questions for how much mail you want to keep on your device, whether to also sync contacts and your calendar, and so on. Make your choices, and you'll be all set.

Note, though, that even if you've configured your Hotmail app to sync your calendar and contacts, there's no calendar or separate contact subapp in it to took at contacts and the calendar. They're easy to find, though. Just head to your Android device's contact app for Outlook.com contacts, and calendar app for Outlook.com calendar.

You can use the app to check multiple Outlook.com accounts. Tap the Home icon, tap "Add Hotmail Account," and then type in the email address and password for any other Outlook.com accounts you have.

Tip: Another way to use Outlook.com on your smartphone or tablet is to launch your browser and head to www.outlook.com, log in, and use it that way. The mobile site doesn't offer as many cool features as the apps outlined here, but it does the trick.

---

iOS Devices

You set up your Outlook.com mail on your iOS device in the same way you would any other Microsoft Exchange account, because it uses Microsoft's Exchange ActiveSync (EAS) service. To do it, go to Settings→Mail, Contacts, Calendars→Add Account→Microsoft Exchange. Enter your email address and password. Leave the Domain field blank. Tap Next, and you'll eventually get to a screen that asks what Outlook.com information you want to sync.

Once you're done, just go to the right individual iOS app—Mail to check your mail, Calendar for your calendar, and Phone and Contacts for your contacts.

HACK 98 Switch Fast Between Outlook.com Accounts

Using more than one Outlook.com mail account is often a kludge. Here's how to make it streamlined and easy.

If you're one of the people who has more than one Outlook.com account, you know how frustrating it can be to check and use your accounts on the Web. Log into an account, then when you want to use another account, you'll have to log out of your account, then log in again using a new account. There must be a better way.

In fact, there is. You can link several Microsoft accounts, and then switch between them on the fly when you're using Outlook.com.

Go to *https://account.live.com* and log in with your Outlook.com mail address. Click Permissions→Manage Linked Accounts→Add linked account. You'll see a screen like that shown in Figure 9-16.

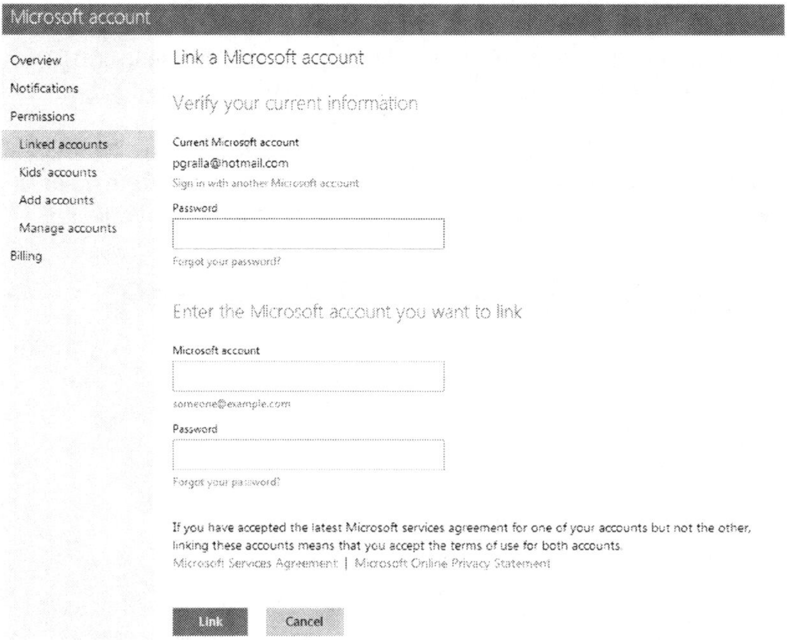

Figure 9-16.
Linking multiple Microsoft accounts

Type the password of your current account, and at the bottom of the screen, the email address and password of the account you want to link. Click the Link button. After a moment or two, your new account will be added to the page you're on, and you'll see both accounts.

Now log in to one of your Outlook.com accounts. When you want to switch to another account, click your user name or picture on the top right of the screen, and you'll see your other Outlook.com accounts. Click the one to which you want to switch.

Turn Outlook.com Into a Universal Inbox

Here's how to consolidate mail from multiple email accounts into Outlook.com.

There's a good chance that you've got more than one email account, and checking them all individually is no picnic. Here's some good news—you can check them all from Outlook.com, as long as they're POP-enabled. And you can also send email from Outlook.com to others, making it look as if it's coming from this account.

Go to www.outlook.com, click the Settings icon (it's a small gear on the upper-right of the screen), and select More mail settings→"Sending/receiving email from other accounts"→"Add an email account." You'll come to a screen like that shown in Figure 9-17.

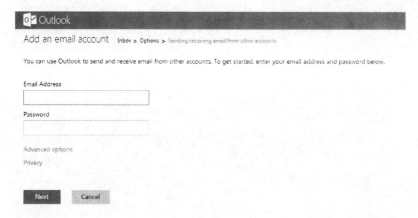

Figure 9-17.
Starting to add a new account for Outlook.com to check

At this point, you have two choices: Simply type your email address and password and hope for the best, or click "Advanced options" and fill in information about your server name and so on. My suggestion is to first type in your email address and password and hope for the best. You have nothing to lose—if Outlook.com can make the connection correctly, you're ready to go.

Because things always don't go according to plan, though, here's how to manually configure Outlook.com to get POP mail:

First, click Advanced Options. From there, you enter information, including the address of your POP server, its port number, and whether to use SSL when retrieving mail. If you don't know that information, check your mail client—its account settings will have that information. If you can't get it there, contact your mail provider or ISP, and be prepared to wait for an hour. However, some providers and ISPs have this information online, so check that first.

Next, enter the information. Pay special attention to the checkbox next to "Leave a copy of my messages on the server." By default, that box is checked, so when Outlook.com grabs your email, it leaves your messages intact on the server, without deleting them. It's a good idea to leave this box turned on, especially if you're going to be also checking the account with your usual mail client. Click Next.

After a moment or two, a new screen appears, asking where you want the email to be kept. You can choose either a new folder (which you can either name yourself or else leave with the default name of your POP mail), or you can have the mail routed to your normal inbox. I prefer to create a new folder, so I can easily distinguish between mail received from different accounts. Make your choice, and then click Save. You're done.

Well, not quite. You're really only half-done. Because now you've got to set up Outlook to let you send mail from the account you've just set up. Go to the Inbox of the POP account you just added to Outlook.com. You'll see an email you've received from Outlook.com with a link verifying that you're setting up the new account. Click that link, and you'll be able to send mail from that account from inside Outlook.com. When you're sending mail, click your name and icon at the upper left of the screen, and choose from which account you want to send it, as shown in Figure 9-18.

Figure 9-18.
Switching between Outlook.com accounts

Getting Mail from Gmail

What if you want to get mail from Gmail? They're both web-based mail, so you might think that you can't have Outlook grab mail from it. But Gmail includes options for POP mail, so you can have this mail be routed to Outlook.com as well.

Log into Gmail, click the Settings icon (it looks like a gear on the upper-right portion of the screen) and select Settings→Forwarding and POP/IMAP. In the POP Download section, select either "Enable POP for all mail (even mail that's already been downloaded)" or "Enable POP for mail that arrives from now on." Click "Save Changes." Now head to www.outlook.com and follow the directions for adding a new account by typing in your Gmail email address and password. You won't need to use the advanced settings.

Note: When you tell Outlook.com to check your Gmail inbox, Gmail may interpret it as a hacker trying to get at your account and block it. If that happens, you'll get a note in your Gmail inbox warning you about it. To tell Gmail to let Outlook grab your mail, click the appropriate link and follow the steps outlined.

Hacking the Hack

If you want, you can set up Outlook.com to send mail from an account, but not to receive any mail. To do this, go to www.outlook.com, click the Settings icon, and select More mail settings→"Sending/receiving email from other accounts"→"Add another account to send mail from." Enter your email address, and in the account where you want to send mail, you'll find an email verifying that you want to be allowed to send mail from the account using Outlook.com. Click the verification link and you'll be set.

See Also

- Hack #91, "Trick the Windows 8 Mail App into Using POP Mail"
- Hack #101, "Turn Gmail into a Universal Inbox"

HACK 100 Great Freebies for Turbocharging Gmail

> Want to make Gmail even more powerful? These free downloads and services will help.

Gmail has plenty of fans who like its simple interface and powerful features. Here's good news: there's plenty of free software and services that make it even more powerful. Here are a few of my favorites.

Smartr Inbox

This free add-on works for Chrome, Firefox, and Safari. Install the add-on, and it adds a sidebar that shows information about the sender or recipient of a given email, including their social media updates, photos, a profile that shows past communications you've had with them, and plenty more. This may be my favorite Gmail add-on of all time. Get it here (*https://www.xobni.com/download/gmail*).

Find Big Mail

Even though Gmail's free 10 GB of space may seem as big as you'll ever need, you may someday run out of room. The problem may be files with big attachments clogging up your inbox. The free service (*http://www.findbigmail.com*) solves the problem for you. Head to the site, type in your Gmail address, and the service goes to work. (You may first receive a pop-up from Gmail asking if you want to allow the site to access your mail.) The service then scans your inbox and shows you a report detailing the 20 largest files.

On the site, you'll see a report detailing its findings (see Figure 9-19), and in Gmail itself you'll get more detailed information, including links to the biggest offenders. Just delete them, and you've regained plenty of space.

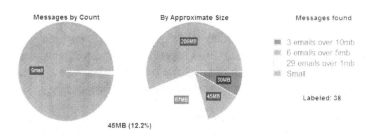

Your scan has finished!

The scan is complete and your mail now has labels identifying the big emails. Below are how many emails were found. A summary email has been sent with more information and charts.

Figure 9-19.
Find Big Mail in action

Cloud Magic

This nifty service and add-on makes it easy to find email, contacts, and documents in the vast ocean that is Gmail. It does a better job of searching and categorizing information than Gmail's own built-in tools. And you can also have the service search through Google Apps and your Twitter account. You can search from the Cloud Magic website (*http://www.cloudmagic.com*), and you can also install an add-on to your browser that lets you search from your browser.

Privicons

This free Chrome extension lets you embed icons and notifications in mail you send to others, alerting them how private you would like your email kept. So you can tell people an email can be shared with the world, kept confidential, deleted after reading, and so on. Download it at *www.privicons.org*.

Minimalist for Everything

Are you a purist who thinks that Gmail is too full of unnecessary frou-frous? Then you'll love this free add-on. Install it and you can strip Gmail of numerous interface features so that it's lean and mean. That means even deleting the annoying sidebar ads that show up in some email. Get it at *http://bit.ly/OKuDY5*.

HACK 101 Turn Gmail into a Universal Inbox

> Have multiple email accounts and are tired of checking them all? Now you can use Gmail as a universal inbox and check all your mail from one interface.

Lots of people have multiple email accounts—one at work, one at home, and perhaps one or more provided by organizations such as an alumni association or civic group. Often, people check these accounts using a mail client. But what if you'd like to be able to see all your mail from all your accounts from a website, in fact from the best web mail program there is—Gmail? It's easy.

Using Gmail as a universal inbox is a good idea for many reasons. Even if you use email software with each account, you can use Gmail to preview mail from all your accounts, without actually downloading the mail into your mail client. So you'll be able to go to Gmail and see all the mail you have from everywhere before downloading.

In addition, you can save copies of all your mail from all your accounts in your Gmail account for easy searching, so you have access to that mail no matter where you are. You can do that even if you use a mail client for your mail. For example, you can have the mail copied into Gmail, and also downloaded into your mail client.

If you like webmail rather than a mail client, you could instead use Gmail to read all your mail. Although it's simple to set up, keep in mind that you can only use Gmail to read mail from other accounts that offer POP3 access. If they don't offer POP3 access, as is the case with many web mail sites, you won't be able to use Gmail as a universal inbox.

To do so, log into Gmail, then click the Settings icon (it's a small gear), then select Settings→"Accounts and Import." In the "Check mail from other accounts (using POP3):" section, click "Add a POP3 mail account you own." Enter the email address of the account you want to add, and click Next Step. A screen like the one in Figure 9-20 will appear.

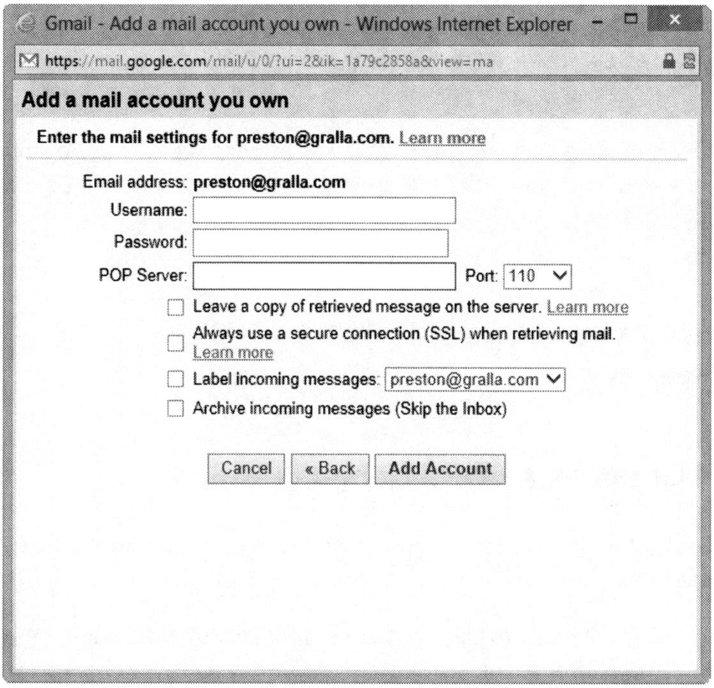

Figure 9-20.
Adding an email account to Gmail

Fill in your username, password, location of the account's POP server and other applicable information. You can get all this info from the account settings in your mail client, or your mail provider or ISP. If you're going to also access the mail from the account you just added through a mail client, or through the account's own web interface account, turn on the "Leave a copy of retrieved message on the server" checkbox. When this setting is turned on, you'll be able to read the email in Gmail, but the email will stay on the server so you can download it with your mail client or read it through the account's web interface. If you're going to access the email for the account only through your Gmail account, leave the box unchecked.

If you want all incoming messages from the account to carry a label—such as the name of the account—turn on the "Label incoming messages" checkbox. In Gmail, a label works much like a folder. When you click a label in Gmail, you can read all email that carries the same label. You'll find there's already a predefined label of the email address of the new account. You can select a different label or create a new one by making a selection from the drop-down list. If you choose, you can have messages bypass your inbox and go straight to your Gmail archive. Use this option if you want to use Gmail primarily for searching through mail. When you've made all your selections, click Add Account.

After your account has been added, you can set it up so that even if you compose mail in Gmail, it'll appear to be from the account you just added. When a message appears asking if you want to create a custom "From address," simply click Yes and follow the instructions.

Gmail will now check your email account and display its messages in Gmail. To stop Gmail from checking that account, click Settings, click Accounts, then click Delete next to the account.

See Also

- Hack #91, "Trick the Windows 8 Mail App into Using POP Mail"
- Hack #99, "Turn Outlook.com Into a Universal Inbox"

HACK 102 Use Gmail as a POP3 Server

> Get the best of both worlds: combine Gmail with your normal email software such as Outlook.

Tempted by Gmail, but aren't ready to give up your email software? No problem. You can use Gmail as a normal POP account, just like the one you have with your workplace or mail service provider.

You'll first have to configure Gmail to let you do it, and then you'll have to tell your email software to retrieve the mail.

In Gmail, click the Settings icon (it's a small gear), then select Settings→"Forwarding and POP/IMAP." The screen shown in Figure 9-21 appears.

If you want your email software to retrieve all the email you've ever received on Gmail, choose "Enable POP for all mail." Be very careful before making this selection. Remember, Gmail gives you over 2 GB of storage, so if you've received a lot of mail, you could end up downloading gigabytes of mail when you make your first connection to Gmail using your email software. Also keep in mind that even if you have only a little mail in your Inbox, that's not all the email you have in your Gmail account. Most of your mail is in the Archive folder, and you might have hundreds or thousands of messages there, even if they're not currently showing in your Inbox.

If you choose "Enable POP only for mail that arrives from now on," only those messages you receive after this point will be downloaded to your email software. It's a much safer choice. If you want some old mail downloaded, you can always go into your Gmail account and forward the mail to yourself. That way, the forwarded mail will be treated as new mail and will be downloaded, while all the rest of your old mail won't.

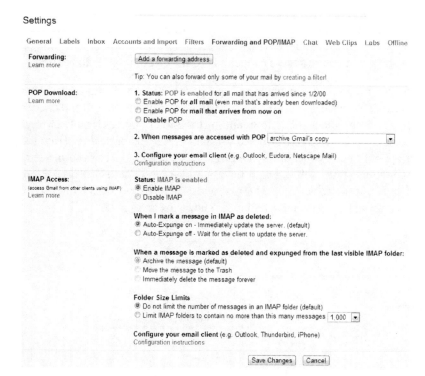

General Labels Inbox Accounts and Import Filters **Forwarding and POP/IMAP** Chat Web Clips Labs Offline

Figure 9-21.
Configuring Gmail for POP3 access

Next, make your choice about what should happen to your Gmail messages: should they be kept on the Gmail server, and if they are, should they be kept in the Inbox or in the Archived mail? Here are your choices:

Keep Gmail's copy in the Inbox

Leaves all new mail on the Gmail server in your Gmail Inbox. That way, even after you download it to your PC, it will stay in the Gmail Inbox on the Web as if you hadn't read it.

Archive Gmail's copy

Leaves all new email on the Gmail server, but instead of putting it into your Inbox, it moves it to your Archived mail. So, whenever you visit Gmail on the Web, if you want to see the mail, go to your Archive.

Delete Gmail's copy

Deletes the mail from Gmail.

Now it's time to configure your email program to get your Gmail email. You set it up as you do any other new mail account. If your email software asks for your POP3 server, use *pop.gmail.com*, and for your SMTP server, use *smtp.gmail.com*. When setting it up, tell your software to use a secure connection (SSL) for both SMTP and POP3.

So, for example, here's how you would set up Outlook 2010 for POP3 Gmail. After you've enabled POP3 access in Gmail, launch Outlook, click the File tab and choose Info→Account Settings→Account Settings and, on the E-mail tab, click New. Click New. On the Add New Account screen, select "E-mail account," and click Next. From the screen that appears, enter your name, your Gmail address, and your password. Select "Manually configure server settings or additional server types," and click Next. From the screen that appears, select Internet E-mail and click Next. You'll come to a screen that asks for a variety of server information, as shown in Figure 9-22.

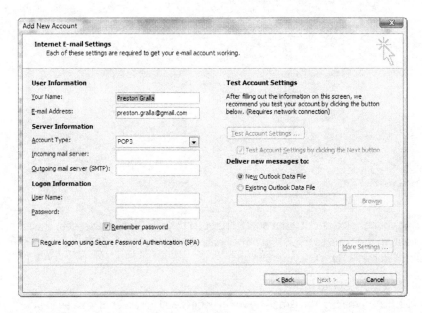

Figure 9-22.
Configuring Outlook for Gmail POP access

In the User Information section, type your name and Gmail address. In the Server information area, choose POP3 for the Account type. In the Incoming mail server box, type *pop.gmail.com* and in the Outgoing mail server box, type *smtp.gmail.com*. In the Logon Information area, enter your Gmail username and password. Turn on the "Remember password" and "Require logon using Secure Password Authentication (SPA)" checkboxes. Click More Settings, choose the Advanced tab, and turn on the "This server requires an encrypted (SSL) connection" checkbox. When you're done, click OK, click Next, and then click Finish.

If you've got Outlook 2007, the instructions are somewhat different. (The instructions provided here are nearly identical for earlier versions of Outlook.) After you've enabled POP3 access in Gmail, launch Outlook and choose Tools→Account Settings. Click New. On the Choose E-Mail Service screen that appears, enter your name, your Gmail address, and your password. Click Next, and you're done.

If that doesn't work, and you can't send and receive email, you'll need to manually enter your server information. Back on the screen where you entered your name, Gmail address, and password, turn on the "Manually configure server settings or additional server types" checkbox. From the screen that appears, select Internet E-mail, and click Next.

In the User Information section, fill in your name and Gmail address. In the Server information area, for the Account type, choose POP3. In the Incoming mail server box, type *pop.gmail.com* and in the Outgoing mail server box, type *smtp.gmail.com*. In the Logon Information area, enter your Gmail username and password. Turn on the "Remember password" and "Require logon using Secure Password Authentication (SPA)" checkboxes. Click More Settings, go to the Advanced tab, and turn on the "This server requires an encrypted (SSL) connection" checkbox. Click OK, click Next, and then Finish.

HACK 103 Stay Off Spam Lists

When it comes to spam, prevention is the best cure. Simple steps can keep you off spam lists.

Unless you enjoy getting lots of mail from friendly Nigerian millionaires willing to share the wealth, or really *do* want to enlarge certain very private body parts, you'd probably prefer to stay away from spam. Sure, built-in spam filters in Outlook and other email software help you avoid it, as do some third-party anti-spam programs. But no matter how good your tools are, spam will always get through.

There's no way to avoid spam completely, but there are ways to cut down on the amount you receive. And one of the best ways to do that is to stay off spam lists in the first place.

First, consider how you end up on spam lists. The most common way, according to a comprehensive study done by the Center for Democracy & Technology, is that your email address is "harvested" by spammers who use programs to automatically scan web pages and gather email addresses from them. Those addresses are then sold to other spammers. The result: you're targeted by dozens of spam lists.

To stay off spam lists, try and keep your email address out of the public eye. If possible, don't put your email address on a public website. If you post to Usenet newsgroups, don't use your real email address. You can instead get a free account at any of the free mail sites, such as Yahoo, Hotmail, or Gmail, and use those to post.

However, if there's a reason you need to have your email address on a public website, you can hide your address from spammers, even when it's in plain view.

At one time, you could get away with spelling out your email address—for example, you could write "preston at gralla dot com" instead of *preston@gralla.com*. Automated harvesting programs weren't smart enough to grab your address when you disguised it that way.

But times have changed, and some spammers have figured out ways to get around that trick. So another solution is to use inline JavaScript to generate your email address when the web page loads. Spam harvester bots see only a `<script>` tag, but people see *bob@bob.com*. Here's an example of the code you can pop in:

```
<script type="text/javascript" language="javascript">
<!--
  {
    document.write(String.fromCharCode(60,97,32,104,114,101,102,61,
    34,109,97,105,108,116,111,58,98,111,98,64,98,111,98,46,99,111,
    109,34,62,98,111,98,64,98,111,98,46,99,111,109,60,47,97,62))
  }
//-->
</script>
<noscript>
<a href = "mailto:%62%6F%62%40%62%6F%62%2E%63%6F%6D">email me</a>
</noscript>
```

To get your own bit of code so that your name is spelled out, go to the JavaScript generator (*http://www.spiderwebmastertools.com/nospamemail.html*). Feed it your email address, and it generates the JavaScript, ready for you to use.

Another solution is to use HTML characters for your address rather than plain-text characters. That way, a person who visits the page can see the email address, because HTML translates the underlying code into a readable address, but an automated harvester won't be able to read it (unless the author of that harvester is reading this book). To use HTML characters, you need to use the ANSI characters and precede each character by &#. Separate each HTML character by a (;) and leave no spaces between characters. So, for example, in HTML, the *preston@gralla.com* address would be:

```
&#112;&#114;&#101;&#115;&#116;&#111;&#110;&#64;&#103;&#114;&#97;&#108;&#108;
&#97;&#46;&#099;&#111;
&#109
```

Keep in mind, though, that if you use HTML characters to spell out your email address, you won't be able to put HTML `mailto:` links; that requires the text to be spelled out the normal way rather than in HTML characters. One solution is to use an email form that doesn't expose your email address, although spambots have found workarounds for this as well. A better solution is to use what is called a CAPTCHA for the form, which requires that someone type in a response to a question in order to complete the task. Whenever you visit a site that asks you type in cryptically displayed text, that's a CAPTCHA. A number of sites offer free CAPTCHA services, including *www.captchas.net* and *www.recaptcha.net* (and by using reCAPTCHA, you're helping to digitize scanned books).

Table 9-1 lists common ANSI codes that you'll need for most email addresses.

Table 9-1. Common ANSI codes

A	65	N	78	a	97	n	110	@	64
B	66	O	79	b	98	o	111	.	46
C	67	P	80	c	99	p	112	0	48
D	68	Q	81	d	100	q	113	1	49
E	69	R	82	e	101	r	114	3	51
F	70	S	83	f	102	s	115	4	52
G	71	T	84	g	103	t	116	5	53
H	72	U	85	h	104	u	117	6	54
I	73	V	86	i	105	v	118	7	55
J	74	W	87	j	106	w	119	8	56
K	75	X	88	k	107	x	120	9	57
L	76	Y	89	l	108	y	121		
M	77	Z	90	m	109	z	122		

For a more comprehensive list of ANSI codes and special HTML characters, go here (*http://www.alanwood.net/demos/ansi.html*).

See Also

- Hack #104, "Prevent Your Newsletter from Being Blocked as Spam"
- Hack #105, "Block International Spam in Outlook"

HACK 104   Prevent Your Newsletter from Being Blocked as Spam

Your newsletter is important, so make sure that it isn't treated like spam.

Spam has become so big a problem that ISPs and mail providers such as Google and Yahoo use spam filters that kill much spam before it ever reaches your inbox. This is a good thing, unless you have a newsletter you send out to customers, friends, or family, and it gets blocked as spam. Making matters even more difficult for newsletter writers is that even if the newsletter makes it through ISP spam filters, spam filters in email programs and security software may filter it out it as well.

There are steps you can take to make it more likely that your newsletter won't get blocked as spam. Spam tends to have certain common characteristics. You can do your best to make sure that your newsletter doesn't have those characteristics and won't be blocked. These tips will help:

Watch your language
Don't use the kind of words that got your mouth washed out with soap as a kid.

Don't overuse capitalization
THIS MIGHT LOOK LIKE SPAM to a spam filter. So use the proper conventions for capitalization.

Don't overuse punctuation marks
Use too many exclamation points and question marks, especially in a row, like this: !!?!, and the newsletter is more likely to be considered spam.

Avoid spam phrases
Some phrases are commonly used by spammers, such as "free investment," "cable converter," or even "stop snoring." Use them, and your newsletter is more likely to be considered spam. For a list of phrases to ignore, head to *http://bit.ly/ yHzbT6*.

Link to domain names instead of IP address
If you have links in your newsletter, always use the domain name, such as *www.oreilly.com*, rather than the IP address, such as 208.201.239.37.

Use simple HTML

A lot of HTML code in a newsletter can set off spam filters, so keep it simple.

Check if you're on blacklists

Many spam filters use blacklists to help determine what's spam. If you end up on a blacklist, your newsletter won't get through to people who use antispam software, and many mail providers and antispam tools use these lists to block spam as well. Here's a list of some of the most common ones: *http://mxtool box.com/blacklists.aspx*, *http://www.spamhaus.org/sbl*, *http://www.abuse.net/ lookup.phtml*, and *http://www.njabl.org/lookup.html*. If you find your IP address or domain on any of the lists, contact the site, and ask how to be taken off the list. Also, if you check the headers of any bounces you receive as a result of blacklist-ing, you may find a URL of the blacklist with a link to instructions for removal.

Encourage your subscribers to whitelist you

Many mail services and applications will let their users add senders to a whitelist; email from anyone on this list will almost always get through. In some cases, putting your email address in their mail program or service's address book is all it takes.

Use their full name

Put the recipient's first and last name at the top of each message ("Dear so-and-so") you send. If there's one thing that most spammers have in common, it's that they only know your email address (unless your email address is an obvious con-catenation of your first and last name). Some spam filters will count on this fact and be more likely to flag as spam messages containing phrases such as "Dear PayPal user" rather than the recipient's full name.

You can also test your newsletter yourself. Subscribe as many email addresses as you have (Gmail, your ISP email address, your school or work address if it won't get you in trouble, etc.). Then, send yourself a copy of the newsletter. When you receive it, look for an option in your email program to view the original message, full headers, raw source, or something along those lines. Some email services will add spam scores/status to the email headers, such as "X-Spam-Status." If your newsletter was cate-gorized as spam, look in the mail headers for cryptic details such as "HOST_MIS-MATCH_COM." Google these terms, and you'll probably find some helpful details that explain what you did to anger the spam filter.

See Also

- Hack #103, "Stay Off Spam Lists"
- Hack #105, "Block International Spam in Outlook"

Annoyed by spam sent to you in foreign languages? No problem—block it forever.

Spam by itself is annoying enough. But getting spam sent to you in a language you can't understand is enough to send you through the roof. And because a good deal of spam comes from overseas, you could be getting a lot of this kind of spam. The Figure 9-23 is an example of increasingly common overseas spam.

Luckily, it's easy to block international spam in Outlook 2010.

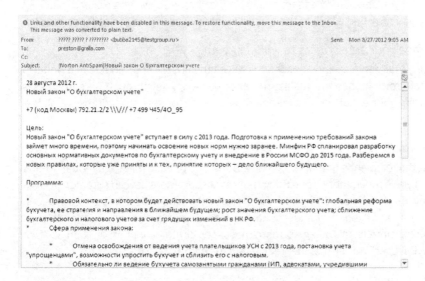

Figure 9-23.
What does this email say? It may well be offering to increase the size of your private body parts.Overseas spam like this is becoming increasingly common.

In Outlook 2010, select Home→Junk→Junk E-mail Options and click the International tab. You'll see a screen like that one in Figure 9-24. (In Outlook 2007, select Actions→Junk E-mail→Junk E-mail Options and click the International tab.)

Click Blocked Encodings List. This panel (Figure 9-25) lets you block mail that is encoded in various language sets. So, for example, if you don't read Japanese, Chinese, Vietnamese, or other languages, there's no point in accepting mail that uses those language sets. Turn on the boxes next to all languages you want to block, and click OK.

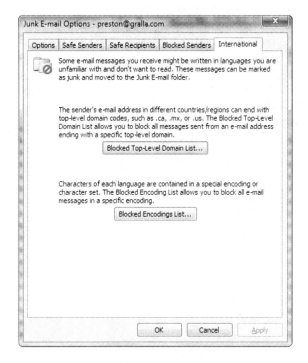

Figure 9-24.
The first step in stopping international spam

Figure 9-25.
This screen lets you block mail that uses a variety of different language sets

Next click Blocked Top-Level Domain List. Here, you can block mail that has email addresses from specific countries (Figure 9-26). Be very careful here: this screen may or may not be of any use to you, and you don't want to block legitimate mail. A lot of spam that appears to originate overseas may not in fact have the domain of the true sender because spammers often use *bots* to send spam—PCs that they've essentially turned into spam-spewing zombies. So using this screen may not offer much help. In addition, it may also block you from getting legitimate email from a foreign country. Still, if you absolutely know you get spam from certain foreign domains and that you'll never receive legitimate mail from there, turn on the checkboxes next to those domains, and then click OK.

You block international spam in Windows Mail and Outlook Express in a similar way. In Windows Mail, choose Tools→Junk Mail. Then choose the International tab, and you'll have options similar to those for Outlook 2007.

Figure 9-26.
This screen lets you block spam that originates from certain countries

See Also

- Hack #103, "Stay Off Spam Lists"
- Hack #104, "Prevent Your Newsletter from Being Blocked as Spam"

HACK 106 Open Blocked File Attachments in Outlook

> Force Outlook to let you open a wide variety of file attachments that it normally blocks.

The world is full of nasty email-borne worms and viruses, and everyone certainly needs to be protected from them. Microsoft, in the latest versions of Outlook, takes a Big Nurse, draconian approach to the problem; it refuses to let you open a large number of file attachments sent to you via email, including those ending in *.exe*, *.bat*, and many other common file extensions. The theory is that it's possible a file with one of those extensions might be dangerous, so you shouldn't be allowed to open *any* file with that extension. That's like banning all cars because some people sometimes get into accidents.

When you try to open a file with one of those blocked extensions, you get the following error message: "Outlook blocked access to the following potentially unsafe attachments." Then you get a list of the attachments in your email that you can't open.

Depending on your version of Outlook and whether you've applied a Service Pack update, your version may or may not exhibit this behavior. Some older versions don't act this way; all newer versions do, including Outlook 2003 and beyond.

The simplest way to know whether your version acts this way is to see what happens when you get one of the blocked file attachments. If it's allowed to go through, there's no need to use this hack. If it's blocked, get thee to the keyboard.

Force Outlook to Let You Open Blocked File Attachments

Outlook assigns a level of risk to every file attachment sent to you. Level 1 is considered unsafe, so Outlook blocks your access to Level 1 attachments; you won't be able to open these files. Level 2 is considered a moderate risk, and you won't be able to open those files directly. Instead, you have to save the files to disk, and then you can open them. Oh, and there's another oddball fact about Level 2: no file types *per se* are considered Level 2 risks. The only way for a file to be considered at that risk level is if you use Outlook in concert with a Microsoft Exchange Server, and the administrator uses his administration tools to put file extensions into that risk category. The administrator is also the only person who can take file extensions out of the category. So, you can pretty much ignore that category, unless you have some convincing official reason for changing your company's policy. Any file types not in Levels 1 and 2 are considered "other," and you can open them normally.

To force Outlook to let you open blocked file attachments, use this Registry hack. Before starting, you need to know the list of Level 1 file attachments that Outlook blocks. They're listed in Table 9-2. Just to make things more confusing, depending on your version of Office and what Service Pack you've installed, not all of these extensions can be blocked.

Table 9-2. Blocked file extensions in Outlook

EXTENSION	FILE TYPE
.ade	Microsoft Access project extension
.adp	Microsoft Access project
.app	Visual FoxPro application

EXTENSION	FILE TYPE
.asx	Windows Media audio/video
.bas	Microsoft Visual Basic class module
.bat	Batch file
.chm	Compiled HTML Help file
.cmd	Windows Command script
.com	MS-DOS program
.cpl	Control Panel extension
.crt	Security certificate
.csh	Unix shell extension
.exe	Executable program
.fxp	Visual FoxPro compiled program
.hlp	Help file
.hta	HTML program
.inf	Setup information
.ins	Internet Naming Service
.isp	Internet Communications settings
.js	Jscript file
.jse	Jscript Encoded Script file
.ksh	Unix shell extension
.lnk	Shortcut
.mda	Microsoft Access add-in program
.mdb	Microsoft Access program
.mde	Microsoft Access MDE database
.mdt	Microsoft Access workgroup information
.mdw	Microsoft Access workgroup information
.mdz	Microsoft Access wizard program
.msc	Microsoft Common Console document
.msi	Microsoft Windows Installer package
.msp	Microsoft Windows Installer patch
.mst	Microsoft Windows Installer transform; Microsoft Visual Test source file
.ops	Office XP settings

EXTENSION	FILE TYPE
.pcd	Photo CD image; Microsoft Visual compiled script
.pif	Shortcut to MS-DOS program
.prf	Microsoft Outlook profile settings
.prg	Visual FoxPro program
.reg	Registry entries
.scf	Windows Explorer command
.scr	Screensaver
.shb	Shell Scrap object
.shs	Shell Scrap object
.url	Internet shortcut
.vb	VBScript file
.vbe	VBScript Encoded script file
.vbs	VBScript file
.wsc	Windows Script Component
.wsf	Windows Script file
.wsh	Windows Script Host Setting file

Decide which file extension you want to be able to open from within Outlook, and close Outlook if it's running. Then launch the Registry Editor by typing *regedit* at the Start Search box or a command prompt (see Chapter 11 for details on the Registry).

Go to **HKEY_CURRENT_USER\Software\Microsoft\Office\14.0\Outlook\Security**, if you're using Outlook 2010. If you're using Outlook 2007, go to **HKEY_CURRENT_USER\Software \Microsoft\Office\12.0\Outlook\Security**. If you're using Outlook 2003, go to **HKEY_CURRENT_USER\Software\Microsoft\Office\10.0\Outlook\Security**. Create a new **String** value called **Level1Remove**. In the **Value Data** field, type the name of the file extension you want to be able to open; for example, *.exe*. You can add multiple file extensions; if you do, separate them with semicolons, but no spaces, like this: **.exe;.bat;.pif**. Use Table 9-2 as a guide for which blocked file extensions you want to be able to open.

When you're done, exit the Registry. Now you'll be able to see and open the file extensions you specified. If you've previously received attachments that you couldn't open, when you go to that old email, you'll see that the attachments are now available to you.

There's also an Outlook add-in that will let you open blocked email attachments without having to edit the Registry, but it's only available for Outlook 2007 and earlier. It's called the Attachment Options add-in, available here (*http://www.slovak-tech.com/attachmentoptions.htm*). It lets you visually change which attachments you can open, and it also lets you set an additional option—having Outlook ask you whether you want to open certain file extensions on a case-by-case basis, instead of blocking them or automatically opening them. (The author asks that you send a $10 donation if you use the add-in.)

Tip: If you know the person sending you a certain attachment, you can also have him zip the file and resend it to you. That way, you're getting a file with a .zip file extension, which will get through. And you can also use SkyDrive to send an attachment. See Hack #95, "Send Large File Attachments in Windows 8 Mail and Outlook.com Using SkyDrive".

HACK 107 Instantly Compress Files You Send via Outlook

Got fat files you need to send via Outlook? Here's a way to zip them in a snap.

When it comes to big files via email, your Internet service provider (ISP) is not your friend. Try to send a file or group of files as attachments over a certain file size, and your ISP or corporate email system won't let you send it—or else the recipient's email system will refuse to accept it.

What to do? Compress the files using built-in ZIP compression. But that can be a tiring process. First find the files, then zip them, then open Outlook, then send the attachment. You've got better things to do with your life.

There's a way, however, to zip them in a single stop, from right within Outlook.

Create your email message as you would normally. Click the attachment icon, highlight all the files you want to send, and right-click the group (or the single file, if you're sending only one). Then select Send To→Compressed (zipped) Folder. The files will be zipped, and the ZIP file will be given the name of the first file in the group. Rename it if you want. Then select the ZIP file, click Insert, and send it on its merry way.

HACK 108 ## Sync Calendar and Contacts Between Google and Outlook

Use Outlook as well as Google for contacts and calendaring? Here's how to make them get along.

Google is Google and Outlook is Outlook and never the twain shall meet.

Until now, that is. If you use Outlook for contacts and calendaring, as well as Google Calendar and Gmail, there are ways to have Google and Outlook syncing their information.

The free Google Calendar Sync synchronizes your Outlook and Google calendars. To get it, head to *http://bit.ly/v8B7eg*. Download it, install it and run it—it's all simple, straightforward, and easy to do. Note that it works with Microsoft Outlook versions 2003, 2007, and 2010.

That takes care of your calendar. As for syncing contacts between Outlook and Gmail, you'll have to buy a piece of software. CompanionLink for Google (*http:// www.companionlink.com/google/outlook*) costs $49.95, and syncs your contacts and calendars. That means that you can add contacts in Gmail and they'll sync to Outlook, or add them to Outlook and they'll sync to Gmail. The same holds true for your calendars.

10

Hardware

What's the whole purpose of an operating system like Windows 8? To run hardware. That's where this chapter comes in. Windows 8 offers plenty of hidden and surprising features to help you get more out of your hardware; for example, for managing hard disk space, using multiple monitors, or getting more juice out of your tablet or laptop. You'll find all that and more in this chapter.

HACK 109   To Infinity and Beyond with Windows 8 Storage Spaces

> Running out of disk space? Who isn't? Windows 8 lets you add multiple types of storage and treats it as one giant hard disk, even though the storage is on different disks.

No matter how much storage space you have, it's never enough. Music collections, downloaded movies and TV shows, photographs...today's PCs suck up hard disk space at an alarming rate.

Windows 8 solves the problem neatly. You can add many different types of storage and mix and match them, including external USB disks, installed hard disks, and more, and make them look like one giant storage pool. To get more disk space, just add another storage source to the pool. No need to rip out an old disk, figure out how to get data from the old disk to a larger one, and then install the new disk.

The feature that solves all that is new in Windows 8, and it's called Storage Spaces. It gives you remarkable capabilities, and yet is surprisingly easy to use.

Note: Some types of drives won't work with Storage Spaces. For example, I haven't found a USB flash drive that works.

First, attach all of the storage devices to your PC that you want to turn into a Storage Space. Again, remember that you can mix and match them.

Once you've done that, launch Control Panel and select System and Security→Storage Spaces (Figure 10-1).

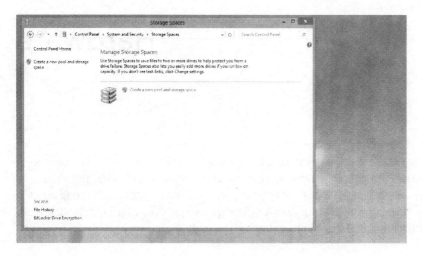

Figure 10-1.
Use Storage Space to combine different types of storage into one giant pool

Click "Create a new pool and storage space." You'll see a list of your drives. Put checkmarks next to those that you want to combine into a Storage Pool. Click Create Pool, and you'll come to a dialog box. First, name the drive and select the drive letter you'd like it to use.

Tip: Make sure that you've taken any data off the drives that you're adding to Storage Spaces. When you add a drive, Windows 8 formats it, destroying whatever files you have on it.

Next comes perhaps the most important decision you'll make when creating a Storage Space—the resiliency type. This setting determines how safe your data is. Several of these options include *mirroring*, which means that if one of the drives goes bad, the data on it isn't lost, because a copy is automatically saved to another one of the drives. Here are your choices:

None

No mirroring is done. The data is stored once on a drive, and if that drive goes bad, the data is lost. But this choice maximizes your storage, because none of the pooled storage is taken up by mirroring.

Two-way mirror

Two copies of your data are stored on separate disks. That way, if one drive goes bad, the data is still available on the other drive. But it means that you need more hard disk space than with the "None" selection, because you're keeping two copies of your data.

Three-way mirror

This option provides even more data security—and requires yet more disk space. The data is kept on three separate disks. If you choose this options, you need at least three disks in your Storage Space.

Parity

When you choose this option, Windows 8 stores what's called *parity* information for your data. This system mirrors your data but uses less disk space. However, it also slows down writing the data. Only choose it if you've got very large files that you use infrequently, such as video files.

After you choose a resiliency type, you choose the "logical size" for your disk. This setting is what the size of the disk looks like to Windows 8 and your applications, and you can set it to be different from the actual total disk size. If you choose a logical size that's larger than the actual physical size, you'll get a warning when you're coming close to running out of physical storage space.

When you're done, click "Create storage space." Your new space is now available to your applications, and it shows up just like any other drive. To manage your Storage Spaces—for example, to add more storage, rename a space, create a new one, and so on—go back to the Control Panel, and you'll see each of your Storage Spaces. Simply click the link next to each to do what you want.

HACK 110 Hack Windows 8's Power Plan

> Here's how to build your own power plan that best balances power use and performance for the way you actually compute.

If you've got a portable Windows 8 device like a tablet or notebook, you know the importance of conserving power. When you're spending time on plane flights and long sessions at Wi-Fi hot spots away from home or the office, how your Windows 8 device handles power becomes increasingly important.

Windows 8 balances performance and power use with several pre-set power plans, but none of them may be quite to your liking. So it also lets you customize how your devices handle power as well.

Let's start with the power basics. By default, Windows 8 uses what it calls a Balanced power plan that conserves battery life, but still gives you the oomph you need to get your work—or fun—done. It's in effect whether your device is plugged in or not.

You can change it when you want, though, for example by using the "Power saver" setting when your device isn't plugged in. Go to the Desktop and click the power icon. You'll find two settings, Balanced and "Power saver." When your device is unplugged, select "Power saver"; when you plug it back in, select Balanced (Figure 10-2).

Figure 10-2.
Windows 8's basic power options

Those aren't the only power plans, though. You can easily create your own power plan or customize an existing one. Click the power icon and select "More power options." Click "Change plan settings" at the bottom of the screen and another power plan appears—"High performance" (see Figure 10-3). It's a good choice when your Windows 8 device is plugged in and you want more performance than you normally get under the Balanced plan.

But you're not stuck with that, either. You can easily customize any plan or create one of your own. On the Power Options screen, click "Change plan settings" next to any of the plans you want to customize.

Your choices are straightforward. From here, choose options for how long your device should be idle before the display is dimmed, the display is turned off, and the computer is put to sleep when plugged in or unplugged (Figure 10-4). You can also select how bright the screen should be when plugged in or unplugged. When you're done, click "Save changes."

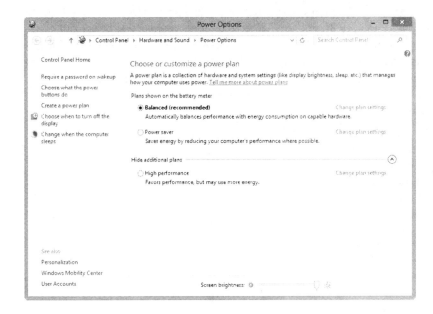

Figure 10-3.
Here's Command Central for all your power options

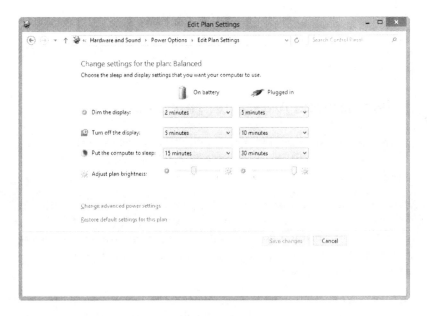

Figure 10-4.
Customize your power options here

But wait, there's more! When you're customizing any plan, click "Change advanced power settings," and you'll come to a screen that offers more power options than you might ever want to use...and more, shown in Figure 10-5. You can choose when to put your wireless card into power saving mode, how long your device should be idle before the hard disk is turned off, power consumption by your processor, and so on.

Figure 10-5.
Changing advanced power options

HACK 111 Two Screens Are Better than One

Windows 8 offers some nifty new features for those who want to use more than one monitor or are giving presentations. Here's how to use that feature to the fullest.

For plenty of people, when it comes to screens, bigger is better. So much better, in fact, that they're not happy with a single monitor. They need at least two, for the biggest workspace possible. And there are those who need to use more than one monitor during presentations, so they can project what's on their monitor onto a larger one—for example, a large projection screen.

Using more than one monitor is simple. First, connect the second monitor to your device. Then press Windows key+P to bring up the Settings pane for multiple monitors, as you can see in Figure 10-6.

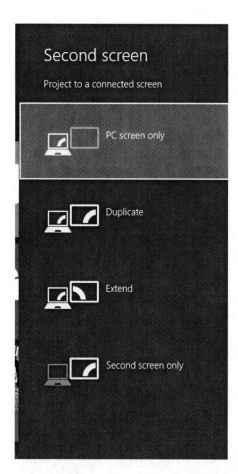

Figure 10-6.
The Settings pane for managing multiple monitors

You have four ways to handle the second screen:

PC screen only

> When you choose this setting, your second screen stays blank. You don't project anything onto it.

Duplicate

> Copies what's on your screen onto a second screen; best for when you're giving a presentation. When you choose this option, the first display and the second display use the same resolution.

Second screen only

With this setting, you project onto the second screen, and your screen goes blank. With this setting, you can make sure that the resolution on the second screen is the best fit. So if you have a notebook, for example, and you're projecting onto a large screen for a presentation, you can choose this setting for maximum impact.

Extend

Makes the two screens work like one large virtual screen; in other words, it extends Windows 8 onto the second screen. So, for example, you can display a single file across both screens, such as a large photograph.

Configuring Both Displays

If you choose to extend your screen onto a second screen, you've got some decisions to make. What resolutions should each monitor be? What orientation? Which should be the main display, and which the secondary one?

To control all that, launch the Control Panel, then click "Adjust screen resolution." The Screen Resolution dialog box appears, as shown in Figure 10-7. Click either screen to change the settings, including its resolution and orientation, and whether to let the screen auto-rotate (for example, if you're using a tablet).

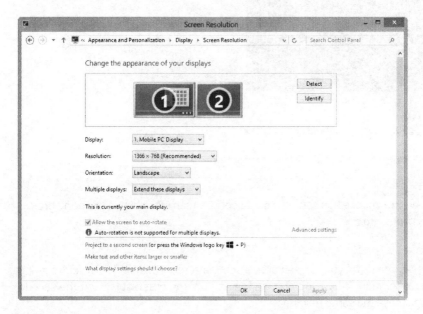

Figure 10-7.
The Screen Resolution dialog box controls the way in which two monitors interact

The dialog box also tells you which is the main display. If you like, you can make another monitor the main display. Just click it and turn on the checkbox next to "Make this my main display." When you're done, click OK.

Configuring the Taskbar on Both Displays

When you extend Windows 8 across multiple monitors, each has the same Taskbar by default. But it doesn't have to be that way. Maybe you want the Taskbar gone from one display, or you want each Taskbar to have only the icons for apps running on that display.

To configure all that, right-click the Taskbar, select Properties, and then click the Taskbar tab. Go to the "Multiple displays section." You'll see a checkmark next to "Show taskbar on all displays." Uncheck it if you want the Taskbar to appear only on the main display.

If you keep the default and have a Taskbar on each display, you can choose how you'd like the Taskbar to behave from the "Show taskbar buttons on" drop-down menu. Here are your choices:

All taskbars

> The same Taskbar runs on all monitors. (This is the default setting.)

Main Taskbar and Taskbar where window is open

> This option sounds more confusing than it is. When you choose it, the Taskbar on your main display shows all of the icons for all of the apps running on both monitors, but on the second monitor, that Taskbar shows only the icons of the apps running on *that* monitor. So, say you've got Internet Explorer and Word running on your main display, and PowerPoint and Excel running on your second display. Your main display's Taskbar will show icons for Internet Explorer, Word, PowerPoint, and Excel. The second monitor will show icons only for PowerPoint and Excel, which are the apps running on it.

Taskbar where window is open

> With this choice, each monitor shows only icons for apps running on it. So in the previous example, the monitor running Internet Explorer and Word shows only icons for those apps, and the monitor running PowerPoint and Excel shows only icons for those apps. With this setting, no one Taskbar shows icons for all apps on all monitors.

Moving Apps Around

If you've chosen to extend Windows 8 across multiple monitors, you can move apps from monitor to monitor quite easily:

Drag and drop Windows 8 native apps

Move apps from monitor to monitor

Press Windows key+Page Up or Page Down

Move a Windows 8 native app or the Start screen from monitor to monitor

Multi-Monitor Slide Shows and Different Desktop Backgrounds

What's the point of using two monitors as a giant extended desktop if both show the same Desktop background? None, as far as I'm concerned. It's much more entertaining to give them different backgrounds.

To do it, press Windows key+W to launch the Search box for settings. Search for Change Desktop Background and launch that applet from the search results. Look for a background you want to use on one of the monitors, and right-click it. From the menu that appears (see Figure 10-8), choose which monitor you want to have that background. Then do the same thing and choose a different background for your other monitor.

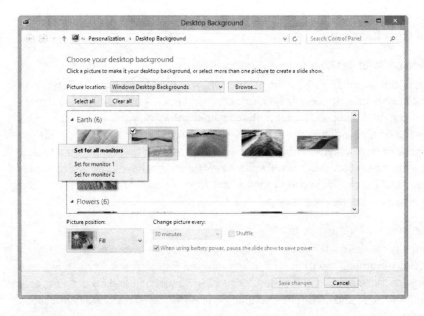

Figure 10-8.
Choosing different background pictures for each monitor is a breeze

Even more entertaining is putting on a slideshow that spans monitors. To do this, simply choose a background that is a slideshow rather than a static image; Windows 8 takes care of the rest.

And you can even have a single Desktop background image that spans both monitors. To do that, when you choose a Desktop background and have it for both monitors, click the "Picture position" drop-down menu and choose Span.

HACK 112 Find Drivers for Windows 8 Fast

> Got out-of-date drivers and can't find the new ones? Here's a quick way to solve the problem.

Because Windows 8 is a new operating system, not all manufacturers had drivers for their hardware ready when it shipped, so you may not be able to use that hardware until you get a Windows 8 driver for it. In theory, Windows Update is supposed to deliver any updated drivers to you; in practice, that may not happen. You'll have to spend time visiting the sites of your hardware manufacturers, and then spend even time trying to find where they've hidden driver information. There's a quicker way, though. Go to the RadarSync Windows 8 Drivers page (*http://www.radarsync.com/windows8*). You'll find links to drivers from many different manufacturers. Simply click the links to head to the right page to download each driver.

HACK 113 Troubleshoot Hardware with Device Manager

> The Device Manager is a great hardware troubleshooting tool, but you'll need this hack to make sense of the error messages it relays to you. Here's how to decode the cryptic messages and—more important—how to use them to solve hardware woes.

If you install and uninstall enough hardware on your system, error messages and system conflicts are a way of life. Luckily, Windows 8 includes a built-in way to resolve system conflicts by hand: using the Device Manager, Windows' best all-around hardware-troubleshooting tool. It's been around for several versions of Windows, and it's still the best hardware tool you'll find.

There are several ways to run it. You can press Windows key+R to open the run box, then type devmgmt.msc and press Enter. You can also, on the Start screen, type *Device Manager*, click Settings, and then click the Device Manager icon that shows up on the left side of the screen. And yes, there's even one more way as well: right-click the left corner of the screen and select Device Manager from the menu that appears. However you get there, the same Device Manager launches, as shown in Figure 10-9.

To find information about any device, right-click it and choose Properties. The multi-tabbed Properties dialog box appears (Figure 10-10). You'll be able to get comprehensive information about the device from here.

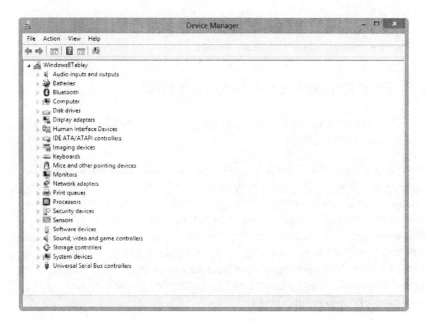

Figure 10-9.
The Device Manager displaying all the devices installed on your system

Figure 10-10.
The Device Manager's General tab

When you open the Device Manager, an icon appears next to any device involved in a system conflict. A yellow exclamation point means the device has a problem or conflict of some sort. A red "X" means the device is disabled. A blue "i" (which stands for *information*) means the device's resource configuration has been altered via the Device Manager.

Note: The blue "i" icon shows up only when you choose one of two views: "Resource by type" or "Resource by connection." To switch to those views, use the View menu.

Only the yellow and red icons mean there's a problem of some sort. To find out more details about the problem, double-click the device that has an icon next to it, and an error message and error code will appear in the "Device status" section of the General tab. Those error messages are supposed to help you solve the hardware problem. Unfortunately, though, they're cryptic at best, and, as a general rule, you won't be any closer to resolving the problem after you read them.

However, armed with the right knowledge, you can resolve the problems based on the error message you see. The advice in Table 10-2 [adapted from Microsoft Knowledge-base Article 125174 (*http://support.microsoft.com/kb/125174*)] tells you how to use the Device Manager to solve the problem.

There are several solutions you might need to employ, and some of the common ones are abbreviated (as shown in Table 10-1).

Table 10-1. The abbreviations in Device Manager error messages correspond to simple solutions

ABBREVIATION	DETAILS
D	Get and install updated drivers from the hardware manufacturer.
I	Uninstall and then reinstall the driver.
M	Check memory and system resources by running Control Panel, then selecting System and Security→System→Advanced System Settings and then clicking Settings under Performance to see whether that is the problem. Change settings here to reduce the amount of memory your system requires, such as eliminating animations. (You may have to install more RAM to solve the problem.)
R	You can try removing the device in the Device Manager and reinstalling the hardware.
U	Update the drivers by choosing Update Driver from the Driver tab, and follow the instructions.

Table 10-2. Device Manager error codes, messages, and potential solutions

CODE	ERROR MESSAGE	RECOMMENDED SOLUTION
1	This device is not configured correctly.	U R
2	The <type> device loader(s) for this device could not load the device driver.	U R

CODE	ERROR MESSAGE	RECOMMENDED SOLUTION
3	The driver for this device might be corrupt or your system may be running low on memory or other resources.	U R M T
4	This device is not working properly because one of its drivers may be bad, or your Registry may be bad.	U R D
5	The device's driver requested a resource that Windows does not know how to handle.	U R
6	Another device is using the resources this device needs.	T
7	The device's drivers need to be reinstalled.	Click Reinstall Driver.
8	This has many associated error messages.	U R
9	This has several associated error messages.	R D Update your system BIOS.
10	This device either is not present, is not working properly, or does not have all the drivers installed. This code may also have a manufacturer-specific error message associated with it, depending on the device.	Make sure the device is physically connected to the computer properly. U
11	Windows stopped responding while attempting to start this device and therefore will never attempt to start this device again.	D
12	This device cannot find enough free <type> resources that it can use. Note that <type> is a resource type, such as IRQ, DMA, Memory, or I/O.	T
13	This device either is not present, is not working properly, or does not have all the drivers installed.	Click Detect Hardware. R
14	This device cannot work properly until you restart your computer.	Restart your computer.
15	This device is causing a resource conflict.	T
16	Windows cannot identify all the resources this device uses.	Click the Resources tab, and manually enter the settings as detailed in the manufacturer's documentation.
17	The driver information file <name> is telling this child device to use a resource that the parent device does not have or recognize. <name> is the .inf file for the device.	U R
18	Reinstall the drivers for this device.	Click Reinstall Driver.
19	Your Registry may be bad.	Click Check Registry.
20	Windows could not load one of the drivers for this device.	U
21	Windows is removing this device.	Wait several seconds, and then refresh the Device Manager view. If the device appears, restart your computer.
22	This device is disabled.	Click Enable Device.

CODE	ERROR MESSAGE	RECOMMENDED SOLUTION
22	This device is not started.	Click Start Device.
23	Several error messages may appear with Code 23.	Click Properties or Update Driver, depending on which button appears.
24	This device is not present, is not working properly, or does not have all its drivers installed.	Click Detect Hardware or Update Drivers, depending on which button appears.
25	Windows is in the process of setting up this device.	Restart your computer.
26	Windows is in the process of setting up this device.	Restart your computer.
27	Windows can't specify the resources for this device.	R D
28	The drivers for this device are not installed.	Click Reinstall Driver. R D
29	This device is disabled because the firmware for the device did not give it the required resources.	Check the device's documentation on how to enable its BIOS. If that doesn't work, enable the device in your computer's CMOS settings.
30	This device is using an Interrupt Request (IRQ) resource that is in use by another device and cannot be shared. You must change the conflicting setting or remove the real-mode driver causing the conflict.	Check the Device Manager to see if another device is using the same IRQ and disable it. If you can't find another device using the IRQ, look for drivers loaded in a Config.sys or Autoexec.bat file, and disable them.
31	This device is not working properly because Windows cannot load the drivers required for this device.	Click Properties. If that doesn't work, remove the device in the Device Manager, and run the Add New Hardware Wizard from the Control Panel. If the device still does not work, get updated drivers or other assistance from the manufacturer.
32	Windows cannot install the drivers for this device because it cannot access the drive or network location that has the setup files on it.	Restart the computer.
33	Windows cannot determine which resources are required for this device.	T Contact the hardware manufacturer, and configure or replace the device.
34	Windows cannot determine the settings for this device. Consult the documentation that came with this device and use the Resources tab to set the configuration.	T Change the hardware settings by following the manufacturer's instructions and then use the Resources tab to configure the device.

CODE	ERROR MESSAGE	RECOMMENDED SOLUTION
35	Your computer's system firmware does not include enough information to configure and use this device properly. To use this device, contact your computer manufacturer to obtain a firmware or BIOS update.	T Update your system BIOS.
36	This device is requesting a PCI interrupt but is configured for an ISA interrupt (or vice versa). Please use the computer's system setup program to reconfigure the interrupt for this device.	Check your computer's docs for instructions on reconfiguring the IRQ settings in the BIOS. T
37	Windows cannot initialize the device driver for this hardware.	I T
38	Windows cannot load the device driver for this hardware because a previous instance of the device driver is still in memory.	Restart the computer. T
39	Windows cannot load the device driver for this hardware. The driver may be corrupt or missing.	TI
40	Windows cannot access this hardware because its service key information in the Registry is missing or recorded incorrectly.	TI
41	Windows successfully loaded the device driver for this hardware but cannot find the hardware device.	I T If the device is an old piece of hardware and is non-Plug and Play, go to Control Panel and choose View Devices and Printers, right-click the device, and select Troubleshoot.
42	Windows cannot load the device driver for this hardware because there is a duplicate device already running in the system.	Restart the computer. T
43	Windows has stopped this device because it has reported problems.	Check the hardware documentation. T
44	An application or service has shut down this hardware device.	Restart the computer. T
45	Currently, this hardware device is not connected to the computer.	Reconnect the device to the computer.
46	Windows cannot gain access to this hardware device because the operating system is in the process of shutting down.	No fix should be necessary; the device should work properly when you start your computer.
47	Windows cannot use this hardware device because it has been prepared for "safe removal" but it has not been removed from the computer.	Unplug the device from your computer, and then plug it in again.
48	The software for this device has been blocked from starting because it is known to have problems with Windows. Contact the hardware vendor for a new driver.	D

CODE	ERROR MESSAGE	RECOMMENDED SOLUTION
49	Windows cannot start new hardware devices because the system hive is too large (exceeds the Registry Size Limit).	Uninstall any devices you are no longer using

See Also

- Hack #114, "Get a Complete History of Troublesome Hardware"
- Hack #115, "Uncover Hidden Hardware with the Device Manager"
- Hack #116, "Get a Comprehensive List of All Your Drivers"

HACK 114 Get a Complete History of Troublesome Hardware

> You might have a piece of hardware that seems to be cursed, and continually causes problems. Here's a way to see the entire history of the device on your system, which may provide clues to its problems.

Some pieces of hardware just seem to be born bad. Something is always going wrong with them and it's not clear why. You're having a hard time troubleshooting the device's problems, and sometimes you feel like you're getting the same problems over and over. Wouldn't it be nice if you could see the entire history of the hardware on your system, including each time a new driver has been installed, and whether it was successful?

Windows 8 has a tool that does exactly that, using the Device Manager. Launch the Device Manager (Hack #113, "Troubleshoot Hardware with Device Manager"), then right-click the device (or any device whose history you want to see) and click the Events tab (Figure 10-11). You'll see the history of the hardware, including dates the device and drivers were installed, updates, and so on. Click any event to see more information about it.

For even more details, click "View all Events," and the Event Viewer launches, providing even more in-depth details about each event (Figure 10-12).

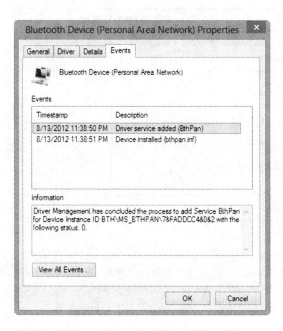

Figure 10-11.
Checking out the history of a piece of hardware

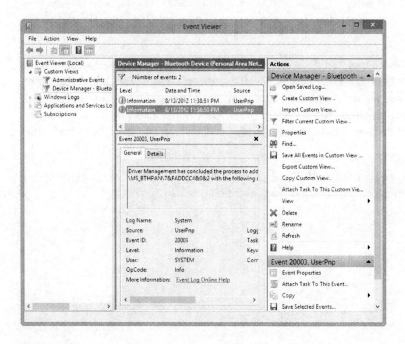

Figure 10-12.
Checking out the history of a piece of hardware

See Also

- Hack #113, "Troubleshoot Hardware with Device Manager"
- Hack #115, "Uncover Hidden Hardware with the Device Manager"
- Hack #116, "Get a Comprehensive List of All Your Drivers"

HACK 115 Uncover Hidden Hardware with the Device Manager

> Hardware ghosts and other hidden devices can cause system conflicts, and the Device Manager won't report on them. This hack forces the Device Manager to uncover all your hidden hardware so you can resolve any conflicts.

One of the strangest hardware problems you'll encounter in Windows involves hardware devices that are invisible to you but that cause system conflicts. You won't see them in the Device Manager, so you can't use that tool to resolve the conflicts.

The Device Manager hides several types of these devices. For example, non–Plug and Play printers and other devices don't show up. Most newer devices are Plug and Play, so you'll likely encounter this problem only if you have old hardware attached to your PC. (Windows 8 automatically recognizes and installs Plug and Play devices.) In this instance, the device is physically present on your PC, but the Device Manager doesn't show you it's there.

Then there are the *nonpresent* or *ghosted* devices—devices you've removed from your system without doing an uninstall, or whose uninstallation didn't work properly. These devices aren't physically present in your system, but Windows treats them as if they were there and devotes system resources to them. For example, if you physically remove an old network card without doing an uninstall, it might cause conflicts because Windows treats it as if it were still in your system.

The Device Manager also might not give you details about USB devices that you frequently attach and remove—for example, MP3 players that you attach to your PC only when you want to add or delete MP3 files from them. Although these devices aren't present in your system, Windows devotes resources to them. Even if you replace one USB device with another of the same model, it's best to go through the uninstall process rather than just swap them.

And then there are devices you may have moved from one PCI slot to another. Windows might believe they are actually present in two slots, so it devotes resources for *both* slots to them.

Displaying these hidden devices can help with troubleshooting. For example, a hidden device could possibly conflict with a nonhidden device. And sometimes you might want to uninstall hidden devices—for example, when you've moved a non-Plug and Play network card from one slot to another and want to uninstall it from one slot.

But to do this kind of troubleshooting, you'll need to force the Device Manager to display information about the devices; otherwise, you won't know how to solve the problem.

Forcing the Device Manager to display non-Plug and Play printers and other devices is a simple matter. Run the Device Manager (Hack #113, "Troubleshoot Hardware with Device Manager") and then choose View→Show Hidden devices.

Displaying ghosted or nonpresent devices takes a little more work. You'll set an environment variable that forces the Device Manager to display them.

At a command prompt, type *set devmgr_show_nonpresent_devices=1*, and press Enter. You won't get a prompt in response; the command prompt will stay blank. At the same instance of the command prompt, type *start devmgmt.msc*, and press Enter. The Device Manager will launch in a separate window.

Keep in mind that you have to run the Device Manager from the same instance of the command prompt in which you typed *set devmgr_show_nonpresent_devices=1*. If you run the Device Manager outside the command prompt, it won't display ghosted devices.

So now you've set the variable properly, but the Device Manager won't display ghosted devices yet. You have to tell it to display them by choosing View→Show Hidden Devices. You should see quite a few devices now, including a lengthy list of non-Plug and Play drivers. Typically, devices that are currently present on your PC are shown in black, and non-present devices in gray. You may also see some devices listed more than once.

Now, use the Device Manager to troubleshoot any of those ghosted devices (Hack #113, "Troubleshoot Hardware with Device Manager"), as shown in Figure 10-13. If you find any ghosted devices you no longer use on your PC, uninstall them from the Device Manager by right-clicking and choosing Uninstall.

Hacking the Hack

You can make the ability to see hidden and ghosted devices *permanent*.

To do that, you need to get to the Environment Variable dialog box. Launch Control Panel, do a search for Environment, and select "Edit the system environment variables"→Environment Variables.

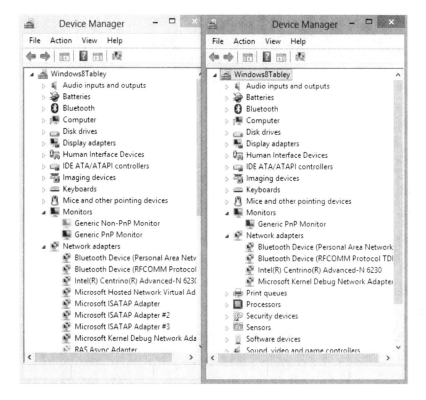

Figure 10-13.
Displaying ghosted devices in the Device Manager. The version of Device Manager on the left shows hidden devices, such as two monitors and many additional network adapters, while the version on the right doesn't show those hidden devices.

The Environment Variables dialog box opens (Figure 10-14). This dialog box lets you set system variables for the entire system or for individual users. Environment variables control a variety of Windows features, such as the location of your Windows directory and TEMP directories and the filename and location of the command processor that launches when you run the command prompt.

The Environment Variables dialog box contains two sections: "User variables" and "System variables." To apply the variable to a single user, use the "User variables" dialog box; to apply the variable to all users, use the "System variables" dialog box. In this case, you'll want to create the variable systemwide, so click New in the "System variables" section. The New System Variable dialog box appears. For "Variable name," type *devmgr_show_nonpresent_devices*. Once you've created the name, you need to give it a value. To turn the setting on, type *1* in the "Variable value" box. Click OK, and then OK again. Run the Device Manager. Now, enable the Device Manager to show ghosted devices in the same way you did previously in this hack.

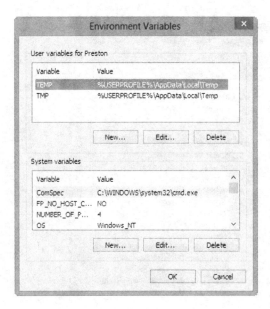

Figure 10-14.
Use this dialog box to tell the Device Manager to always show ghosted devices

See Also

- Hack #113, "Troubleshoot Hardware with Device Manager"
- Hack #114, "Get a Complete History of Troublesome Hardware"
- Hack #116, "Get a Comprehensive List of All Your Drivers"

HACK 116 Get a Comprehensive List of All Your Drivers

Not sure what drivers you've got on your system and when they were installed? Use this command-line tool.

The Device Manager (Hack #113, "Troubleshoot Hardware with Device Manager") lists drivers for you, one by one, as you navigate your way through it. But that's an awful lot of work if you're looking to get a list of all the drivers in your system.

Why get a list of all your drivers? You may want to print them out, so in the event of a system crash, you'll know all the drivers you need to reinstall. Or if you have multiple systems at home or are a system administrator, you may want to make sure that all the drivers on all your PCs are up-to-date. If you have lists to compare, you can see at a glance, for example, that one system has a newer driver than another for the same piece of hardware, so the older one needs updating.

The command-line tool DriverQuery lists all your drivers, along with information about each, including file size and more.

To see a list of all drivers, type *driverquery* at a command prompt, and press Enter. You'll see a long list of drivers, along with basic information about each. Here's an excerpt of what you might see:

```
Microsoft Windows [Version 6.2.9200]
(c) 2012 Microsoft Corporation. All rights reserved.


C:\Users\Preston>driverquery


Module Name   Display Name            Driver Type    Link Date
============  ======================  =============  ======================
1394ohci      1394 OHCI Compliant Ho  Kernel         7/25/2012 10:26:46 PM
3ware         3ware                   Kernel         3/8/2012 3:33:45 PM
ACPI          Microsoft ACPI Driver   Kernel         7/25/2012 10:28:26 PM
acpials       ALS Sensor Filter       Kernel         7/25/2012 10:28:02 PM
acpiex        Microsoft ACPIEx Drive  Kernel         7/25/2012 10:25:57 PM
acpipagr      ACPI Processor Aggrega  Kernel         7/25/2012 10:27:16 PM
AcpiPmi       ACPI Power Meter Drive  Kernel         7/25/2012 10:27:33 PM
acpitime      ACPI Wake Alarm Driver  Kernel         7/25/2012 10:27:37 PM
adp94xx       adp94xx                 Kernel         12/5/2008 6:54:42 PM
adpahci       adpahci                 Kernel         5/1/2007 1:30:09 PM
adpu320       adpu320                 Kernel         2/27/2007 7:04:15 PM
AFD           Ancillary Function Dri  Kernel         7/25/2012 10:24:27 PM
agp440        Intel AGP Bus Filter    Kernel         7/25/2012 10:29:13 PM
AmdK8         AMD K8 Processor Drive  Kernel         7/25/2012 10:26:48 PM
AmdPPM        AMD Processor Driver    Kernel         7/25/2012 10:26:48 PM
amdsata       amdsata                 Kernel         6/11/2012 6:19:56 PM
amdsbs        amdsbs                  Kernel         2/21/2012 1:15:43 PM
amdxata       amdxata                 Kernel         6/11/2012 6:36:48 PM
AppID         AppID Driver            Kernel         7/25/2012 10:25:12 PM
arc           arc                     Kernel         3/19/2012 1:49:21 PM
arcsas        Adaptec SAS/SATA-II RA  Kernel         3/19/2012 1:51:00 PM
AsyncMac      RAS Asynchronous Media  Kernel         7/25/2012 10:28:25 PM
atapi         IDE Channel             Kernel         7/25/2012 10:30:33 PM
b06bdrv       Broadcom NetXtreme II   Kernel         5/14/2012 5:42:24 PM
BasicDisplay  BasicDisplay            Kernel         7/25/2012 10:29:08 PM
BasicRender   BasicRender             Kernel         7/25/2012 10:28:51 PM
```

```
Beep          Beep                       Kernel       7/25/2012 10:30:19 PM
bowser        Browser Support Driver File System      7/25/2012 10:28:01 PM
BthAvrcpTg    Bluetooth Audio/Video Kernel            7/25/2012 10:28:27 PM
BthEnum       Bluetooth Enumerator S Kernel           7/25/2012 10:25:17 PM
```

Some basic information is missing, though; notably, the filename and size of the driver. To see that additional information and more, add the /v switch:

```
driverquery /v
```

You'll get the extra information, but it will be hard to read on the screen. So to display the output in a list format, type this:

```
driverquery /v /fo list
```

You'll see output like this:

```
Module Name:       vga
Display Name:      vga
Description:       vga
Driver Type:       Kernel
Start Mode:        Manual
State:             Stopped
Status:            OK
Accept Stop:       FALSE
Accept Pause:      FALSE
Paged Pool(bytes): 20,480
Code(bytes):       4,096
BSS(bytes):        0
Link Date:         11/2/2006 4:53:56 AM
Path:              J:\Windows\system32\DRIVERS\vgapnp.sys
Init(bytes):       4,096
```

You can even save the results to a text file with the redirection operator (>):

```
driverquery /v /fo list > drivers.txt
```

For extra security (in case your system crashes and you need a list of drivers to help you troubleshoot the problem), print it out, and keep it in a safe place.

Hacking the Hack

DriverQuery has other switches as well. Here's how to use them:

/fo format

Specify the format of the display: /fo table (the default) for a formatted table, /fo list for a plain-text list, or /fo csv for a comma-separated report, suitable for importing into a spreadsheet or database.

/nh

If using the /fo table or /fo csv format (above), the /nh option turns off the column headers.

/v

Display additional details about drivers other than signed drivers.

/si

Display additional details about signed drivers.

/s system

Connect to a remote system, where system is the name of the computer.

/u user

Specify a user account (include an optional domain before the username) under which the command should execute.

/p password

The password for the user account specified with /u; prompts for the password if omitted.

See Also

- For more information about how to use DriverQuery, see *http://bit.ly/ROyhho*.
- Hack #112, "Find Drivers for Windows 8 Fast"
- Hack #114, "Get a Complete History of Troublesome Hardware"
- Hack #115, "Uncover Hidden Hardware with the Device Manager"

11

The Registry and Group Policy Editor

When it comes to hacking Windows, you need to know how to use the Registry. It contains the underlying organization of the entire operating system, and its often-incomprehensible settings hold the key to countless hacks. In simpler days, you could hack Windows without bothering with the Registry; a solid knowledge of such things as .*ini* files would suffice. But no longer. If you want to get hacking, the Registry holds the key—literally, since it's organized by way of keys.

Even if you've edited the Registry before, you'll find a lot in this chapter to help. It not only teaches the mechanics of using the Registry, but also explains its underlying organization. You'll find ways to keep your Registry safe, learn how to back it up, and find downloadable tools to make the most of the Registry. As a bonus, this chapter includes a grab bag of other great hacks.

This chapter also covers Group Policy Editor. Don't be confused by its name; it's not just a tool for system administrators looking to handle file permissions, centrally manage settings across users and computers, and the like. In fact, it's an exceedingly powerful tool for hacking many parts of Windows. It comes with Windows 8 Professional and Windows 8 Enterprise, so if you've got other versions of Windows 8, you're out of luck.

`HACK 117` Don't Fear the Registry

> The Registry is a great tool for hacking Windows 8. Here's an introduction to how it's organized and how to use it.

If you haven't spent much time in the Registry, you can easily be cowed by it. At first glance, it's a maze of apparently incomprehensible settings. In fact, though, there's a method to the madness. The Registry is a hierarchical database of information that defines exactly how your system works, including virtually every part of Windows and its applications. Editing the Registry database is often the best way to hack Windows. In fact, it's the only way to make certain changes to the operating system.

Even if you've never used the Registry directly before, you've changed it without realizing it. Whenever you change a setting using the Control Panel, for example, behind the scenes a Registry change puts that new setting into effect. The menus and dialog boxes you see in Windows 8 are often little more than a visual front end to the Registry.

If you want to optimize Windows and master every part of it, you'll have to use the Registry. Windows contains so many different settings and customizations that it simply wasn't possible for Microsoft to build a graphical interface for every conceivable option. And many times it's easier, and you get more options, when you edit the Registry instead of using the graphical Windows interface. You can use Windows without ever editing the Registry—many users do—but advanced users understand its power tool status.

The way to edit the Registry is by using the *Registry Editor*, also called Regedit, which is shown in Figure 11-1.

Before you edit the Registry, though, first you should get a basic understanding of its structure.

Warning: Sometimes, power users like to jump in without reading the manual. The Registry is not the best place to experiment and learn as you go until you understand at least a little of what's going on. You could render your system useless and unrecoverable with just a few changes. So, we recommend making a backup (Hack #120, "Better Registry Backups") and reading most of this chapter first. You'll be glad later if you do this now.

The Five Logical Registry Hives

The Registry has many thousands of settings; in fact, it often has tens of thousands of them. They are organized into five main Registry sections, called *Registry hives*. Think of each hive as a root directory. Each hive has a different purpose. When you start to delve into the Registry, you may notice that many of the settings seem to be exact duplicates of one another; in other words, the settings in one hive mirror the settings in another hive. In fact, frequently one set of settings is merely an alias (called a *symbolic link*) of another, so when you change those settings in one hive, the changes are made in both hives.

Note: Most of the information about the hives and files that support them are stored in the C:\Windows\system32\config. You won't be able to see the hives there. Instead, you'll see files such as System, System.log, Security, and others. And you can't edit the Registry from those files.

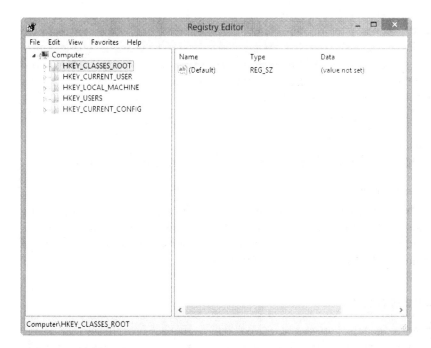

Figure 11-1.
Controlling Registry settings by using the Registry Editor

Following are the five hives and what each does:

HKEY_CLASSES_ROOT

This hive contains information about file types, filename extensions, and similar information. It instructs Windows on how to handle every different file type and controls basic user interface options, such as double-clicking and context menus. This hive also includes class definitions (hence the word CLASSES in its name) of unique objects, such as file types or OLE objects. Frequently, classes associated with file types contain the Shell subkey, which defines actions, such as opening and printing, that can be taken with that file type.

HKEY_CURRENT_USER

This hive contains configuration information about the system setup of the user that is currently logged in to Windows. It controls the current user's desktop, as well as Windows' specific appearance and behavior for the current user. This hive also manages network connections and connections to devices such as printers, personal preferences such as screen colors, and security rights. Also included in this hive are Security Identifiers (SIDs), which uniquely identify users of the PC and which have information about each user's rights, settings, and preferences, and which are the computer representation of users and groups.

HKEY_LOCAL_MACHINE

This hive contains information about the computer itself, as well as the operating system. It includes specific details about all hardware, including keyboard, printer ports, storage—the entire hardware setup. In addition, it has information about security, installed software, system startup, drivers, services, and the machine's specific configuration. (Note: You need to have administrative privileges on the system to change values in keys in this hive.)

HKEY_USERS

This hive contains information about every user profile on the system.

HKEY_CURRENT_CONFIG

This hive contains information about the current hardware configuration of the system, in the same way HKEY_CURRENT_USER contains information about the current user of the system. (You will need to have administrative privileges on the system to change values in keys in this hive.)

Using Keys and Values

Each hive is at the top of the hierarchy, and underneath each hive are keys, which can in turn contain subkeys, and those subkeys can contain subkeys, and so on, organized in folderlike fashion, much like files on a hard drive.

Keys and subkeys contain a value, which controls a particular setting. For example, this key:

```
HKEY_CURRENT_USER\Control Panel\Mouse\DoubleClickSpeed
```

determines the amount of time between mouse clicks that must elapse before Windows won't consider it to be a double-click. To set the amount of time, you change the key's value. In this case, the default value is 500, measured in milliseconds, and you can edit the Registry to change it to whatever value you want, as shown in Figure 11-2. You can also make the changes using the Mouse Properties dialog box (Control Panel→Hardware and Sound→Mouse). When you make changes to that dialog box, the changes are in turn made in the Registry, which ultimately controls the setting. In essence, the dialog box is merely a convenient front end to the Registry.

A Registry key can contain several types of values. Here are the six primary datatypes of values in the Registry:

REG_SZ *(string value)*

This datatype is easy to understand and edit because it's made up of plain text and numbers. It's one of the most common datatypes in the Registry. The value for DoubleClickSpeed, mentioned earlier in this hack, is of this type.

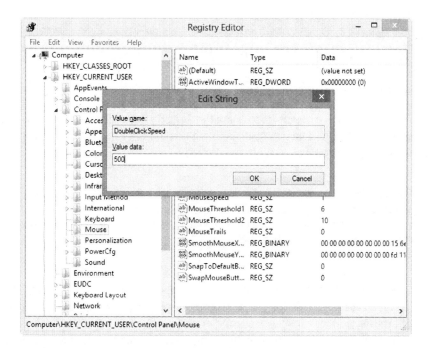

Figure 11-2.
Editing a Registry key's value

REG_MULTI_SZ *(multi-string value)*

This datatype contains several strings of plain text and numbers.

REG_EXPAND_SZ *(expanded string value)*

This datatype contains variables that Windows uses to point to the location of files.

REG_BINARY *(binary value)*

This datatype is made up of binary data: *0*s and *1*s. As a general rule, you won't edit binary values; instead, you'll edit string values because they're made up of text and numbers.

REG_DWORD *(DWORD values)*

This datatype is represented as a number. Sometimes a `0` turns on the key or a `1` turns off the key, though it can use other numbers as well. While you see and edit the value as a number, such as `456`, the Registry itself views the number as a hexadecimal number, `1C8`. You can switch between both views in the Registry editor when you change the value.

`REG_QWORD` *(QWORD values)*
> This is like REG_DWORD, except that it can hold larger values. A DWORD holds 32 bits (D stands for double, and Q stands for quad), and a QWORD holds 64 bits.

Launching the Registry Editor

There's an upside and a downside to using the Registry Editor. The upside is that it's relatively simple to use. The downside is that it doesn't offer much functionality beyond basic Registry editing.

> Note: *In some instances, when you make changes using the Registry, the changes take effect as soon as you exit the Registry. In other instances, they'll take effect only after you log out and then log back in. And, in yet other instances, they'll take effect only after you restart Windows.*

To run the Registry Editor, press Windows key+R, type *regedit*, and press Enter. (You can also type *regedit* at the Command Prompt, or type *regedit* on the Start screen, highlight the Regedit icon that appears and press Enter.) If this is the first time you've run the Registry Editor, it will open, highlighting the HKEY_CURRENT_USER hive, as shown in Figure 11-3. If you've previously used the Registry Editor, it will highlight the last key you edited or the last place you were in the Registry.

You can browse through the Registry with the Registry Editor in the same way you browse through a hard disk using File Explorer. Clicking a rightward-facing triangle opens a key to reveal the next level down the hierarchy. Clicking the triangle again (it will have turned into a downward-facing triangle) closes the key.

The Registry can be several levels deep in keys and subkeys, so navigating it using a mouse can take a substantial amount of time. (Every time you open it, it jumps to the last-used key.) You can use shortcut keys, though, to more easily navigate through the Registry. The right-arrow key opens a Registry key to reveal subkeys; the left-arrow key closes a key and moves one level up in the key hierarchy. To jump to the next subkey that begins with a specific letter, press that letter on the keyboard.

You use the Registry Editor to edit existing keys and values, create new keys and values, or delete existing keys and values. Again, sometimes the changes take effect as soon as you make the change and exit the Registry Editor; other times, you'll have to reboot for them to take effect. Keep in mind that there is no Save button. When you modify a value, it changes right then and there. There is also no Undo button, so make your changes carefully.

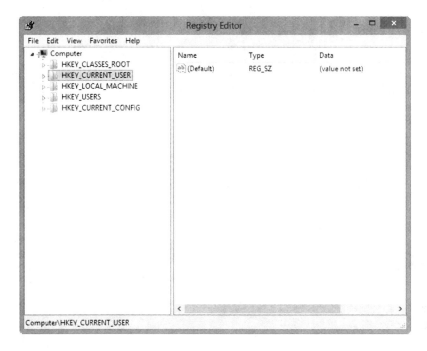

Figure 11-3.
Using the Registry Editor for the first time

If you want to edit a particular key, an even faster way to navigate is to use the Find command from the Edit menu. (You can also use the Find command by pressing Ctrl +F.) To find successive keys with the same value, press the F3 key.

To edit the data associated with a value, double-click the value in the right pane of the Registry Editor; a box appears that lets you edit the value.

When you're editing the Registry, it's often hard to tell what key you're editing because the Registry Editor doesn't highlight that key. Instead, it shows only an open folder icon next to it, but it's easy to miss that icon. Check the status bar at the bottom of the Registry Editor; it should display the key you're editing. If it doesn't, choose View→Status Bar from the Registry Editor menu. Figures 11-4 through 11-7 are examples of what you'll see when you edit various types of Registry keys.

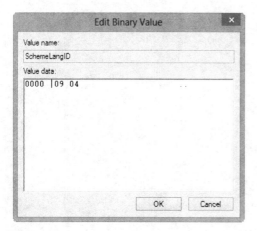

Figure 11-4.
Binary values

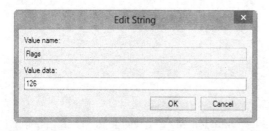

Figure 11-5.
Editing string values

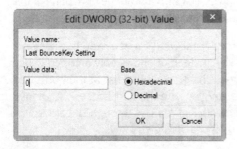

Figure 11-6.
Editing DWORD values

Figure 11-7.
Editing an expanded string value

To rename a key or value, select it, and choose Edit→Rename from the menu. You can also right-click the key and choose Edit→Rename, or select it and press F2.

Adding and Deleting Keys and Values

Editing the Registry often requires that you add and delete keys and values. To add a new key, select its parent key in the left pane. Then, choose Edit→New→Key from the menu. Type in the new key's name. You can also right-click the new key's parent key and choose Edit→New→Key. To delete a key, select it, and press the Delete key.

Very often, you need to add values to a key for its changes to take effect. To add a value to a key, select the key's parent key in the left pane. From the menu, choose Edit→New, and from the submenu, select the type of value you want to create. See Table 11-1 for the values you can create.

Table 11-1. Values you'll encounter in the Registry

VALUE NAME	REGISTRY DATATYPE
String value	REG_SZ
Binary value	REG_BINARY
DWORD (32-bit value)	REG_DWORD
QWORD (64-bit value)	REG_QWORD
Multi-string value	REG_MULTI_SZ
Expandable string value	REG_EXPAND_SZ

To create a new value, type in the name of the new value, and press Enter. Press Enter again. Add your data, and press Enter.

See Also

- For an excellent collection of Registry hacks, go to the Registry Guide for Windows (*http://www.pctools.com/guides/registry*).

Here are some great hacks that use the Registry to do their magic.

You'll find dozens of Registry hacks sprinkled throughout this book, but to give you a sense of the breadth of the kinds of hacks you can accomplish using the Registry, I've included a wide-ranging sample of Registry hacks here as well.

Turn Off Mouse-Over Charm Launcher

In Windows 8, when you move your mouse to the upper right or lower right of the screen, you launch the Charms Bar. The Charms Bar is a nifty feature, but what if that causes problems for you? What if, for example, you're using an app that has an important button or other tool in any of those areas? Every time you try to use it, you'll instead trigger the Charms Bar.

It's not as if you can't get at the Charms Bar without your mouse. Just press Windows key+C to display it. You can turn the mouse trigger for the Charms Bar using a Registry hack. Here's how to do it.

To turn off the Charms Bar, run the Registry Editor and go to `HKEY_CURRENT_USER\Soft ware\Microsoft\Windows\CurrentVersion\ImmersiveShell`. Create a new key and name it `EdgeUI`. Create a new `DWORD` value for `EdgeUI` and name it `DisableCharmsHint`. Give it a value of `1`. Exit the Registry. Move your mouse to the upper-right or lower-right corner of your device, and the Charms Bar won't appear. (Pressing the Windows key-C makes it appear.) If you'd like to enable the mouseover, either delete the key and DWORD that you've just created, or edit `DisableCharmsHint` and give it a value of `0`.

Auto Log On into Windows

Tired of having to log into Windows? Would you prefer that when you started the machine, you logged in automatically? Here's a simple Registry Hack to do it. Launch the Registry and go to `HKEY_LOCAL_MACHINE\SOFTWARE\Microsoft\Windows NT\CurrentVer sion\Winlogon`. You'll see a string value underneath it called `DefaultUserName`, which will be the user name for your account. (If you are using a Microsoft ID to log in, it should look something like *MicrosoftAccount\yourname@hotmail.com*, or whatever your Microsoft ID is.) You'll also see an `AutoAdminLogon` string value. Edit it by and change its value to `1`. Next, create a new `string value` for `Winlogon` called `DefaultPass word`. Edit its value—type in your password and press Enter. Exit the Registry. You won't need to log on to Windows any more—you'll log in automatically. To turn off auto login, give the `AutoAdminLogon` a value of `0`.

Disable Shutdown

There might be times when you want to make sure Windows 8 can't be inadvertently shut down. You can use a Registry hack to disable the normal shutdown. Run the Registry Editor, and go to `HKEY_CURRENT_USER\Software\Microsoft\Windows\CurrentVersion\Policies\Explorer`. Create a new `DWORD` value named `NoClose` with a data value of 1. Exit the Registry. You won't be able to shut down Windows in the normal manner from now on. If you turn on Settings from the Charms Bar and click Power, you'll have no options available to you, as shown in Figure 11-8.

Figure 11-8.
Turning off Windows 8 shutdown

To sign out of Windows 8 or log in as another user, press Ctrl-Alt-Delete and make a selection. However, to turn off Windows 8, you'll have to resort to an ancient piece of technology—the on/off button.

If you want to reenable normal shutdowns, delete the `NoClose` value, sign out of Windows by pressing Ctrl+Alt+Delete, and then log back on again.

Change the Names of the Registered User and Company

When you install Windows or when it comes factory-fresh on a PC, a username and company name are entered as the owner of the system. And that's the way it stays, like it or not. But a Registry hack will let you change both. Run the Registry Editor, go to `HKEY_LOCAL_MACHINE\SOFTWARE\Microsoft\Windows NT\CurrentVersion`, and look for the values `RegisteredOwner` and `RegisteredOrganization`. Edit their value data to whatever username and company name you want.

Change the Default Location for Installing Programs

Windows uses the *C:\Program Files* directory as the default base directory into which new programs are installed. However, you can change the default installation drive and/or directory by using a Registry hack. Run the Registry Editor, and go to `HKEY_LO CAL_MACHINE\SOFTWARE\Microsoft\Windows\CurrentVersion`. Look for the value named `ProgramFilesDir`. By default, the value will be `C:\Program Files`. Edit the value to any valid drive or folder; Windows will use that new location as the default installation directory for new programs. Don't forget to change the ProgramsFilesDir (x86) key too, when using a 64-bit Windows installations.

HACK 119 Safely Edit the Registry Using .reg Files

> Forgo the dangers and inconvenience of editing the Registry directly. Instead, use plain-text *.reg* files.

When you're editing the Registry, it's easy to make small errors that cause major repercussions. You might inadvertently edit the wrong key, put in a wrong value, or— given how confusing the Registry is—make changes without realizing it. The Registry is unforgiving when this happens. It doesn't keep a backup, so you're stuck with the new setting unless you've made backups yourself (Hack #120, "Better Registry Backups").

When you edit the Registry directly, you're also apt to make errors if you're making multiple changes, because you have no chance to look at all the changes you're making at once.

There's a way to solve both problems: use *.reg* files to edit the Registry. These are plain ASCII text files you can create or read with Notepad or any text editor, and merge into the Registry to make changes. You can create a *.reg* file from scratch, or you can export it from a portion of the Registry, edit it with Notepad or another text editor, and then merge it back into the Registry. You'll find that *.reg* files are particularly useful if you're going to make changes to the Registry of several computers or if you are leery about editing the Registry directly.

You should also consider creating *.reg* files to copy the parts of the Registry you're about to edit using the Registry Editor (Hack #117, "Don't Fear the Registry"). Then, if you make a mistake with the Registry Editor, you can revert to the previous version of the Registry by merging the *.reg* file into the Registry. They're also useful if you need to do search-and-replace operations on parts of the Registry, because the Registry Editor doesn't include search-and-replace functionality. You can do the search-and-replace operation in your text editor and then merge the edited file back into the Registry.

To create a *.reg* file from an existing portion of the Registry, run the Registry Editor, highlight the key or portion of the Registry you want to export, and choose File→Export. Choose a name and location for the file. You can export an individual key, a branch of the Registry, a hive, or the entire Registry. Here is an example of a *.reg* file exported from the `HKEY_CURRENT_USER\Control Panel\Accessibility` branch:

```
Windows Registry Editor Version 5.00

[HKEY_CURRENT_USER\Control Panel\Accessibility]
"MessageDuration"=dword:00000005
"MinimumHitRadius"=dword:00000000

[HKEY_CURRENT_USER\Control Panel\Accessibility\AudioDescription]
"On"="0"
"Locale"=""

[HKEY_CURRENT_USER\Control Panel\Accessibility\Blind Access]
"On"="0"

[HKEY_CURRENT_USER\Control Panel\Accessibility\HighContrast]
"Flags"="126"
"High Contrast Scheme"=""
"Previous High Contrast Scheme MUI Value"=""

[HKEY_CURRENT_USER\Control Panel\Accessibility\Keyboard Preference]
"On"="0"

[HKEY_CURRENT_USER\Control Panel\Accessibility\Keyboard Response]
"Last Valid Wait"=dword:000003e8
"Last Valid Delay"=dword:00000000
"Last Valid Repeat"=dword:00000000
"Last BounceKey Setting"=dword:00000000
"Flags"="126"
"DelayBeforeAcceptance"="1000"
"AutoRepeatRate"="500"
"AutoRepeatDelay"="1000"
"BounceTime"="0"

[HKEY_CURRENT_USER\Control Panel\Accessibility\MouseKeys]
"Flags"="62"
```

```
"MaximumSpeed"="80"
"TimeToMaximumSpeed"="3000"

[HKEY_CURRENT_USER\Control Panel\Accessibility\On]
"On"=dword:00000000
"Locale"=dword:00000000

[HKEY_CURRENT_USER\Control Panel\Accessibility\ShowSounds]
"On"="0"

[HKEY_CURRENT_USER\Control Panel\Accessibility\SlateLaunch]
"ATapp"="narrator"
"LaunchAT"=dword:00000001

[HKEY_CURRENT_USER\Control Panel\Accessibility\SoundSentry]
"FSTextEffect"="0"
"Flags"="2"
"TextEffect"="0"
"WindowsEffect"="1"

[HKEY_CURRENT_USER\Control Panel\Accessibility\StickyKeys]
"Flags"="510"

[HKEY_CURRENT_USER\Control Panel\Accessibility\TimeOut]
"Flags"="2"
"TimeToWait"="300000"

[HKEY_CURRENT_USER\Control Panel\Accessibility\ToggleKeys]
"Flags"="62"
```

Edit a *.reg* file as you would any other text file. As you can see, the first line of the *.reg* file starts with `Windows Registry Editor Version 5.00`. Don't change this; Windows uses it to confirm that the file does in fact contain Registry information. Previous versions of Windows have a different first line; for Windows 95/98/Me and Windows NT 4.0, the first line reads either `REGEDIT4` or `Registry Editor 4`.

The names of Registry subkeys are surrounded by brackets, and they include the full pathname to the subkey, such as [`HKEY_CURRENT_USER\Control Panel\Accessibility \Keyboard Response`]. Following each subkey are the subkey values and data. Values and data are both surrounded by quotation marks. Here is the full section of a subkey, along with its associated values and data:

```
[HKEY_LOCAL_MACHINE\SYSTEM\CurrentControlSet\Services\mouclass]
"ImagePath"=hex(2):5c,00,53,00,79,00,73,00,74,00,65,00,6d,00,52,00,6f,00,6f,
00,\
  74,00,5c,00,53,00,79,00,73,00,74,00,65,00,6d,00,33,00,32,00,5c,
```

```
00,64,00,72,\
 00,69,00,76,00,65,00,72,00,73,00,5c,00,6d,00,6f,00,75,00,63,00,6c,
00,61,00,\
 73,00,73,00,2e,00,73,00,79,00,73,00,00,00
"Type"=dword:00000001
"Start"=dword:00000003
"ErrorControl"=dword:00000001
"Group"="Pointer Class"
"Tag"=dword:00000002
"DisplayName"="@msmouse.inf,%mouclass.SvcDesc%;Mouse Class Driver"
"Owners"=hex(7):74,00,65,00,72,00,6d,00,6d,00,6f,00,75,00,2e,00,69,00,6e,
00,66,\
 00,00,00,6d,00,73,00,6d,00,6f,00,75,00,73,00,65,00,2e,00,69,00,6e,
00,66,00,\
 00,00,00,00

[HKEY_LOCAL_MACHINE\SYSTEM\CurrentControlSet\Services\mouclass\Enum]
"0"="HID\\VID_045E&PID_0773&MI_01&Col01\\8&2d02998f&0&0000"
"Count"=dword:00000002
"NextInstance"=dword:00000002
"1"="HID\\VID_056A&PID_00EC&Col01\\7&223a98b2&0&0000"
```

Quotes surround data for String values. DWORD values, however, are preceded by dword: and don't have quotes surrounding them. Similarly, binary values are preceded by hex: and don't have quotes surrounding them.

Edit the value and data, and save the file. When you've made your changes, import the file back into the Registry by choosing File→Import in the Registry Editor and opening the file. An even easier way to import it is to double-click the file. Windows will ask whether you want to import it; when you answer yes, Windows will import it and make the changes to the Registry. This is somewhat counterintuitive and can be confusing; at first you might think double-clicking a .reg file will open it for editing. But it won't; it will merge it into the Registry. To edit a .reg file, open Notepad or another text editor, and then open the .reg file. Alternatively, you can right-click the .reg file and choose Edit.

Note: Because double-clicking a file merges it back into the Registry, it's easy to mistakenly make Registry changes when you really just want to edit a .reg file. I explain how you can protect yourself against this kind of mistake later in this hack.

Delete Registry Keys and Values Using .reg Files

You can use a *.reg* file not only to create new keys or values or to modify existing ones, but also to delete keys and values. To delete a key with a *.reg* file, put a minus sign in front of the key name, inside the bracket, like this:

```
[-HKEY_CURRENT_USER\Control Panel\Accessibility\Keyboard Response]
```

When you import the *.reg* file, that key will be deleted. Keep in mind that you won't be able to delete a key this way unless all of its subkeys have been deleted, so you'll have to delete them first.

To delete a key's value using a *.reg* file, put a minus sign after the equals sign in the *.reg* file:

```
"BounceTime"=-
```

When you import this into the Registry, the value will be deleted but the key will still stay intact.

Protect the Registry by Changing the Default Action for .reg Files

As mentioned earlier in this hack, when you double-click a *.reg* file, the file doesn't open for editing; instead, it gets merged directly into the Registry via the Registry Editor. This can cause serious problems, since most of us are used to double-clicking to open files in Windows. But the file will end up merging into the Registry and making Registry changes you perhaps didn't want to make.

To solve the problem, change the default action so that a *.reg* file is opened for editing in Notepad rather than merged when you double-click it. Head to the Start menu, type *Default Programs*, and then select the Default Programs icon that appears on the left side of the screen and press Enter. Click "Associate a file type or protocol with a program," and scroll down until you find the *.reg* entry. Highlight it and click "Change Program...." Click "More Options," select Notepad (Figure 11-9), and then click Close. (If Notepad is not shown as an available program, click the "More options" link and scroll down until you reach Notepad. Click it. When Windows is done, click "Close" in the "Set Associations" window.) From now on, any *.reg* files will be opened with Notepad rather than by the Registry itself when you double-click them.

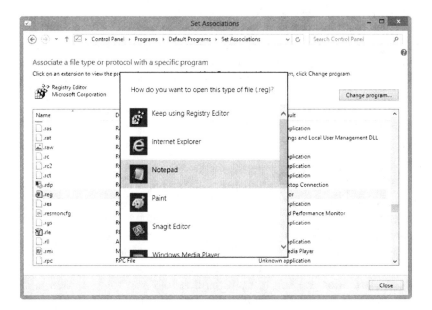

Figure 11-9.
Telling Windows 8 to open .*reg* files with Notepad

To change the default back to the Registry Editor, return to the Default Programs screen, highlight the .*reg* entry and click Change Program. Under Notepad, you'll see Registry Editor listed; click it.

Warning: Never use a word processor like Word to edit .reg files (unless you make sure to save it as a plain-text file from within the word processor). Word processors add extra codes that the Registry can't understand. Always use a text editor like Notepad or WordPad.

HACK 120 Better Registry Backups

> Avert disaster by backing up the Registry so you'll always be able to revert to a clean copy.

The Registry is unforgiving; once you make a change to it, the change is permanent. There is no Undo. To get the Registry back to the way you want it, you'll have to remember and revert the often arcane and complicated changes you make—if you can. And, unlike most Windows applications, the Registry Editor doesn't ask you whether you want to save your changes. Changes happen instantly. To paraphrase F. Scott Fitzgerald, there are no second acts when you edit the Registry.

For this reason, you should take precautions to keep your Registry safe and ensure that you can restore it to its previous safe settings whenever you want to. The best way to do that is to back up your Registry before you edit it. You should make copies of your Registry not only to protect against accidentally doing damage while you're editing it, but also to ensure that you can restore your system in the event of a system crash.

Here are the best ways to back up your Registry:

System Restore

One of the simplest ways to back up and restore the Registry is by using System Restore. System Restore creates a snapshot of your entire system, including the Registry, and lets you revert your system to that snapshot. To use System Restore, before editing the Registry, run Control Panel, then select System and Security→System→System Protection, then click the link System protection in the left pane, and click Create at the bottom of the screen. Then follow the wizard to create a restore point (Figure 11-10). If you want to restore the Registry to its pre-edited state after you edit it, from the Control Panel select System and Security→System→System Protection, click System Restore, and follow the prompts.

Tip: If, after a bad Registry edit, you can't boot Windows properly anymore, you can use the Windows Recovery Environment (Windows RE) or the Windows 8 DVD to perform a System Restore from a recovery point.

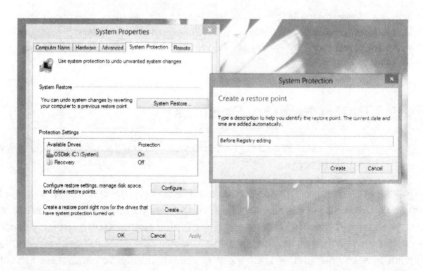

Figure 11-10.
Creating a restore point

Registry Editor

You can also use the Registry Editor to back up the Registry. This is probably the easiest way to back up the Registry, but it's not failsafe, because you cannot import a registry export when a system is unbootable.

Run the Registry Editor, then highlight Computer. (If you highlight an individual Registry hive instead, only that hive will be backed up.) Next, choose File→Export. The Export Registry File dialog box appears, as shown in Figure 11-11. Give the file a name, choose a location, and save it. For safety's sake, also make backups to another machine and to a CD. To restore the Registry, run the Registry Editor, choose File→Import, and then import the file.

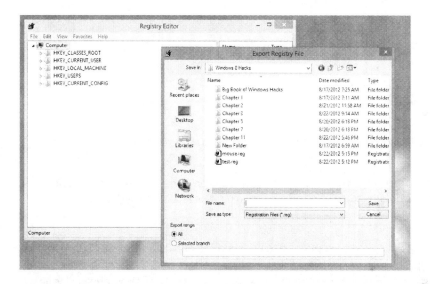

Figure 11-11.
Backing up the Registry

HACK 121 Hack Away at Windows with the Group Policy Editor

This tool offers simple but powerful ways to hack Windows.

The Group Policy Editor was primarily designed for system administrators on networks, but is also a powerful tool for single machines as well, not only for creating policies for every user of the single computer, but also for offering access to settings and controls not otherwise accessible (Figure 11-12). To start the Group Policy Editor, press Windows key+R to open the Run box, type *gpedit.msc*, and press Enter. (You can also type *gpedit.msc* at the Start screen, and then click the icon that appears.)

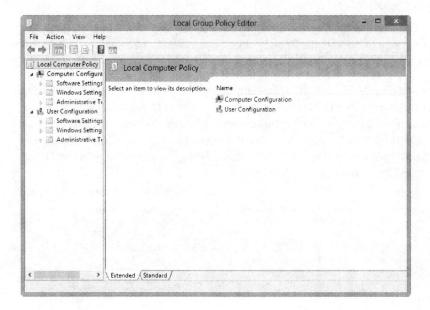

Figure 11-12.
The Group Policy Editor gives you complete administrator's access to Windows' deepest settings

---

Note: The Group Policy Editor is typically found only on Windows 8 Pro and Windows 8 Enterprise, so you may not have it on your version of Windows 8.

The Group Policy Editor's options can be found in a handful of folders in (sometimes) plain English, such as "Hide Add New Programs Page" and "Turn off the Store application." (And there are obscure ones as well, such as "User Group Policy loopback processing mode.")

Warning: Be very careful when using the Group Policy Editor. It makes it possible to restrict or reconfigure almost every security setting on your computer, so it's very easy to break something. And there's no undo feature.

There are two major folders in the Group Policy Editor: Computer Configuration and User Configuration. Computer Configuration lets you set policies computer-wide (or network-wide), while User Configuration lets you set them for individual users, although it will apply to all users on a standalone Windows 8 installation. To some extent, the folders mirror one another, with the same subfolders and settings in each. However, there are some policy settings available only in Computer Configuration, and others available only in User Configuration.

When you're doing editing, the Group Policy Editor has two views: Extended and Standard. The Extended view (Figure 11-13) shows a description of the policy you're considering editing, while the Standard view doesn't. In the Standard view (Figure 11-14), you typically see the entire name of the policy, while in the Extended view, it tends to get cut off unless you expand the Group Policy Editor to full screen.

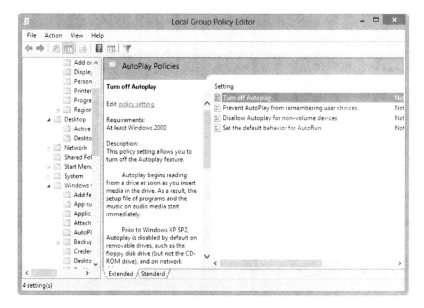

Figure 11-13.
The Extended view in Group Policy Editor

Note: Looking through the descriptions of various settings in the Extended view is a bit like a trip down memory lane. You'll find many settings and their descriptions that aren't designed for or available for Windows 8, which you can safely ignore. For example, there's a setting for Aero Windows Shake, even though it isn't available on Windows 8; the Active Desktop, which was killed after Windows XP; the Start button, which was killed after Windows 7; and many more old settings.

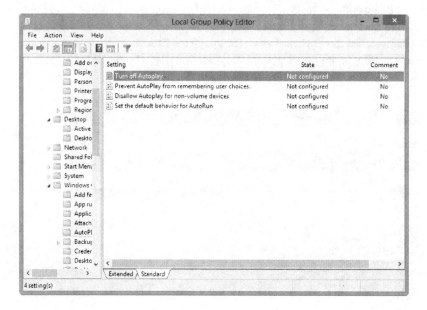

Figure 11-14.
The Standard view in Group Policy Editor

To change a setting, double-click it, and select Enabled or Disabled, as you can see in Figure 11-15. There are plenty of things you can do with the Group Policy Editor; here are a few of the more entertaining and useful ones:

Ban adding new features to Windows 8

Windows 8 has an option that lets you add new features to it. As I write this, the only "new feature" it offers is buying a different version of Windows 8 than the one currently installed. It's possible that Microsoft will add other options as well, such as buying add-ons, not just upgrading the entire operating system. When you choose this option, a wizard launches that walks you through the process of adding features. You may not want this wizard available, though, because it means that anyone with administrative privileges can make a drastic change to your copy of Windows. So you can disable it with the Group Policy Editor. Go to *User Configuration\Administrator Templates Windows Components\Add features to Windows 8*, and double-click "Prevent the wizard from Running." Select Enabled, and the wizard won't run when people try to add new features to Windows 8.

Choose Places for your Places Bar

Go to *User Configuration\Administrative Templates\Windows Components\File Explorer\Common Open File Dialog*, and double-click the Items Displayed in Places Bar option. Click Enabled, and then type the full pathnames of up to five folders on your hard disk. Click OK, and these folders will appear in the gray "Places" bar on the left side of most File→Open and File→Save dialog boxes.

Figure 11-15.
Change settings from this screen

Note: There aren't any Browse buttons in this dialog, but you can specify folder paths without typing by opening Windows Explorer, navigating to the folders you want, highlighting the text in the Address bar, copying it, and pasting the text into the Group Policy Editor's dialog box. Alternatively, you can use the Places Bar in Microsoft Office file dialogs to customize your Places Bar. Doing that, of course, will affect only Office applications. And you can use environmental variables, like %username% in these input fields.

Turn off CD/DVD Autoplay

Go to *Computer Configuration\Administrative Templates\Windows Components \AutoPlay Policies*, and double-click the Turn off Autoplay option on the right. If you enable this option, Windows will no longer play CDs and DVDs automatically when you insert them.

Disable User Tracking

Go to *User Configuration\Administrative Templates\Start Menu and Taskbar*, double-click the "Turn off user tracking" entry to the right, and click Enabled. This will stop Windows from recording every program you run, every document you open, and every folder path you view, thus hobbling such features as "personalized" menus and the Recent Documents menu.

Index

Symbols

/? command, 17

A

abbreviations, Device Manager, 353
access points, wireless, 247, 249
accessories
    displayed in Desktop group, 43
    pinning to Start screen, 43
Action Center (Control Panel), 116, 146, 264
ActiveX plug-ins, 227
Add columns (File Explorer), 111
Add Counters (Performance Monitor), 125
administrative templates
    autoplay policies, 389
    banning new features, 388
    bypassing Lock screen, 2
    disabling user tracking, 390
    hiding Control Panel applets, 98, 99
    Internet settings for, 212
    locking Lock screen image, 4
    Places Bar settings for, 388
    start menu and taskbar settings for, 101
    Windows 8 syncing, 170
administrator
    administrative tools, 53, 116
    Administrator account, 272, 274, 291
    approval settings for unrecognizable apps, 264
    changing password for, 291

    and elevated command prompt, 16, 106–109, 273
    and file extension risk levels, 335
    and hive keys, 370
    secret account, 274
    and UAC, 269, 269–274
Advanced Attributes dialog box, 65
advanced power settings, changing, 346
Advanced properties, 66
Advanced Security, 279
All Apps screen, 40
Allowed apps (Firewall), 276–278
Android devices
    Hotmail on, 315
    LogMeIn on, 228
    Outlook.com on, 314, 316
    SkyDrive on, 154, 163
anonymous ftp servers, 237
ANSI codes, 329
antenna orientation, 249
Apache OpenOffice, 152
App history tab (Task Manager), 63, 130, 233
app tiles, 188
Apple Boot Camp, 18
applets, hiding unused
    with Group Policy Editor, 97
    with Registry, 96
Applications and Services Logs (Event Viewer), 149
Applications Folder, 35
apps
    advanced attributes for, 65

We'd like to hear your suggestions for improving our indexes. Send email to index@oreilly.com.

About the Author

Preston Gralla is the author of more than 40 books that have been translated into 20 languages, including *Big Book of Windows Hacks*, *Windows XP Hacks*, *NOOK Tablet: The Missing Manual*, *How the Internet Works*, and *How Wireless Works*. He is a contributing editor to *Computerworld*, a founder and editor-in-chief of Case Study Forum, and was a founding editor and then editorial director of *PC/Computing*, executive editor for *CNet/ZDNet*, and the founding managing editor of *PC Week*.

He has written about technology for many national newspapers and magazines, including *USA Today*, *Los Angeles Times*, *Dallas Morning News* (for whom he wrote a technology column), *PC World*, and numerous others. As a widely recognized technology expert, he has made many television and radio appearances, including on the CBS Early Show, MSNBC, ABC World News Now, and National Public Radio. Under his editorship, *PC/Computing* was a finalist for General Excellent in the National Magazine Awards. He has also won the "Best Feature in a Computing Publication" award from the Computer Press Association.

Gralla is also the recipient of a Fiction Fellowship from the Massachusetts Cultural Council. He lives in Cambridge, Massachusetts with his wife; his two children have flown the coop. He welcomes feedback about his books by email at *preston@gralla.com*.

Colophon

The text, heading, and title font is Benton Sans; the code font is Ubuntu Mono.

Have it your way.

O'Reilly eBooks

- Lifetime access to the book when you buy through oreilly.com
- Provided in up to four DRM-free file formats, for use on the devices of your choice: PDF, .epub, Kindle-compatible .mobi, and Android .apk
- Fully searchable, with copy-and-paste and print functionality
- Alerts when files are updated with corrections and additions

oreilly.com/ebooks/

Safari Books Online

- Access the contents and quickly search over 7000 books on technology, business, and certification guides
- Learn from expert video tutorials, and explore thousands of hours of video on technology and design topics
- Download whole books or chapters in PDF format, at no extra cost, to print or read on the go
- Get early access to books as they're being written
- Interact directly with authors of upcoming books
- Save up to 35% on O'Reilly print books

See the complete Safari Library at safari.oreilly.com

O'REILLY®

Get even more for your money.

Join the O'Reilly Community, and register the O'Reilly books you own. It's free, and you'll get:

- $4.99 ebook upgrade offer
- 40% upgrade offer on O'Reilly print books
- Membership discounts on books and events
- Free lifetime updates to ebooks and videos
- Multiple ebook formats, DRM FREE
- Participation in the O'Reilly community
- Newsletters
- Account management
- 100% Satisfaction Guarantee

Signing up is easy:

1. **Go to: oreilly.com/go/register**
2. **Create an O'Reilly login.**
3. **Provide your address.**
4. **Register your books.**

Note: English-language books only

To order books online:
oreilly.com/store

For questions about products or an order:
orders@oreilly.com

To sign up to get topic-specific email announcements and/or news about upcoming books, conferences, special offers, and new technologies:
elists@oreilly.com

For technical questions about book content:
booktech@oreilly.com

To submit new book proposals to our editors:
proposals@oreilly.com

O'Reilly books are available in multiple DRM-free ebook formats. For more information:
oreilly.com/ebooks

O'REILLY®

Spreading the knowledge of innovators   oreilly.com